CRITICAL INCIDENTS IN MANAGEMENT

Fourth Edition

Critical incidents in management

JOHN M. CHAMPION, Ph.D.

JOHN H. JAMES, D.B.A.
both of the
University of Florida

69164

1980

RICHARD D. IRWIN, INC. Homewood, Illinois 60430

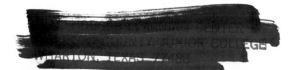

ISBN 0-256-02269-0
Library of Congress Catalog Card No. 79–88784

Printed in the United States of America

3 4 5 6 7 8 9 0 ML 7 6 5 4 3 2

Dedicated to

Our Contributing Professors

PREFACE

SINCE PUBLICATION of the first edition of *Critical Incidents in Management* in 1964, the value of incidents as an instructional tool in management development has become increasingly recognized. Analysis and discussion of critical incidents appear to stimulate students in all stages of professional development. While the level of professional maturity and background of students obviously varies, the purpose of the incident-study method remains the same. As we complete the materials for this fourth edition, the rationale basic to the development of this and preceding editions remains as follows.

First, it is felt that the most characteristic task of the manager is decision making. The typical manager is often confronted with decisions for which there exist no precedent, no formula, no procedural manual, no established principles, and few, if any, factual premises. Decisions of this type call for a knowledge of managerial principles as well as a philosophy of thought, a personal system of values, a professional code of ethics, and a view of what constitutes business morality. Thus, in a method of instruction which incorporates use of this book, students of management are encouraged to develop their own perspective, frame of reference, or method of thinking necessary to cope effectively with the value premises needed in making managerial decisions. In effect, each reader is motivated to formulate a personal "philosophy" of management.

Second, experience indicates that greater student interest in assigned reading materials and increased classroom participation can be achieved when theoretical concepts are related to practical situations of the type likely to confront the manager in day-to-day operations. Therefore, in this book a series of managerial situations, or incidents, is presented, each involving some management principle, concept, or practice. For most of the incidents there are two commentaries or analytical critiques written by outstanding academicians from leading universities across the country. These critiques analyze in depth the basic issues involved in the incident. In most instances they present differing views and opinions regarding the issues and actions to take. Conflicting expressions were sought from those contributing critiques, since this helps to achieve the basic purpose for which they were written, which is to encourage students to develop their own philosophies of management, to exercise their own judgment, and to lead them to a decision-making position. For most of the incidents, comprehensive reading lists are included from which supplementary assignments in books and professional journals can be drawn. Students, ordinarily, are intrigued by the issues in the incident, stimulated by the views expressed in the critiques, and find enjoyable the reading of material necessary for the justification of the position which they take regarding the incident.

In this fourth edition an attempt has been made to incorporate suggestions and comments from university instructors and industrial trainers having experience with earlier editions. An introduction is included for the purpose of acquainting readers with the rationale basic to the book's usage, with the values to be accrued from use of its contents, and with suggested ways in which it can be used. There are 58 incidents drawn from a variety of organizational settings including business, government, hospitals, and education. Supplementary reading lists have been revised and updated to include only the latest available editions of books and many of the most recently published articles in professional journals. Finally, 20 incidents have been included for which analytical critiques have not been provided, for use as preferred by the instructor in situations where it is desired to present the student with an incident unstructured by the formal analysis of other persons.

This book can be used as a basic text with assigned readings from the reading lists, or as a supplement to some standard textbook. It can easily be adapted for use in any course concerned with management development, but in particular for use in such courses as principles of management, personnel administration, human relations, administrative practices, policy formulation, or industrial psychology. (This is particularly true in instances where no cases or incidents are included in the textbook used, where the instructor is not happy with the cases included in the textbook being used, where it is desirable to emphasize the behavioral problems the typical executive can expect to face, or where the instructor desires to utilize the pedagogical power of analytical critiques of the incidents prepared by outstanding professionals in the field.) Additionally, business organizations conducting management training programs have found an application for the contents of this book. Whether the student is a business trainee or a college enrollee, the study of incidents provides experience in diagnosing managerial situations and making decisions.

The development and presentation of these concepts and materials leaves us with an indebtedness to many. In particular, we owe a debt of gratitude to those who so enthusiastically responded when asked to write critiques for the incidents. The incidents are based on real world situations we have encountered in our consulting activities or on situations related by managers who have been participants in various management training programs which we have either conducted or in which we have participated. Names, of course, have been changed to avoid the possibility of connection with actual persons or organizations. The critiques were contributed by 77 different distinguished university professors from many of the leading universities and colleges in the United States and Canada. Most are professors of management and are instructing courses in such diverse disciplines as management, organizational behavior, economics, health care administration, psychology, sociology, labor relations, industrial engineering and business ethics. All have written and published widely, and most have consulting and administrative experience. Without their depth of insight, the basic philosophy inherent in this approach to education for the management process could not have been achieved. Their biographical sketches appear in a special section at the end of the book. To them we dedicate this book.

December 1979   **John M. Champion**
                                                  John H. James

CONTENTS

Incidents without Critiques

INTRODUCTION

SINCE *Critical Incidents in Management* is a unique book, unlike any other existing to date, a few remarks in addition to those found in the Preface seem to be in order. In particular, it appears appropriate to point out the basic philosophy of the book, acquaint the reader with its format, and discuss various characteristics of its usage. The basic unit of the book consists of *(a)* the description of an incident, *(b)* two or more critiques of the decisions and issues reported in the incident, *(c)* a comprehensive list of suggested readings from leading textbooks and professional journals, and *(d)* thought-provoking questions for discussion.

The incident-study approach

Any review of basic management textbooks will probably reveal the emphasis currently placed on the manager's role as a decision maker. In fact, many authors, in their attempt to define management, state that decision making is the most characteristic task of the executive. This being the case, it follows that the purpose of any program of managerial development should be not only to provide for the comprehension of established principles and concepts of professional management but also to develop among participants the perspective, mental set, or method of thinking needed to cope effectively with the premises, especially value premises, present in most executive decisions. For many of the decisions which a manager must make each day, there exist no precedent, no formula, no procedural manual, no ten tried-and-true principles. Yet, a manager's ability to cope with such situations effectively may determine to a large extent his or her status and progress in an organization.

Decisions of this type require a knowledge of managerial principles and concepts and, in addition, a philosophy of thought, or a personal system of values. Attempts to instill in the student of management an appreciation for a self-developed philosophy concurrent with the comprehension of managerial principles and concepts through the traditional lecture method on assigned topics have not always been successful.

During recent years various attempts have been made to supplement the lecture approach to management development; witness the use of visual aids, role-playing exercises, case discussions, simulated problems, and in-basket techniques. A method of instruction utilizing the materials in this book represents still another approach. This method, in the absence of a better term, will be referred to hereafter as "incident-study."

Using the incident-study method of instruction, this book presents the student with a series of situations, or incidents, each involving some management principle, concept, or topic which the instructor desires to be discussed. Along with most of the incidents, the student is given two or more commentaries or critiques written by recognized university professors. These critiques provide the student with scholarly views and recommended courses of action relative to the issues involved in the incident. For most of the incidents the student also receives a comprehensive reading list from which reading assignments can be drawn.

Students read the incident and the accompanying critiques, and then, on the basis of assigned supplementary reading, are required to give their own views and recommended course of action. In doing so, they are encouraged to focus attention on good management principles and concepts, to recommend steps to take in avoiding similar incidents, and to formulate policies to serve as guides for the future. Thus, an incident dealing with a violation of policy provides the basis and incentive for a study of basic concepts of policy formulation, written versus verbal policies, flexible versus nonflexible policies, and so on; the failure of a subordinate to assume his or her responsibilities provides an excellent beginning for a study of organizational principles.

The increase in acceptance and use of critical incidents in manager instruction and development has coincided with the emergence of situational and contingency theories of management. Contingency theories explicitly recognize that organization designs, models of leadership, models of behavioral change, and other management-related concepts become appropriate or inappropriate in relation to the situation to which they are applied. Contingency approaches to management include methods for identifying, classifying, and weighting those dimensions of the situation that are significant for managerial decisions. Through use of the incident-study method, the student improves the ability to analyze situations, balance conflicting requirements, identify and combine options, select a course of action, and design plans for effectively implementing the desired action. Faced with the realities of specific job situations presented in the incident, students recognize that any theory must be adapted for application to specific needs of the situation. Thus, the use of the incident approach brings realism to situational and contingency theories of management, provides an opportunity for students to practice situational analysis, and therefore aids in developing managerial skill for making decisions and taking decisive action.

Students almost unanimously acclaim the incident-study method of instruction as one that attracts their attention, holds their interest, and stimulates reading and study. It is often stated by students that exposure to the incidents creates a new interest in orthodox textbook material. The incidents require decision making, and sound decision making requires basic knowledge and factual information. An instructor using this method of instruction should require students proposing certain courses of action to justify their decisions. The justification provides the real basis for careful preparation and stimulating classroom discussions and analyses. The students, intrigued by the incidents and critiques, enjoy reading assigned material which will assist in the formulation and defense of their own views and recommendations. Students without a strong background in management subject matter are forced to read and prepare themselves extensively or else admit that they cannot justify their recommendations. Thus, incident-study can be viewed as a means of holding students' attention throughout the discussion of basic concepts necessary to the development of a perspective which will serve them well when confronted with their own "real" incidents. In this way the concept that increased student interest results in accelerated incentive to read assigned material and greater retention of subject matter is served.

Student participation and involvement in the learning process can be further increased by dividing members of the class in accordance with their views and conducting debates; by assigning readings for oral reports; and by culminating discussion of an incident in a role-playing exercise. The incidents can be used along with any method of instruction which emphasizes class discussion and classroom participation, and where the objectives are the comprehension of professional management subject matter, awareness with regard to subject matter sources (textbooks, journals, periodicals, leading authors), and skill in the art of management. It should be pointed out, also, that the incidents can be used at either the graduate level or the undergraduate level, depending on the knowledge instructor and students have of the subject matter. In certain instances an incident is more usable than a case because of its brevity, and more interesting because of the decision-making situation that has been established.

Incidents

The incident itself, based on an actual situation, is short in length, generally three or four paragraphs, but so precisely stated and to the point that in most instances a decision can be made from the information given. The typical incident begins with a brief history of the situation, immediately develops a decision-making environment, and concludes with the responsibility for a decision to be made by the reader or central figure in the incident. The decision to be made does not necessarily represent a crisis, or even mean success or failure for the enterprise, but it does usually involve the manager in a delicate situation. Such incidents face the manager daily and require an attitude and an analytic process that hopefully can be developed through an instructional method such as the one suggested in this book.

There are 58 incidents illustrating situations that have developed from managerial efforts to plan, organize, control, and direct others in organizational situations. Fundamental subjects in the incidents range from "employee resistance to change" to "violation of company policy." Every effort has been made to include incidents that typify decision-making problems facing key operating managers. In practically every incident the key figure is faced with making a decision regarding a situation that has no precedent in that organization.

No attempt has been made to classify any of the incidents in terms of functional areas, such as planning, controlling, and so forth. Each incident will ordinarily relate more to one particular managerial function than another, but in the accompanying critiques many issues and concepts are raised that create overlap between functions. Many are deceptive in appearance and much like icebergs, that is, more is hidden underneath than appears on the surface. Actual choice of an incident should, therefore, be a result of the instructor's own analysis of course objectives, student sophistication, the incidents, critiques, supplementary reading lists, and the subject matter areas listed for each incident.

Critiques

Previous classroom experience with incidents and cases has revealed that students have a tendency to seek opinions of "authorities" or "experts" with regard to issues and concepts presented. When confronted with practical situations in the form of an incident, and faced with the task of formulating a recommended course of action, students will often seek publications of academicians known for their work in organization, if it is an organization problem, or policy if it is a policy problem. A result is that students are often guilty of viewing an authoritative opinion as representing the last word on the matter. They too readily accept the judgment of a learned writer as beyond question. However, if they read further and their thought processes begin to mature, they slowly realize other authorities have different opinions; there are different ways to view the issues and alternative approaches to a problem, each usually having some degree of merit. Students are impressed with the fact that there is no "correct" answer, necessarily. They become aware of the concept that management is an "art" as well as a "science," and realize the necessity of developing their own philosophy of management. They discover that seldom is there one, and only one, alternative in the actual situation either. Otherwise a standard operating manual could be developed and used as a substitute for the interpretation of the situation, which is the real contribution of the manager. There would be no need for management development programs, academic work at the collegiate level, or experience on the "firing line."

The incident-study method facilitates this maturation process through the use of critiques. For 38 of the incidents, 77 recognized university professors of business administration and related disciplines have written short critiques giving their views on the basic issues in the incident, opinions with respect to the action that should be taken, explication of how the incident might have been avoided, and recommendations regarding future policy. Intentionally, the critique writers were brief in order to provide the students with latitude in their own discussion. The critiques are, however, thoughtfully written and focus on some of the concepts, issues, and perceptions involved in the incident, serving to intrigue and interest the student. There is no intent that a critique necessarily represents a desirable pattern of analysis. It, instead, represents one possible approach or interpretation. Thus, there are always many assumptions, problems, and points of elaboration not included in the critiques. Many of the critique writers have conflicted in their views with respect to a particular issue. To see two "authorities" in disagreement on an issue has a profound effect on the student. The result is a realization that in the final analysis each of us must develop a personal managerial attitude, perception, value structure, or philosophy.

A critique should not be construed to suggest a right answer or the correct way of doing things. It represents a point of view, often in conflict with the point of view someone else has taken or might take. It may be, however, that a critique serves to structure a discussion and the resulting point of view which the student formulates for himself. In order to permit free discussion and exploration of issues, 20 incidents lack critiques or reading lists. This avoids any structuring, other than for information provided in the incident.

Suggested readings

For most of the incidents a comprehensive reading list has been prepared. These readings can be used to develop the students' own critical potentials and lead them to a decision-making position. The suggested readings have been taken from basic textbooks and representative journals and periodicals and involve the reader in basic issues and concepts of the incident. It should be pointed out that for each incident there are probably more readings on the list than the instructor might wish to assign. However, by including references from some of the more popular textbooks, *Critical Incidents in Management* can more easily be adapted by an instructor wishing to use it as supplementary material in the course for which a particular textbook is used. For example, at one time or another most of the material in *Principles of Management* (Terry) is assigned as supplementary reading. The same is true for *Management: A Systems and Contingency Analysis of Managerial Functions* (Koontz and O'Donnell), *Human Behavior at Work* (Davis), *Personnel and Human Resources Administration* (Megginson), and others. Thus, instead of using a standard textbook and assigning it chapter by chapter in a way that sometimes becomes monotonous, the instructor can choose an incident from *Critical Incidents in Management* that includes in the reading list the material he wishes the student to read. The student then reads the same material that would have been read anyway, but with interest and purpose, all the while focusing attention on good management principles and concepts.

To summarize, then, *Critical Incidents in Management* consists of a series of managerial incidents, most with critiques written by recognized academicians from many colleges and universities, and suggested reading lists to supplement the student's knowledge of the concepts involved in the incident. Student responsibility becomes clear when reading an incident: (1) analyze the incident as well as views provided in the critique, (2) make a decision or recommendation, and (3) justify the views taken. In doing so, the student will define the problem, state the primary and secondary issues, recommend an action to be taken, specify how this problem could have been avoided, make recommendations relative to ways of avoiding similar incidents, and formulate a policy to be used as a guide in future situations. The instructor's responsibility also is clear: to lead the discussion in such a way that all fundamental points, principles, and concepts of good management are brought forth and examined. In this manner, the fundamental process of self-education will be advanced.

All incidents, as all decision-making issues, have alternative courses of action. The analysis and discussion of alternative courses of action, the additional reading for the purpose of justifying a course of action, and further consideration of the facts, issues, and concepts of an incident make the experience dynamic and challenging.

1

A POWER CAGE PROTEST

Motivating productive human behavior, grievance handling, control, decision making, power

Incident

ON TUESDAY MORNING at 6:30 A.M., two young auto workers, disgruntled over failing to get their supervisor fired, scaled the ten-foot fence of a power control area, shut off the power, and closed down a Transpower Corporation assembly line. They simply took matters into their own hands when the union's grievance procedure did not work fast enough to satisfy them. For 13 hours thereafter, William Strong and Larry Kane carried on their protest in the six-by-seven-foot facility known as the power cage, as fellow workers shouted encouragement.

This dramatic protest ended in victory with the delivery to the power cage of a signed statement from the plant manager, officially reporting that the supervisor had been fired and that there would be no reprisal against the protesters. Strong and Kane were carried from the plant on the shoulders of their fellow workers. They were back in the plant working as spot welders the next day, but the fired supervisor, Sam Winfare, was out of his job, although he hoped to get another job with the company.

Winfare, who has four children and who was fired for "personnel violations," claimed the action was unjust. In explaining the events that led up to the power cage protest and his subsequent firing, Winfare said that production on the assembly line had been chronically below quota before he was named supervisor. At the time Winfare was made supervisor, the plant manager had plainly told him that his job was to improve the production rate, and production had, in fact, improved markedly in the short time that he was supervisor.

Winfare said his firing would set a damaging precedent. "The company's action creates a situation where the operations of the plant are subject to the whims of any employee with a grudge," he said. This possibility was emphasized by the comment of a union steward who said there were other conditions in the plant that needed improving—such as the cafeteria food and relief from the more than 100-degree heat in the metal shop. Moreover, the steward said, there was at least one other supervisor who should be fired. His manner implied that the successful power cage protest would facilitate attaining these ends, too. The union steward's final comment was that two men on an unauthorized, wildcat strike had clearly accomplished the same thing as a full blown strike.

While commenting to a news reporter about the power cage strike, the two auto workers reportedly said, "We knew we were going to win. When you cut the power, you've got the power. Every minute we were in there was costing the company money, and we weren't going to leave. It showed the power of the workers to control the company."

The protest at the Transpower plant cost the company the production of 900 to 950 automotive units valued at $5,000 each and one reliable supervisor, according to newspaper accounts.

As the plant manager began to prepare a report on the power cage protest for his supervisor, the division vice president, he reviewed the events of the day, the decisions he had made, and the implications for the future. He wondered if the situation might not have been dealt with more effectively.

Critiques

LARRY L. CUMMINGS

Professor of Organizational Behavior
University of Wisconsin

There are two basic managerial and behavioral themes underlying this incident. Both represent significant and recurring issues in the management of persons and organizations.

The first centers on the bases of *influence and power* within organized systems. The second focuses on the *motivational bases or origins* of behavior within organizations.

Strong and Kane exhibit power-seeking behaviors growing out of implicit frustration with their lack of ability to exert influence upward within the organization. Their behavior illustrates one of the basic propositions of psychology; that is, aggression is a frequent consequence of frustration (blockage of goal-directed behavior). It is likely that Strong and Kane either found the legitimate appeal system provided by the company and the union to be ineffective or, perhaps, failed to perceive that such a system could be used to seek redress against a supervisor. Control over resources is the fundamental mechanism underlying the development and use of power within organizations. Organizations allocate this control through their formal structures, reward allocations, and status systems. Lower-level participants (like Strong and Kane) frequently are allocated little or no power through these means. Thus, some sort of upward-influence or upward-power mechanism becomes necessary to integrate the participants into the organization. Frequently, management provides such a system (grievance procedures, open-door policies, suggestion systems, and so forth) and/or relies upon the unions representing the organization's employees to provide such a system. So the appropriate questions to ask on this issue as they relate to this incident are:

1. Who has the primary responsibility to provide upward channels of influence in large, bureaucratic unionized organizations—management or union?
2. What possible reasons might be suggested for why the management *and* union channels failed to function effectively in this case?

The second theme prevalent in this incident concerns the range of motivations reflected in the behaviors of the participants—particularly Strong, Kane, Winfare, the plant manager, and the steward. The motivational bases for willing cooperation and self-control *within* a large organization are quite complex and, in many cases, precarious. Organizations assume that participants will either identify with the goals of the larger system and/or see the goals or objectives of the system as logical means to the achievement of individual goals or objectives. In other words, if participants act in their own self-interest, organizational aims will be achieved. In most large organizations, this model is unrealistic for one or more of the following reasons:

1   The goals of the organization are not clear or are misperceived by participants.
2.   The goals of the organization are inconsistent with those of the participant.
3.   The paths or means provided by the organization for the attainment of participant aims are not clear.
4.   The organization's structure and technology cause the participant to feel that his personal efforts are unrelated to the achievement of organizational goals and performance.

How would you analyze and "explain" the behaviors of Strong, Kane, Winfare, the plant manager, and the steward, utilizing the above four reasons?

HENRY L. TOSI
*Professor and Chairman of
Management
University of Florida*

It is very easy in this situation to say what the plant manager *should* have done. There can be little question that his decision to remove Winfare and acquiesce to the demands of the two employees will raise debates about the responsibility and the authority of managers and resource allocation decisions.

When those two employees were in the power cage holding the rest of the plant as hostage it was no different from someone's holding a gun to another person's head and making extreme demands. An immediate solution was needed in this crisis situation. There is no question about the very high costs of shutting down the plant for any extended period of time to negotiate. What other ways were there to deal with this problem? Let's speculate. Could we get the union involved in talking these two workers out of the power cage? Should we make concessions to the two workers that were vague and ambiguous, which we later would claim to be unlawful?

Instead of asking what should have been done, the more relevant question now is what are the issues involved for the future? There are basically two questions that must be considered. The first one is, What should be the fate of Winfare? There is a serious question of equity here. Apparently there was a set of problems which existed when Winfare took the supervisory position. I believe it is irresponsible to take an inexperienced or untrained person, put him or her under pressure, not provide much assistance, and then hold the person responsible. Sinking or swimming is not an acceptable way to operate a firm. It may well be that in this case, Winfare was the victim of many previous unfair circumstances and events. If that is true, then every effort should be made to place him in another, similar position without prejudice.

There is another important dimension that should not be overlooked. The act of taking over the power cage is an extreme one. It is equivalent to holding a gun to management's head. Unless there is some reason to believe that the two workers are seriously and emotionally disturbed, such an act suggests that there are very serious problems to which the management must attend. It is time to look hard at the circumstances in which the workers must perform. An evaluation of working conditions, eating facilities, pay systems, and supervisory practices is clearly in order. If there are more hazardous and extreme working conditions that precipitated this act of aggression against management, they must be removed. If not, there will be another retaliatory event at some unpredictable time in the future that may be more serious.

Discussion items

1. On what basis can the firing of Winfare by the plant manager be justified, since Winfare had achieved marked improvements in the production rate as he had been instructed to do by the plant manager?

2. What other optional courses of action were open to the plant manager during the 13 hours that passed before he decided to fire Winfare? Consider the potential costs and benefits of each.

3. Who should bear the cost of the wildcat power cage protest: the company? The union? Strong and Kane? Winfare? Others? Why?

Suggested reading list

BOOKS

Burack, Elmer H. *Organizational Analysis: Theory and Applications.* Hinsdale, Ill.: The Dryden Press, 1975. Chap. 8.

Carroll, Stephen J., and **Tosi, Henry L.** *Organizational Behavior.* Chicago: St. Clair Press, 1977. Chap. 4.

Davis, Keith. *Human Behavior at Work.* 5th ed. New York: McGraw-Hill Book Co., 1977. Chaps. 3–5.

Dressler, Gary. *Personnel Management: Modern Concepts and Techniques.* Reston, Va.: Reston Publishing Co., 1978. Chaps. 8–9.

Duncan, W. Jack. *Organizational Behavior.* Boston: Houghton Mifflin Co., 1978. Chap. 7.

Flippo, Edwin B., and **Munsinger, Gary M.** *Management.* 4th ed. Boston: Allyn and Bacon, Inc., 1978. Chap. 14.

Jucius, Michael J. *Personnel Management.* 9th ed. Homewood, Ill.: Richard D. Irwin, Inc., 1979. Chaps. 24–27.

Koontz, Harold, and **O'Donnell, Cyril.** *Management: A Systems and Contingency Analysis of Managerial Functions.* 6th ed. New York: McGraw-Hill Book Co., 1976. Part 5.

Longnecker, Justin G. *Principles of Management and Organizational Behavior.* 4th ed. Columbus, Ohio: Charles E. Merrill Publishing Co., 1977. Chaps. 8, 16, 22.

Megginson, Leon C. *Personnel and Human Resources Administration.* 3d ed. Homewood, Ill.: Richard D. Irwin, Inc., 1977. Chaps. 21, 22.

Terry, George R. *Principles of Management.* 7th ed. Homewood, Ill.: Richard D. Irwin, Inc., 1977. Chaps. 17–19.

JOURNALS

Albanese, Robert. "The Management of Authority." *Advanced Management Journal* vol. 39, no. 1 (January 1974):57–63.

Clutterback, David. "Getting to Grips With Employee Grievances." *International Management* vol. 30, no. 3 (March 1975):14–18.

Fox, Edna B.; Turner, Jim L.; and **Fox, Vriel G.** "Response Generalization in Aggression." *Human Relations* vol. 25, no. 4 (August 1972):337–50.

Goldstein, S. G. "A Structure For Change." *Human Relations* vol. 31, no. 11 (November 1978):957–82.

Henle, Peter. "Worker Dissatisfaction: A Look at the Economics Effects." *Monthly Labor Review* vol. 18, no. 2 (Winter 1975):59.

Paine, Frank T., and **Gannon, Martin J.** "Job Attitudes of Supervisors and Managers." *Personnel Psychology* vol. 26, no. 4 (Winter 1973):521–29.

Prince, George M. "Creative Meetings Through Power Sharing." *Harvard Business Review* vol. 50, no. 4 (July/August 1972):47–54.

Reesor, Clayton. "Can Behavioral Science Really Change Management?" *Management Review* vol. 62, no. 1 (January 1973):52–54.

Revans, R. "Alienation and Resistance To Change." *Management Decision* vol. 3, no. 1 (Spring 1969):10–14.

Rossel, Robert O. "Required Labor Commitment, Organizational Adaptation and Leadership Orientation." *Administrative Science Quarterly* vol. 16, no. 3 (September 1971):316–20.

Rousseau, Denise M. "Technological Differences in Job Characteristics, Employee Satisfaction and Motivation: A Synthesis of Job Design Research and Sociotechnical Systems Theory." *Organizational Behavior and Human Performance* vol. 19, no. 1 (June 1977):18–42.

Sherwin, Douglas S. "Strategy for Winning Employee Commitment." *Harvard Business Review* vol. 50, no. 3 (May/June 1972):37–47.

Shull, Fremont A., Jr., and **Cummings, L. L.** "Enforcing the Rules: How Do Managers Differ?" *Personnel* vol. 43, no. 2 (March/April 1966):33–39.

2

A STRINGLESS GIFT?

The importance of organizational policy, ethical considerations, personal value structure, extralegal activity

Incident

ONE OF THE CHARGES leveled against Hugh Springfield last week when he was dismissed from his state job of Beverage Control Agent was the charge of "gift taking." His attorney won reinstatement for Springfield after a brief hearing in which he established that both the executive director of the Department of Business Regulation, which oversees the Beverage Department, and the director of the State Highway Patrol had accepted gifts from commercial firms and others.

The Business Regulation director said that originally he saw nothing wrong in accepting gifts from businesses under his regulation but that they had become "a public embarrassment." He admitted that he had in the past been given free motel rooms and other gifts by businesses regulated by his department.

Col. Rutledge Seashore, the Highway Patrol Director, acknowledged that he had received gift certificates from a grocery chain at Christmas for several years. "I see nothing wrong with it," said Seashore, who last year admitted receiving nearly $1,000 in cash and other gifts from troopers under his command in appreciation for a pay raise that he had won for them. "We don't do anything for the donors and I don't intend to stop my men from accepting gifts from friendly businesses," Seashore emphatically announced. "They're underpaid as it is."

As Hugh Springfield was drinking his second cup of coffee before leaving home for his first day back at work in his reinstated job, he scanned the morning newspaper, a leading one in the state. His eye focused on the editorial. It said in part:

It is human to feel kindly toward someone who has done you a favor.

A psychological thread attaches to the gift. As the gifts are repeated, the threads twine into a string. One day the giver pulls the string and asks for just a small favor in return—can the beneficiary refuse?

There is also the matter of public confidence. Say a public official is absolutely incorruptible. But it becomes known that he takes a handout here, a handout there from those who come under the authority of his office. Who is going to believe that he is dealing impartially with the gift-givers?

During the 20-minute drive to his office, Springfield reflected upon the rapid-fire events in which he had been a central figure: dismissal from his job, the legal hearing, revelation of gift-taking on a scale greater than he had previously imagined, reinstatement, the thought-provoking editorial. While trying to organize his thoughts and derive a personal policy regarding gifts, other questions came to his mind. What was the essential difference between gifts, bribes, and graft? Where was the problem in accepting gifts if the public interest did not suffer? Was there a distinguishable line between a gift that was acceptable and one that was unacceptable? Was it acceptable for persons highly placed in the organization to receive large gifts and for persons lower in the organization to receive small gifts? What was the clue to gift acceptability—size, frequency, source, or recipient? Springfield was still uncertain as he parked his car and headed toward the elevator that would take him to his familiar office and surroundings.

As he walked through the office door, Springfield was greeted by a person well-known to him as a holder of a beverage license in the area under his official jurisdiction. The license holder said, "Welcome, Hugh. Here's a little something to help you forget your worries of the last few days—a country-cured 12-pound ham!"

Critiques

WILLIAM C. FREDERICK

*Professor of Business
Administration
University of Pittsburgh*

Consider the incident first from an *ethical* point of view. Since Hugh Springfield occupies a position of public trust that requires him to regulate the activities of beverage license holders, it would appear to be unethical for him to accept favors from those he regulates for fear that he would be lax in his enforcement. But shouldn't that rule also apply to his boss, to the Highway Patrol Director, and to all others holding similar regulatory powers? And if the practice of accepting gifts is so widespread, who is to say what is ethical and what isn't? Springfield might wind up being ethical and poor, while others around him are lining their pockets through practices that seem commonly condoned. Whose ethical standards should be applied?

We are not told who brought the charges against Springfield, but he appeared to be exonerated simply because others had also accepted gifts as a regular practice. Is that a sufficiently good ethical standard to apply in such cases?

Consider the incident now from an *individual* point of view. Where gift-giving is an established precedent in an organization, can a conscientious person refuse to accept a gift without seeming to be "holier than thou," therefore risking ostracism from his fellow employees? In this case, if Springfield turns down the gift ham, he'll run the risk of making his own boss (who also accepts gifts) look bad. Do you suppose that will threaten his job?

Where gifts have become an informal part of the pay structure of an organization, is it really immoral to accept them? Refusing to accept gifts is then equivalent to taking a voluntary pay reduction.

Now consider the incident from a *management* point of view. Some important management principles are at stake. First, if Springfield refuses to take the ham and all other future gifts, he is, in effect, saying that his decisions from now on will be made on a professional, not a personal, basis. Refusing gifts—or having them prohibited by law—is a way to clear the decision process of considerations of friendship and organizational obligations, thus putting decision making on a more rational, objective basis.

A second principle concerns salary levels. If pay is too low, what is the solution? Backdoor gifts that may weaken the regulatory system? Or does this signal the need for top officials to bring political and legal pressures to bear to gain more adequate salaries for the regulatory personnel? Substituting shady pay practices for legitimately established pay levels is nothing but a type of managerial default.

The third management principle to consider is the importance to management of having an image of public confidence and trust-worthiness. Since managers are usually the most visible representatives of an organization, their actions are often seen as typical or symbolic of the entire organization. If they are known or even strongly suspected of being involved in under-the-table dealings, their effectiveness as organizational decision makers will be impaired because no one—stockholders, consumers, employees, nor the general public—will trust them.

VINCENT P. LUCHSINGER
*Professor of Administration
and Human Resources
Texas Tech College of Business Administration*

Hugh Springfield is in trouble. We might view this situation in two different perspectives: the immediate and the overall. In the immediate situation, Hugh cannot afford to accept the offered gift for several reasons. The precedent of accepting gifts must be repudiated. Too much unfavorable attention has come to the practice of accepting any offering.

In the overall setting, the office should adopt policy guides for situations in which gifts are offered. Ethical issues, instances of personal gratuities, and the general aura of obligation inferred from accepting gifts must be resolved. With the unfortunate background of this incident, special care should be exercised to eliminate any reason for believing that the agency is not free to act without the constraint of obligations, real or perceived, to donors. Guidelines may be established that prohibit acceptance of any gift. Possibilities exist for upper limits on gifts in terms of value, size, or significance. Perhaps the rule might indicate a top value of one dollar, a coffee (but no meal), or possibly a small promotional item such as a pot holder or ash tray that could remain as inconspicuous as possible in the office. Not only the fact but the appearance of acceptance should be avoided. The intent is to remain independent of outside influence, to permit open and unfettered transactions, and to maintain public confidence that public agencies are being operated in the best interests of the public, uncomplicated by self-serving motives and actions.

Discussion items

1. What is the basis of gift acceptability? Is it size? Frequency? Source? Recipient? Other?
2. What ethical principles are likely to be violated by gift taking?
3. Draft a workable policy for governing the acceptance of gifts by organization members.

Suggested reading list

BOOKS

Carroll, Stephen J., and **Tosi, Henry L.** *Organizational Behavior.* Chicago: St. Clair Press, 1977. Chap. 14.

Davis, Keith. *Human Behavior at Work.* 5th ed. New York: McGraw-Hill Book Co., 1977. Chap. 15.

Duncan, W. Jack. *Organizational Behavior.* Boston: Houghton Mifflin Co., 1978. Chap. 10.

Flippo, Edwin B., and **Munsinger, Gary M.** *Management.* 4th ed. Boston: Allyn and Bacon, Inc., 1978. Chap. 3.

Hicks, Herbert G., and **Gullett, C. Ray.** *The Management of Organizations.* 3d ed. New York: McGraw-Hill Book Co., 1976. Chap. 4.

Jucius, Michael J. *Personnel Management.* 9th ed. Homewood, Ill.: Richard D. Irwin, Inc., 1979. Chap. 27.

Kast, Fremont E., and **Rosenzweig, James E.** *Organizations and Man-*

agement: A Systems Approach. 3d ed. New York: McGraw-Hill Book Co., 1979. Chaps. 1, 2.

Koontz, Harold and **O'Donnell, Cyril.** *Management: A Systems and Contingency Analysis of Managerial Functions.* 6th ed. New York: McGraw-Hill Book Co., 1976. Chap. 10.

Longnecker, Justin G. *Principles of Management and Organizational Behavior.* 4th ed. Columbus, Ohio: Charles E. Merrill Publishing Co., 1977. Chap. 7.

Miner, John B. *The Management Process.* 2d ed. New York: Macmillan Publishing Co., Inc., 1978. Chap. 30.

Terry, George R. *Principles of Management.* 7th ed. Homewood, Ill.: Richard D. Irwin, Inc., 1977. Chaps. 3, 11, 22.

JOURNALS

Baker, Henry G., Sr. "Identity and Social Responsibility Policies." *Business Horizons* vol. 16, no. 2 (April 1973):23–28.

Brenner, Steven N., and **Molander, Earl A.** "Is the Ethics of Business Changing?" *Harvard Business Review* vol. 55, no. 1 (January/February 1977):57–71.

Byron, William J. "The Meaning of Ethics in Business." *Business Horizons* vol. 20, no. 6 (November 1977):31–34.

Duncan, R. B. "Environments and Uncertainty." *Administrative Science Quarterly* vol. 17, no. 2 (June 1972):313–27.

Eilbert, Henry, and **Parket, I. Robert.** "The Current Status of Social Responsibility." *Business Horizons* vol. 16, no. 4 (August 1973):5–14.

England, George W. "Personal Value Systems of American Managers." *Academy of Management Journal* vol. 10, no. 1 (March 1967):53–68.

Handy, Charles B. "The Problem of Attitude Change in Management." *Journal of Management Studies* vol. 7, no. 1 (February 1970):37–44.

Kaikati, Jack G. "The Phenomenon of International Bribery." *Business Horizons* vol. 20, no. 1 (February 1977):25–37.

Moyer, Charles. "Toward a Specification of Business Social Responsibility." *Management Decision* vol. 11, no. 3 (Summer 1973):195–203.

Owens, James. "Business Ethics: Age Old Ideal, Now Real." *Business Horizons* vol. 21, no. 1 (February 1978):26–30.

Sherman, V. C. "Business Ethics: Analysis and Philosophy." *Personnel Journal* vol. 47, no. 4 (April 1968):271–77.

Sullivan, A. M. "Business Ethics: Policy or Principle?" *Dun's Review and Modern Industry* vol. 74, no. 5 (November 1959):67–74.

Wright, Maurice. "The Professional Conduct of Civil Servants." *Public Administration* vol. 51 (Spring 1973):1–15.

3
ABSENTEE OFFICE FORCE

Gaining acceptance for changes: coordination, use of consultants, attitudes, morale

Incident

AS OFFICE MANAGER of the Duncan Paper Products Corporation, Robert Hale was responsible for the work of approximately 45 employees, of whom 26 were classified as either stenographers or file clerks. Acting under pressure from the company president, he agreed to allow a team of outside systems analysis consultants to enter his realm of responsibility and to make a time study and work method analysis in an effort to improve the efficiency and output of his staff.

The consultants began their study by observing and recording each detail of the work of the stenographers and file clerks. After two days of observation, they indicated that they were prepared to begin their time study on the following day.

The next morning five of the office employees participating in the study were absent. On the following day ten employees were absent. In concern Robert Hale investigated the cause of absenteeism by telephoning several absentees. Each employee related approximately the same story. Each was nervous, tense, physically tired after being viewed as a "guinea pig" during a period of several days. One stenographer told Mr. Hale that her physician had advised her to ask for a leave of absence if working conditions were not improved.

Shortly after the telephone calls, the chief of the systems analysis team explained to Mr. Hale that, if there were as many absences on the next day, his team would necessarily have to drop the study and proceed to another department. He elaborated that a scientific analysis would be impossible to formulate with ten employees absent. Realizing that he would be held responsible for the failure of the systems analysis, Mr. Hale began to create and evaluate alternative courses of action that would provide the conditions necessary for the study.

Critiques

ALAN C. FILLEY
Professor of Management
University of Wisconsin

An outside group of consultants has been imposed upon Robert Hale and his subordinates. The result has been absenteeism, lower performance, and pressure on Hale to avoid displeasing his own superior. The case may exemplify one of two common errors in the consulting process. First, top executives sometimes identify and attempt to solve the wrong problem. For example, the president might have discovered that profits were down, identifying the problem as a need for more productivity and the solution as a need for time and methods analysis. Second, consultants with fixed solutions sometimes attempt to apply them universally. For example, the president may have obtained consultants whose chief skills are the ones employed here. After all, auditors will audit, surgeons will operate, and time study specialists will do time studies.

At present, assuming that the right solution is being employed to solve the right problem, the process has still ignored the fact that an effective outcome depends both on the quality of the solution and its acceptability to those affected by it. Furthermore, neither we nor Hale know whether the product of the consultants' efforts will be facts that Hale and his people can use to develop their own improved work methods or whether the consultants will be imposing their own prescriptions upon Hale and others.

It is time for Hale to get some facts. He should find out what considerations led top management to employ the consultants in the first place. He should determine the intended role of the consultants, whether it is to provide data and aid in problem solving or to prescribe solutions unilaterally. It would be useful for top management to meet with all personnel involved to clarify the facts of the situation. If this is not practical, then at least the consultants and Hale should meet with his own people to discuss the nature of the project and action to be taken.

In some companies faced with a situation like this, a decision would be made by those affected about whether or not to proceed with the study. In others, the work study would be dictated by management but its purpose and processes would be clarified. If Hale can determine the outcomes sought by the study, for example, increased productivity, and if the consultant data can be used for joint problem solving, then further study may be acceptable to Hale and his subordinates.

Hopefully, the group might agree that: (a) the work methods study would be continued, (b) the results of the study would be provided to the group, and (c) the group would use the data and suggestions from the consultant to arrive at improvements that are both effective and acceptable.

If the above actions are not possible, then at least Hale can demonstrate more initiative in dealing with both his subordinates and his superior. His subordinates expect him to represent their interests with the president. Hale can provide his subordinates with more information than he has to date. Hale might well alert management to the fact that actions that create dissatisfaction will generally result in greater absenteeism and turnover. If the employees to be lost under mandatory work evaluation are poor performers in the first place, then the results need not be bad. If the lost employees include top performers, then well-intended actions on the part of management will have resulted in negative rather than positive consequences.

JAMES P. LOGAN

Professor of Management
University of Arizona

My critique is built on five questions:

a.   What are the present pressures on Hale?

b. What behavior on Hale's part contributed to the situation?

c. What does the incident reveal of the organization of the office?

d. What might Hale reasonably do now?

e. What stereotypes or traps for the unwary is a reader likely to find in the incident?

Present pressures on Hale: Hale has to now: (1) maintain current output in the office, (2) find out what conditions would lead to the absentees' return, (3) find a way to have the systems analysis work done soon, (4) have an answer to these problems that will satisfy himself as an effective office manager and also satisfy the president.

With almost 40 percent of his stenographic and filing force absent, Hale has a major problem of work load and output on his hands. The easiest way to take care of this would probably be to get the regular employees back to work. Hale knows why they are gone, but not what inducements would persuade them to return.

Further, Hale has to see eventually that the systems analysis work is done to satisfy the president's desires. Postponement or proceeding at once will depend upon the outcome of talks with the chief of the systems team and with the absentees. It should be noted that Hale's situation is complex and that he has to respond to several forces, not just one.

Hale's behavior: The surprises about Hale's actions as an executive are: (1) Why does the president have to pressure for a study? Is something remiss with office productivity? Or has Hale not educated him as to its effectiveness? (2) Why has Hale taken two days to discover difficulties? On such a major project it would seem that Hale would be acquainted with his workers' condition and the analysts' behavior at least twice each day. (3) Why did Hale not explain the project to his employees and observe it from the beginning? The office is his responsibility. As the key supervisor, Hale is considerably distant from the events.

Organization of the office: Are there other office supervisors and had they roles in the incident? If Hale is attempting to manage the employees directly, he has too much work—as is shown by his lack of knowledge about the study and perhaps by the pressure from the president. If Hale has other supervisors, he is not using them effectively. He makes the phone calls and notices the absences himself. He hears nothing through or from any supervisors. The organization can only be speculated about, but it influences the kind of action suitable for Hale. For example, further information on inducing the employees to return to work should be obtained by and with the supervisors. Also the problem of maintaining output should be worked out with the supervisors. If there are none, Hale has a question of organization, selection, and promotion.

What might Hale reasonably do now? First, talk to his supervisors, if he has any, for their help is important in getting the work out, in finding out why people are absent, and in getting the employees back to work in a proper atmosphere. Second, find out how the systems team operated so that he can *judge* whether the team's methods of work contributed to the problem. This might or might not be so. Hale doesn't know yet. Finally, when he has the information, set up a program to restore output and the confidence of the work force and to get the systems analysis done eventually. He might also be prepared to explain to the president what has happened and what the most reasonable next steps are.

Stereotypes and traps for the unwary: Readers should check their thinking for any of the following common errors: *(a)* Concluding that the stenographers were "wrong" because they were opposing change or because they were staying out sick when they really weren't. Did you blame the employees? *(b)* Concluding that the systems team was "wrong" because it was ineptly using time study techniques. Did you blame "unfeeling engineers"? *(c)* Hale was wrong because he did not "correctly" prepare the employees for the study. Did you try to pin the whole thing down to some *one* error by Hale? *(d)* "Searching for a villain"—did you look for one person to blame for everything? *(e)* Substituting value judgments for investigation—did you jump to conclusions that actions were "good" or "bad" when really Hale seems to be mostly in the dark and in need of more information rather than judgments? *(f)* Identification—did you immediately think you were Hale? or one of the stenos? or the chief analyst? or the president? You will learn most by looking at the incident from all these points of view. Do not automatically identify with one.

Discussion items

1. What course of action do you think Mr. Hale should adopt? Justify your response.

2. Mr. Hale's subordinates appear to be exercising sanctions in the form of absenteeism. Examine the various means by which sanctions can be applied by both superiors and subordinates.

3. What is your evaluation of Professor Logan's recommendation regarding what Mr. Hale might reasonably do?

Suggested reading list

BOOKS

Carroll, Stephen J., and **Tosi, Henry L.** *Organizational Behavior.* Chicago: St. Clair Press, 1977. Chap. 13.

Davis, Keith. *Human Behavior at Work.* 5th ed. New York: McGraw-Hill Book Co., 1977. Chaps. 10, 13.

Filley, Alan C.; House, Robert J.; and **Kerr, Steven.** *Managerial Process and Organizational Behavior.* 2d ed. Glenview, Ill.: Scott, Foresman and Co., 1976. Chaps 19, 20.

Flippo, Edwin B., and **Munsinger, Gary M.** *Management.* 4th ed. Boston: Allyn and Bacon, Inc., 1978. Chaps. 18, 21.

Jucius, Michael J. *Personnel Management.* 9th ed. Homewood, Ill.: Richard D. Irwin, Inc., 1979. Chaps. 24, 28.

Kast, Fremont E., and **Rosenzweig, James E.** *Organizations and Management: A Systems Approach.* 3d ed. New York: McGraw-Hill Book Co., 1979. Chaps. 23, 24.

Longnecker, Justin G. *Principles of Management and Organizational Behavior.* 4th ed. Columbus, Ohio: Charles E. Merrill Publishing Co., 1977. Chaps. 16–18.

Luthans, Fred. *Introduction to Management.* New York: McGraw-Hill Book Co., 1976. Chaps. 14, 15.

McCormick, Ernest J., and **Tiffin, Joseph.** *Industrial Psychology.* 6th ed. Englewood Cliffs, N.J.: Prentice-Hall, Inc., 1974. Chaps. 8, 11, 16–18.

Miner, John B. *The Management Process.* 2d ed. New York: Macmillan Publishing Co., Inc., 1978. Chaps. 24–27.

Terry, George R. *Principles of Management.* 7th ed. Homewood, Ill.: Richard D. Irwin, Inc., 1977. Chaps. 4, 6.

JOURNALS

Fiedler, Fred E. "Job Engineering for Effective Leadership: A New Approach." *Management Review* vol. 66, no. 9 (September 1977):29–31.

Gordon, Michael E., and **Kleiman, Lawrence S.** "The Prediction of Trainability Using a Work Sample Test and an Aptitude Test: A Direct Comparison." *Personnel Psychology* vol. 29, no. 2 (Summer 1976):243–58.

Ilgen, Daniel R., and **Hollenback, John H.** "The Role of Job Satisfaction in Absence Behavior." *Organizational Behavior and Human Performance* vol. 19, no. 1 (June 1977):148–61.

Kovack, Kenneth A. "Improving Employee Motivation in Today's Business Environment." *MSU Business Topics* vol. 24, no. 4 (Fall 1976):5–12.

Levinson, Robert E. "How to Conquer the Panic of Change." *Management Review* vol. 66, no. 7 (July 1977):20–24.

Martin, Richard. "How Companies Are Using Office Work Measurement." *Management Review* vol. 55, no. 7 (July 1966):69–72.

Nance, Harold W. "Four Myths of Office Work Measurement." *Personnel* vol. 42, no. 6 (November/December 1965):8–16.

Pfeffer, Jeffrey. "Interorganizational Influence and Managerial Attitudes." *Academy of Management Journal* vol. 15, no. 3 (September 1972):317–30.

Porter, Lyman W., and **Lawler, Edward E., III.** "What Job Attitudes Tell about Motivation." *Harvard Business Review* vol. 46, no. 1 (January/February 1968):118–26.

Quick, Thomas L. "The Many Uses of a Task Force." *Personnel* vol. 51, no. 1 (January/February 1974):53–61.

Reif, William E., and **Tinnell, Ronald C.** "A Diagnostic Approach to Job Enrichment." *MSU Business Topics* vol. 21, no. 4 (Autumn 1973):29–37.

Stone, Morris. "If You Were the Arbitrator: Suspicious Absences." *Supervisory Management* vol. 22, no. 5 (May 1977):25–31.

Woody, Robert H., and **Woody, Jane D.** "Behavioral Science Consultation." *Personnel Journal* vol. 50, no. 5 (May 1971):382–91.

4

ADVANCED STUDY

The engineer or scientist as a manager: university management development programs

Incident

WHILE ATTENDING A REUNION of his class at a small midwestern college, a classmate remarked to John Washburn, president of Washburn Instruments, that his company was sending him to a large northeastern university to attend a six months' executive program entitled "Advanced Study in Dynamic Philosophic Concepts." Upon returning home, Mr. Washburn asked the personnel department to recommend someone to attend the advanced studies program. The name of Donna Russell, a physicist, was submitted. The personnel director explained, upon Mr. Washburn's inquiry, that Ms. Russell, who was being considered for an executive position, would profit from the program.

Mr. Washburn stated that he had always felt that anyone such as a physicist, a chemist, or an accountant, trained to cope with factual premises, would never learn to deal with value premises of the type encountered in executive positions. He said that statistics proved that someone with scientific training often fails as an executive. He argued that it would be a waste of money to send such a person to the university because someone with that background would always be searching for a formula, truly defined steps and principles, or situations that are either black or white. Mr. Washburn did say, however, that he would abide by the decision of the personnel director and asked for his recommendation after reconsideration.

Critiques

LYNN H. PETERS
Professor of Management
San Diego State University

As in most problems, there are here several possible levels of approach. One could take the "macro" view and discuss the kinds of corporate problems that result from the random behavior pattern exhibited by Mr. Washburn. At the other extreme, one could examine the matter of Ms. Russell's probable attitude toward the company as a result of the evident lack of confidence in her managerial potential. Between these two approaches to the situation lies the matter of the personnel director, the nameless entity who is really the person with a problem. He is caught between the proverbial rock and a hard place.

What action should the personnel director take in this situation? Let us assume, *arguendo,* that the personnel director had previously made inquiries into the nature of the "Advanced Study in Dynamic Philosophic Concepts." Let us assume, further, that he has information about the kinds of persons who have been attending the program and their companies' expectations of them. If he had not done these things before making the original recommendation, he most certainly would have failed his professional duty, and no further discussion would really be necessary.

How then to deal with Mr. Washburn in this new charge? Clearly, the personnel director is on the spot, since Mr. Washburn had agreed to abide by his decision. If Ms. Russell is again nominated, attends the program, and subsequently gives less than satisfactory managerial performance, there is a double negative outcome: Mr. Washburn's prejudice is confirmed, and the personnel director's professional competence is put into question.

The focus of the immediate problem, of course, is on Mr. Washburn's perception of cause (training in objective or scientific professions) and the effect (incapacity to exercise necessary managerial judgment). It would seem that the personnel manager has at least two courses of action, not mutually exclusive, if he really believes in his own judgment. First, he can do some research into the professional backgrounds of managers by type of industry. The statistics cited by Mr. Washburn about "failure" of scientifically trained managers would be helpful to reference if available or in existence. Much more to the point are the readily available statistics showing the high percentage of managers in science-based industry with scientific backgrounds. The other possible course of action would be an explanation to Mr. Washburn of the nature of the program; that clearly it is a program in the humanities that is designed to introduce the scientist to the qualitative, "it depends" orientation that the humanities provide so splendidly for management. One must confess that these two approaches are not in themselves totally logically consecutive. Operationally, that luxury is rarely available.

If the personnel director did his homework thoroughly in the first instance, he should have no hesitation at all in renominating Ms. Russell. Not to do so would indicate either that he had not acted professionally or that he is afraid for his own job.

THOMAS E. MILLER
*Professor of Business and
Human Relations
University of Missouri at
Kansas City*

This incident primarily concerns John Washburn's evaluations of the necessary qualifications for executives. According to Washburn, physicists, chemists, and accountants, because of their particular factual training, do not have these special qualifications and are, therefore, not executive material. Now, it is very possible that Donna Russell is a "factually oriented" scientist and, thus, would never be acceptable to Mr. Washburn in an executive position. This, however, is not the issue here.

It is my belief that John Washburn needs to review and reconsider his basic evaluations of scientific personnel. An effective conclusion to this situation can result only from improved evaluations on the part of the company president. This is not to suggest that Washburn should *not* act in accordance with his considered views. It is to suggest that there are crucial factors that he is overlooking and that he may need some assistance in recognizing. In particular, he is responding to a generalized image of all scientists, not to Donna Russell, a unique individual. The technical misevaluation from the point of view of general semantics concerns Washburn's failure to index, namely, to differentiate among physicist 1 who has a factual orientation, physicist 2 who does not, and physicist 3, Russell, who may, in all likelihood, differ considerably from both physicists 1 and 2. When we fail to index, we tend to evaluate present situations totally in the light of past situations without recognizing any differences.

If I were the personnel director, I would not point out this misevaluation to Washburn, particularly now that he has indicated his willingness to accept my decision. I would simply listen to him in as skillful a manner as possible. When a favorable opportunity arose, I would explore with him his past experiences (successes and failures) with physicists and other scientists in relation to his present evaluation of Donna Russell. As I listened to Washburn, I would try to help him to "see" Donna Russell, physicist 3.

Let me be perfectly clear that I would not try to "change" Washburn's mind—the listening approach is not a persuasive device—nor would I try to outmaneuver him. My approach does not promise an immediate and/or easy solution. (John Washburn, like all of us, will probably not alter his cherished evaluations with alacrity.) However, this approach seems the most effective in view of the fact that the problem may arise soon again with the proposed promotion of Donna Russell. If John Washburn continues to view Russell solely as a "factually oriented" scientist, then it is possible that the company may lose a promising future executive.

Discussion items

1. Does the specialized training of the engineer, scientist, or accountant somehow generally reduce their capacity for managerial thinking and decision making? Why?

2. Is there a significant difference between the abilities required for being a successful engineer and those required for being a successful manager? Explain your position.

3. Should the personnel director attempt to change President Washburn's mind? Justify your answer.

Suggested reading list

BOOKS

Carroll, Stephen J., and **Tosi, Henry L.** *Organizational Behavior.* Chicago: St. Clair Press, 1977. Chap. 17.

Davis, Keith. *Human Behavior at Work.* 5th ed. New York: McGraw-Hill Book Co., 1977. Chaps. 11, 19.

Donnelly, James H.; Gibson, James L.; and **Ivancevich, John M.** *Fundamentals of Management.* 3d ed. Dallas, Tex.: Business Publications, Inc., 1978. Chaps. 1, 2.

Flippo, Edwin B., and **Munsinger, Gary M.** *Management.* 4th ed. Boston: Allyn and Bacon, Inc., 1978. Chap. 9.

Jucius, Michael J. *Personnel Management.* 9th ed. Homewood, Ill.: Richard D. Irwin, Inc., 1979. Chap. 14.

Koontz, Harold, and **O'Donnell, Cyril.** *Management: A Systems and Contingency Analysis of Managerial Functions.* 6th ed. New York: McGraw-Hill Book Co., 1976. Parts 1, 4.

Longnecker, Justin G. *Principles of Management and Organizational Behavior.* 4th ed. Columbus, Ohio: Charles E. Merrill Publishing Co., 1977. Chaps. 1–4, 19.

Megginson, Leon C. *Personnel and Human Resources Administration.* 3d ed. Homewood, Ill.: Richard D. Irwin, Inc., 1977. Chaps. 12, 13.

Miner, John B. *The Management Process.* 2d ed. New York: Macmillan Publishing Co., Inc., 1978. Chaps. 3, 29, 32.

Terry, George R. *Principles of Management.* 7th ed. Homewood, Ill.: Richard D. Irwin, Inc., 1977. Chap. 21.

JOURNALS

Bowen, Charles P., Jr. "Let's Put Realism into Management Development." *Harvard Business Review* vol. 51, no. 4 (July/August 1973):80–87.

Ernest, R. G. "Training an Engineer for Management." *Chemical Week* vol. 81, no. 20 (November 16, 1957):27, 30.

Fournes, Ferdinand F. "Why Management Appraisal Doesn't Help Develop Managers." *Management Review* vol. 63, no. 1 (January 1974):19–24.

Handschumacher, Albert G. "The Scientist: Is He Equipped for Managing?" *Office Executive* vol. 36, no. 4 (April 1961):20–21.

Hill, Norman C. "Increasing Managerial Effectiveness." *Training and Development Journal* vol. 31, no. 7 (July 1977):16–20.

Kearney, William J. "Management Development Programs Can Pay Off." *Business Horizons* vol. 18, no. 2 (April 1975):81–88.

Larwood, Lauri; Wood, Marion M.; and **Inderlied, Sheila Davis.** "Training Women for Management: New Problems, New Solutions." *Academy of Management Review* vol. 3, no. 3 (July 1978):584–93.

Lundberg, Craig C. "Planning the Executive Development Program." *California Management Review* vol. 15, no. 1 (Fall 1972):10–16.

Mandt, Edward. "Managing the Knowledge Worker of the Future." *Personnel Journal* vol. 57, no. 3 (March 1978):138–43.

Simpson, Karl F., Jr. "Management Development: Full Spectrum Training." *Training and Development Journal* vol. 29, no. 5 (March 1975):3–7.

Tosi, Henry L., Jr., and **House, Robert J.** "Continuing Management Development beyond the Classroom." *Business Horizons* vol. 9, no. 2 (Summer 1966):91–101.

Vod der Embse, Thomas J. "Choosing a Management Development Program: A Decision Model." *Personnel Journal* vol. 52, no. 10 (October 1973):907–12.

Watson, Charles E. "Getting Management Training to Pay Off." *Business Horizons* vol. 17, no. 1 (February 1974):51–58.

5

AIR-CONDITIONED CAFETERIA

*Factors important in job satisfaction: relation between
productivity and job satisfaction*

Incident

IN DECEMBER 1977, the executive-management committee of
the Berkshire Stove and Range Company made a recommendation to the president of the company that the employee cafeteria
be air-conditioned. Their recommendation was based upon the
fact that the temperature in the foundry area and other production areas was often over 100 degrees Fahrenheit. In addition,
since company profits for the fiscal year had been good, the
committee felt that employees were entitled to share in the profits. The air-conditioned cafeteria would represent management's
appreciation of the employees' good work.

At the end of another fiscal year, December 1978, the executive-management committee held a meeting and reviewed the
company's operation for the past year. Again, profits were high,
labor productivity had been good, and labor turnover had been
low. The committee unanimously agreed that the employees deserved additional recognition for their fine work, and the group
considered what might be done to show management's appreciation. Since the company cafeteria had been air-conditioned
during the past year on the recommendation of the committee,
several of its members wondered if this sort of action was appreciated by the employees. In the course of discussion, the
committee asked Oscar Thompson, the personnel director, to
send a questionnaire to a sample of 50 employees and obtain
their reaction to the air-conditioned cafeteria. The committee
agreed to meet again in a month and hear a report from the
personnel director.

The personnel director mailed a simple form to 50 employees

containing the following request: "Please state your reaction to the recently air-conditioned cafeteria."

Of the 50 forms mailed, 46 were returned. The answers could be classified generally as follows:

	Reaction	Total Number
a.	"I didn't know it was recently air conditioned."	16
b.	"I never eat there."	8
c.	"If management can spend money like that, they should pay us more."	6
d.	"I wish the entire plant were air-conditioned."	8
e.	"That is a cafeteria for management people."	4
f.	"It's OK."	2
g.	Miscellaneous comments.	2

Critiques

KEITH DAVIS
Professor of Management
Arizona State University

First, let us make some observations on the action that management took with regard to air conditioning the cafeteria in December, 1977.

1. Management made the decision without any participation from employees or any effort to determine specifically what the most pressing employee needs were.
2. The underlying causes for management's action seem to have no direct relation to the action taken.
   a. The fact that production areas are hot does not necessarily require refrigerated eating areas. As a matter of fact, the opposite may be true. The contrast between the hot work areas and the cool area where one relaxes may be so great as to cause chilling, discomfort, and colds.
   b. A good profit year is not necessarily a proper reason for installing air conditioning.

Generally, action should be rationally related to causes.

Now, let us look at management's action in December 1978.

1. The personnel director apparently is not carrying out his responsibilities, because he has nothing particular to recommend and has to be instructed to follow up on what happened last year. He will be more effective if he offers professional personnel leadership and initiative.

2. Neither the personnel director nor the other executives seem to be sure how employees reacted to last year's expression of "appreciation." What has happened to communication?

3. The open-end questionnaire is effective in disclosing several different types of responses that probably were not expected. The proportion of returns was high for this sort of survey, but responses were overwhelmingly negative, suggesting that there may be some problems with employee attitudes and job satisfaction. (For details on job satisfaction surveys, see Keith Davis, *Human Behavior at Work*, New York: McGraw-Hill Book Co., 1977, Chapter 5, "Job Satisfaction.")

In general, management planning is weak, employee communication is deficient, and decision making is not rationally related to causes or employee needs. As a consequence of these problems, satisfaction with the cafeteria (and probably other employment conditions) is poor. Although low job satisfaction does not guarantee declining productivity, it may have long-run negative effects unless management improves in quality.

PAUL J. GORDON
Professor of Management
Indiana University

What recognition can management provide to show appreciation for employee contribution to a successful year? Should the sharing take place only in years of success? Should employees share if it can be demonstrated that the circumstances leading to success had little to do with employee behavior as such? If some award is to be made, either as a recognition of past accomplishment or as a likely anticipation of accomplishment yet to come, why and how do consultation or at least a declaration of intention fit into the picture? These are some of the questions that place the case of the air-conditioned cafeteria into a larger context for diagnosis and disposition.

If management were more fully developed as a science, it might be possible to say that the selection of utilities (U) as desirable should lead to the choice of actions (A) to be taken under conditions (C) and that these should produce outcomes (O) with probabilities (P) and risks (R). Then, in cases such as the present, the rational manager would have little difficulty in making a highly rational decision. As in real life, however, rationality, information, prediction, and control, especially in the area of human behavior, are not fully developed.

Without getting into technical criticism of the questionnaire technique, there might have been ways to avoid what is now potentially a source of irritation for employees and embarrassment for management. The recognition given with neither consultation nor declaration of intention by management apparently has not received the interpretation that management would have preferred. Unfortunately, without some reasonable meeting of expectations, one or both parties can become aggrieved. Consultation might have avoided the 1977 gap and might have provided better understanding generally on the use of the cafeteria and the allocation of money for improvements such as air conditioning. This earlier experience, however, can provide learning for management for the coming year.

The important issues now are to learn, if possible, why things are going so well; to assure continuity of a good situation; and to find policies and means for continued improvement in the future. Information given in the case suggests that profits, productivity, and turnover are in good shape. If management can clarify the objectives (the future conditions that management seeks to create), and tie employee performance through some means and standards to these objectives, it may be started on a more adequate policy and system for incentives. The objectives, the standards, and the necessary details of administration will have to be well understood if the intended results are to be achieved. This means adequate communication and may mean consultation and participation in the developmental stages and possibly in the administration of the plan. The ad hoc, unilateral decision may have done no harm, but there is nothing to suggest that repetition will do any special good.

Discussion items

1. What is your evaluation of the reasons that Professors Davis and Gordon give for the employee reaction to air-conditioning their cafeteria? What is your analysis of the reaction?

2. How should the management of the Berkshire Stove and Range Company use the information they have obtained from the opinion survey?

3. In what way is the issue of "resistance to change" relevant in this incident?

Suggested reading list

BOOKS

Carroll, Stephen J., and **Tosi, Henry L.** *Organizational Behavior.* Chicago: St. Clair Press, 1977. Chap. 13.

Davis, Keith. *Human Behavior at Work.* 5th ed. New York: McGraw-Hill Book Co., 1977. Chap. 5.

Flippo, Edwin B., and **Munsinger, Gary M.** *Management.* 4th ed. Boston: Allyn and Bacon, Inc., 1978. Chap. 16.

Jucius, Michael J. *Personnel Management.* 9th ed. Homewood, Ill.: Richard D. Irwin, Inc., 1979. Chaps. 21, 24.

Koontz, Harold, and **O'Donnell, Cyril.** *Management: A Systems and Contingency Analysis of Managerial Functions.* 6th ed. New York: McGraw-Hill Book Co., 1976. Chap. 23.

Longnecker, Justin G. *Principles of Management and Organizational Behavior.* 4th ed. Columbus, Ohio: Charles E. Merrill Publishing Co., 1977. Chap. 22.

Megginson, Leon C. *Personnel and Human Resources Administration.* 3d ed. Homewood, Ill.: Richard D. Irwin, Inc., 1977. Chap. 24.

Miner, John B. *The Management Process.* 2d ed. New York: Macmillan Publishing Co., Inc., 1978. Chaps. 24–27.

Reitz, H. Joseph. *Behavior in Organizations.* Homewood, Ill.: Richard D. Irwin, Inc., 1977. Chap. 11.

Terry, George R. *Principles of Management.* 7th ed. Homewood, Ill.: Richard D. Irwin, Inc., 1977. Chaps. 17, 18, 25.

JOURNALS

Bergerson, Allen W. "Employee Suggestion Plan Still Going Strong at Kodak." *Supervisory Management* vol. 22, no. 5 (May 1977):32–36.

Budd, J. Mark. "Employee Motivation through Job Enrichment." *Journal of Systems Management* vol. 25, no. 8 (August 1974):34–38.

Cooper, M. R.; Margon, B. S.; Foley, P. M.; and **Kaplan, L. B.** "Changing Employee Values: Deepening Discontent." *Harvard Business Review* vol. 57, no. 1 (January/February 1979):117–25.

Hawk, Donald L. "Effective Attitude Surveys." *Personnel Journal* vol. 57, no. 7 (July 1978):384–89.

Herzberg, Frederick. "One More Time: How Do You Motivate Employees?" *Harvard Business Review* vol. 46, no. 1 (January/February 1968):53.

Hood, John M., Jr. "The Company Man in Crisis." *Personnel Journal* vol. 54, no. 1 (January 1975):93–96.

Kempner, T., and **Wild, Ray.** "Job Design and Productivity." *Journal of Management Studies* vol. 10, no. 1 (February 1973):62–81.

Kirchner, Wayne K. "Ways to Boost Individual and Group Morale." *Research Management* vol. 28, no. 4 (July 1978):30, 31.

Kornhauser, Arthur. "Psychological Studies of Employee Attitudes." *Personnel* vol. 21, no. 3 (November 1944):170–89.

Palmer, Robin. "A Participative Approach to Attitude Surveys." *Personnel Management* vol. 9, no. 12 (December 1977):26, 27 ff.

Prewitt, Lena B. "Discontent in the Ranks: Is the Operative Worker Really Trapped?" *Personnel Journal* vol. 52, no. 10 (October 1973):879–84.

Roach, John M. "Managing Psychological Man." *Management Review* vol. 66, no. 6 (June 1977):27–31.

Scobel, Donald N. "Doing Away With the Factory Blues." *Harvard Business Review* vol. 53, no. 6 (November/December 1975):132–42.

Sexton, William P. "Organization and Individual Needs: A Conflict?" *Personnel Journal* vol. 46, no. 6 (June 1967):337–43.

Walton, Richard E. "How to Counter Alienation in the Plant." *Harvard Business Review* vol. 50, no. 6 (November/December 1972):70–81.

6

AN EXAM FOR MRS. SMITH

Personality tests: value of tests, influence of wives on managers, ethical considerations

Incident

THE PRESIDENT OF LINCOLN, INC., asked the director of development to recommend within the organization itself the person most suitable for promotion to position of plant manager. Lincoln, a producer of textile fabrics, controlled 16 plants throughout 11 states. The position to be filled involved a plant employing 2,300 individuals in Dallas, Texas.

Extensive evaluation of personnel records revealed the name of Mr. John Smith, assistant manager of a company plant in Little Rock, Arkansas. Mr. Smith was a graduate of a leading university with a master's degree in business administration. He had six years of industrial experience and four years of military service at the time he joined the company. During his seven years with Lincoln, Inc., he had progressed rapidly and was highly regarded throughout the company.

An invitation was extended Mr. Smith to visit the central office in Philadelphia, Pennsylvania. Company officials requested him to bring along his wife so that they might meet her. The president welcomed the Smiths at the airport and escorted them to his club for dinner and conversation. He was quite impressed by Mr. Smith, and with a single qualification he was inclined to offer the post of plant manager. His qualification was a recommendation to the director of development that Mrs. Smith should be requested to submit to a psychological examination before Mr. Smith was tendered a definite offer. It was the president's belief that Mrs. Smith exhibited certain traits of a neurotic or psychotic nature.

Mr. Smith was obviously offended and disturbed when he

33

learned of this suggestion. He thereupon stated that he had no intention of following the president's request. He stated further that not only did he believe that his wife's health did not bear upon his employability, but also that an apology for a serious breach of decorum was due from the president of the company. If he received no such apology, he felt he would have to submit his resignation immediately, before returning to Little Rock.

The director of development was faced with the decision of either approaching the president for an apology or of supporting him in his contention that Mrs. Smith required a psychological examination. The director decided that his personnel philosophy was closely attuned to that of the president. He accepted Mr. Smith's resignation.

Critiques

JOHN M. CHAMPION

Professor of Management and
Health Services Administration
University of Florida

Confronted with an immediate decision, the director of development chose the correct and proper course of action. The president of Lincoln, Inc., was fearful that Mrs. Smith was suffering from some mental disturbance, and he was thus within his rights in requesting a psychological examination for her. Psychologists have based much of their work on the premise that human behavior is the product of various influences such as heredity, religious and home environment, and education. Hence John Smith's wife is an influence that, conceivably, could adversely affect his performance as plant manager. It is also questionable whether Mrs. Smith is at this time capable of performing her function as a plant manager's wife.

One must also consider that Mr. Smith's behavior, upon learning of the president's request, may represent to some extent an immature reaction. To consider as insulting the president's view that Mrs. Smith is ill, and dogmatically to demand an apology, must have suggested to the director of development the undesirability of placing Mr. Smith in a position of trust, responsibility, and leadership.

Some may feel that the president created an undesirable and embarrassing incident in requiring of Mrs. Smith an examination not asked of others in the past and that, as a layman, he was not qualified to designate Mrs. Smith as neurotic. It appears, too, that the company should have anticipated the possibility of an incident such as that of Mrs. Smith and formulated a policy for this eventuality. Nevertheless, the president had no alternative course of action if, sensitive to the responsibility of his post, he was fearful that Mrs. Smith's health might affect her husband's performance as plant manager.

It is emphatically recommended that the director of development immediately reexamine and evaluate the company policy of such visits. Before another interview is planned, he should minutely examine the practices and procedures of other companies in an effort to formulate his organization's policy. The requirement of a psychological evaluation of both husband and wife by a qualified examiner should be seriously considered as a routine step in the Philadelphia visit.

WILLIAM M. FOX

Professor of Industrial
Relations and Management
University of Florida

There are several dimensions to this problem that deserve special attention. The first has to do with the inadequacy of evidence with which the president jumped to his conclusion about Mrs. Smith and the possible misinterpretation of what little evidence he had. Mr. Smith had been with the company for seven years and it is most unlikely that during this time his wife had been in limbo. Probably, discreet contact with appropriate company personnel and others would have yielded important information as to her adjustment and standing in Little Rock and elsewhere.

Even if her behavior in Philadelphia were unquestionably neurotic (and we may question the president's competence to classify it), was it the result of serious maladjustment or merely temporary anxiety based upon a different social background and overconcern for her husband's promotional chances? The president does not seem to realize that her everyday behavior in Little Rock would probably provide a much better basis for judging her stability and personality. Certainly, he has given us strong reason to suspect rashness and insensitivity to the needs of others on his part by his seeming disregard for his offense to Mr. and Mrs. Smith and failure to realize that, were he right about Mrs. Smith, he would jeopardize his chances of retaining Smith in the Little Rock position where, evidently, Mrs. Smith's qualifications were relatively irrelevant to her husband's performance!

If a discreet investigation had been conducted and the president's suspicions confirmed, and *if* it were clear that her role as a plant manager's wife would make demands upon her that would be significant to the company's interests, then a tactful discussion of the problem with Smith might have been fruitful. Such a discussion could have explored Smith's awareness of his wife's condition, the relevance of this to his present position, and its possible relevance to the proposed position, and so on. Presumably, this approach would have left an acceptable "out" to maintain the status quo as well as an opportunity to explore various courses of action . . . all without offending Smith, if handled with perception and tact (this is quite hypothetical, of course, for the president, from the little we know of him, seems incapable of this role!).

It is interesting to speculate as to whether or not the president and his chief lieutenants have ever really analyzed the basic policy issue in the case: What demands can and should the company reasonably make with regard to wives? And should certain demands be made across the board or merely with respect to certain specific positions, or both?

We are told that the director of development was faced with the decision of either approaching the president for an apology or of supporting him in his contention that Mrs. Smith require a psychological examination. What about the alternative of making the president aware of Mr. Smith's reactions, to see if he might wish to reexamine his position? There is an obvious need here to develop sound policy for present and future action.

In any event, the director of development appears oblivious to the sizable costs of losing a valuable employee and of having unfavorable publicity concerning the president's action spread throughout the company and beyond. It is unlikely that Smith will refrain from letting the cat out of the bag before his departure from the company. The insecurities and resentment this will engender will probably go a long way toward making even a reasonable approach to the questions of "wife qualifications," as well as other matters, very difficult to sell to company personnel in the future. Esprit de corps is hard to attain initially and, once forfeited, doubly hard to regain.

ALLEN R. SOLEM
Professor of Management
University of Minnesota

Frankly, I think the president should be told to go to hell, in whatever words the director chooses as long as the meaning is unmistakable. I base this on the grounds that *(a)* the president is in no sense qualified to judge the mental health of anyone and *(b)* Mrs. Smith's health is none of his business unless she or her husband ask for help, and judging from the case, the president is the last person he should go to.

Discussion items

1. In his critique Professor Champion indicates that management should have the prerogative to investigate any factor relating to the employability of a candidate for a managerial position. Do you agree or disagree? Why?

2. What responses do you have to Professor Fox's questions regarding the basic policy issues in this incident? They are:

   a. What demands can and should a company reasonably make with regard to spouses?

   b. Should certain demands be made across the board or merely with respect to certain specific positions, or both?

3. Do you think that the director of development was correct in accepting Mr. Smith's resignation? Justify your response on the basis of your own philosophy of management.

Suggested Reading List

BOOKS

Carroll, Stephen J., and **Tosi, Henry L.** *Organizational Behavior.* Chicago: St. Clair Press, 1977. Chap. 3.

Davis, Keith. *Human Behavior at Work.* 5th ed. New York: McGraw-Hill Book Co., 1977. Chaps. 11, 19, 23.

Flippo, Edwin B., and **Munsinger, Gary M.** *Management.* 4th ed. Boston: Allyn and Bacon, Inc., 1978. Chap. 9.

Jucius, Michael J. *Personnel Management.* 9th ed. Homewood, Ill.: Richard D. Irwin, Inc., 1979. Chaps. 6–10.

Kast, Fremont E., and **Rosenzweig, James E.** *Organizations and Management: A Systems Approach.* 3d ed. New York: McGraw-Hill Book Co., 1979. Chap. 16.

Koontz, Harold, and **O'Donnell, Cyril.** *Management: A Systems and Contingency Analysis of Managerial Functions.* 6th ed. New York: McGraw-Hill Book Co., 1976. Chaps. 4, 10, 19–21.

Longnecker, Justin G. *Principles of Management and Organizational Behavior.* 4th ed. Columbus, Ohio: Charles E. Merrill Publishing Co., 1977. Chap. 19.

McCormick, Ernest J., and **Tiffin, Joseph.** *Industrial Psychology.* 6th ed. Englewood Cliffs, N.J.: Prentice Hall, Inc., 1974. Chaps. 5–7.

Megginson, Leon C. *Personnel and Human Resources Administration.* 3d ed. Homewood, Ill.: Richard D. Irwin, Inc., 1977. Chaps. 11, 13.

Miner, John B. *The Management Process.* 2d ed. New York: Macmillan Publishing Co., Inc., 1978. Chap. 28.

Terry, George R. *Principles of Management.* 7th ed. Homewood, Ill.: Richard D. Irwin, Inc., 1977. Chaps. 13–16, 21.

JOURNALS

Bell, Theodore D. "Corporate Wives Can Win Friends in a New Community." *Personnel Journal* vol. 56, no. 1 (January 1977):8–10.

Business Week "Personnel Widens its Franchise" no. 2574 (February 26, 1979):116, 124.

French, Wendell L. "Psychological Testing: Some Problems and Solutions." *Personnel Administration* vol. 29, no. 2 (March/April 1966)19–24.

Ivancevich, J. H. "Control and Satisfaction in an Organizational Setting." *Academy of Management Journal* vol. 13, no. 4 (December 1970):427–36.

Kay, Emanuel. "New Alternatives for Middle Managers." *Management Review* vol. 62, no. 10 (October 1973):4–10.

Lipsett, Laurence. "What Rights of Privacy Should Job Applicants Have?" *Supervisory Management* vol. 22, no. 10 (October 1977):30–36.

Mayfield, Harold. "Executive Selection: How Much for Charm?" *Management Review* vol. 55, no. 2 (February 1966):4–10.

Moreau, David. "When War Breaks Out in the Company." *Management Review* vol. 67, no. 3 (March 1977):35, 36.

Root, W. E. "Ten Commandments of Upper Level Recruiting." *Administrative Management* vol. 34, no. 9 (September 1973):61, 62.

Stoess, Alfred W. "Conformity Behavior of Managers and Their Wives." *Academy of Management Journal* vol. 16, no. 3 (September 1973): 433–41.

Tracy, Lane. "The Control Process in Personnel Management." *Personnel Journal* vol. 55, no 9 (September 1976):446–50 ff.

Trietal, Joanne. "Your Wife: A Prisoner of Your Success?" *Management Review* vol. 61, no. 10 (October 1972):46–50.

Veiga, John F. "The Mobile Manager at Mid-Career." *Harvard Business Review* vol. 51, no. 1 (January/February 1973):115–19.

Whyte, William H., Jr. "The Fallacies of 'Personality' Testing." *Fortune* vol 50 (September 1954):117–21, 204–10.

———. "The Wives of Management." *Fortune* vol. 44 (October 1951):86–88, 204–13.

Winkler, Ronald C., and **Mathews, Theodore W.** "How Employees Feel about Personality Tests." *Personnel Journal* vol. 46, no. 8 (September 1967):490–92.

7

CHIEFLAND MEMORIAL HOSPITAL

Organization objectives and policies, authority distribution, responsibility, resolving managerial grievances

Incident

MR. JAMES A. GROVER, retired land developer and financier, is the current president of Chiefland Memorial Hospital Board of Trustees. Chiefland Memorial is a 200-bed voluntary short-term general hospital serving an area of approximately 50,000 persons. Mr. Grover has just begun a meeting with the administrator of the hospital, Mr. Edward M. Hoffman. The purpose of the meeting is to seek an acceptable solution to an apparent conflict-of-authority problem within the hospital between Hoffman and the Chief of Surgery, Dr. Lacy Young.

The problem was brought to Mr. Grover's attention by Dr. Young during a golf match between the two men. Dr. Young had challenged Mr. Grover to the golf match at the Chiefland Golf and Country Club, but it turned out that this was only an excuse for Dr. Young to discuss a hospital problem with Mr. Grover.

The problem that concerned Dr. Young involved the operating-room supervisor, Geraldine Werther, R.N. Ms. Werther schedules the hospital's operating suite in accordance with policies that she "believes" to have been established by the hospital's administration. One source of irritation to the surgeons is her attitude that maximum utilization must be made of the hospital's operating rooms if hospital costs are to be reduced. She therefore schedules in such a way that operating-room idle time is minimized. Surgeons complain that the operative schedule often does not permit them sufficient time to complete a surgical procedure in the manner they think desirable. More often than not, insufficient time is allowed between operations for effective preparation of the operating room for the next procedure. Such scheduling, the surgical staff maintains, contributes to low-quality patient care. Furthermore, some of the surgeons have complained that Ms. Werther shows favoritism in her scheduling, allowing some doctors more use of the operating suite than others.

The situation reached a crisis when Dr. Young, following an explosive confrontation with Ms. Werther, told her he was firing her. Ms. Werther then made an appeal to the hospital administrator, who in turn informed Dr. Young that discharge of nurses was an administrative prerogative. In effect, Dr. Young was told he did not have authority to fire Ms. Werther. Dr. Young asserted that he did have authority over any issue affecting medical practice and good patient care in Chiefland Hospital. He considered this a medical problem and threatened to take the matter to the hospital's board of trustees.

As the meeting between Mr. Grover and Mr. Hoffman began, Mr. Hoffman explained his position on the problem. He stressed the point that a hospital administrator is legally responsible for patient care in the hospital. He also contended that quality patient care cannot be achieved unless the board of trustees authorizes the administrator to make decisions, develop programs, formulate policies, and implement procedures. While listening to Mr. Hoffman, Mr. Grover recalled the position belligerently taken by Dr. Young, who had contended that surgical and medical doctors holding staff privileges at Chiefland would never allow a "layman" to make decisions impinging on medical practice. Young also had said that Hoffman should be told to restrict his activities to fund raising, financing, maintenance, housekeeping—administrative problems rather than medical problems. Dr. Young had then requested that Mr. Grover clarify in a definitive manner the lines of authority at Chiefland Memorial.

As Mr. Grover ended his meeting with Mr. Hoffman, the severity of the problem was unmistakably clear to him, but the solution remained quite unclear. Grover knew a decision was required—and soon.

Critiques

DAVID B. STARKWEATHER
Professor of Hospital
Administration
University of California
at Berkeley

Given the basic organizational characteristics of hospitals, this situation is quite plausible: a power structure shared by professionals invoking the authority of knowledge, administrators invoking the authority of office, and a board with the semblance of ultimate power but no practical way of making it directly operative. The situation is also typical of most organizational conflict in that there are two elements inextricably entwined: a substantive, immediate issue and a larger, longer-run contest over power. Any attempts at resolution must deal with both.

As for the immediate problem at hand, management should *attempt to bring increased rationality* to the situation.

1. Werther's statement that she is operating within policies that she "believes" to have been established by the hospital's administration suggests that there is imprecision in hospital policies that should be cleared up.
2. The allegation by surgeons that there is insufficient time to complete operations is a serious clinical matter that should be referred to the surgical department of the medical staff for review and comment to Hoffman. Likewise, the charge that scheduling practices "contribute to low-quality patient care" should be carefully documented (if possible) and investigated.
3. Even the charge of favoritism is subject to objective analysis.

As for the larger question of organizational power, management's efforts should be aimed at *clarifying authority and making it operative*. That large gray zone in hospitals between medical and administrative jurisdictions is (1) sometimes a no-person's land left to nurses and (2) more commonly a constantly shifting battlefield where both physician and administrator try to redefine organizational prerogatives into their own sphere. The contest goes on constantly and cannot be eliminated altogether. Yet it is important to clarify authority *as much as possible* (granting at the same time that it may be necessary to have some few remaining vague areas). There is a place in organizational dynamics for tacit agreement to avoid formal precision on a certain few points, on the grounds that to force the issue too far would negatively affect desired organizational relationships.

The confusion over authority between Hoffman and Chiefland's board must be clarified before the confusion between Hoffman and Young and the others can be addressed. Features of the case that make this apparent include (1) the conduct of essential hospital business on the golf course, (2) the categorical statement by Young that he has authority over any activity at Chiefland affecting medical practice, as if it were not true that virtually all activities of an administrator have such effect, and (3), most notably, the recall by Grover that physicians had previously prescribed a narrow maintenance function for the administrator, without apparent further clarification by the board at the time of Hoffman's appointment.

In the last paragraph of the incident it is unclear as to who is going to make the required decision; yet the way seems to be open for Hoffman to take the initiative. He should do so in the following way:

1. Propose a statement for board action that would both generally establish his management authorities and make clear his responsibility for Werther's employment.
2. Schedule a meeting with Young, or if not Young then with the chief of surgery and the chief of staff, at which he should outline and seek agreement on a method of inquiry into the charges of Werther's contribution to declining quality—which method should start with a commitment to writing of the complaints by Young in a memorandum to Hoffman.
3. Indicate to Werther his sole authority for her employment. (If this is not sustained by the board, Hoffman should resign, as there is no real opportunity for him at Chiefland without this recognition.)
4. Undertake a careful review of the scheduling practices regarding the use of the operating room, preferably in concert with the chief of surgery or another respected surgeon ac-

ceptable to both the chief and Hoffman. Any favoritism should be corrected immediately through new scheduling procedures.

5. Finally, once having taken this initiative, Hoffman should (1) locate a friend, in or out of the hospital, with whom he can personally discuss the whole matter and (2) maintain his sense of perspective about the whole situation regardless of the outcome.

STUART A. WESBURY, JR.

President, American College of
Hospital Administrators
Chicago

This incident describes a classic problem in hospital administration. Conflicts involving the board of trustees, medical staff, and administrator are common and an inherent characteristic of the division of authority in a hospital. However, the seriousness of the situation described in the above incident indicates that the problem is somewhat out of control.

Two basic issues must be addressed. First, Mr. Hoffman should begin a thorough investigation of the specific operating-room incident in order to seek a satisfactory resolution of the scheduling problem. Secondly, immediate steps must be taken with representatives of the board, the medical staff, and the administrator to come to an understanding as to the administrator's role in managing the affairs of the institution. No order of priority is intended by the sequencing of these two steps. In fact, both should be started immediately and carried on concurrently.

Any attempt to identify the specific problem involved carries back to the occasion of the appointment of Mr. Hoffman as administrator. Why was there not a better clarification of roles at that time? The fault lies both with the board and the administrator himself. If an understanding had been reached and made part of the operational procedures of the institution, the issue of operating-room scheduling would never have been blown up to such extensive proportions. This mistake must be rectified by carefully examining this problem and developing clear-cut policies with regard to operating authority. Of course the medical staff must be involved in this process in order that resolution of the problem be effectively communicated to and understood by all parties involved. Mr. Hoffman's integrity as administrator is certainly an issue that will pervade all discussions. The implication is present that other serious problems exist similar to the operating room situation, which makes one feel that Mr. Hoffman has not been very effective in clarifying the authority issue from his own point of view. Very simply stated, can he survive as administrator?

Much time could be spent in discussing the steps to be taken to straighten out the operating-room scheduling problem. It is obvious that the "real facts" of the case are not fully known. In fact, the description of the incident itself indicates that nothing seems to be in writing and that the nurse follows policies that she "believes" to have been established by the hospital's administration. It would appear that this is not an insurmountable problem if only the parties involved will sit down and begin working on it.

In the incident description, Mr. Hoffman was reported as stating that he is legally responsible for patient care in the hospital. This is not literally true. The responsibility for patient care rests with the board. The board through its delegation of authority will certainly place a great deal of this responsibility upon the administrator. However, again we are faced with the need to clarify this issue to the mutual satisfaction of the board, the medical staff, and the administrator.

In summary, the two primary problems of delegation of authority and the specific operating-room scheduling must be dealt with immediately and simultaneously. These steps should assure everyone that there is interest in resolving these current issues as well as in establishing long-range policies and practices that will prevent the occurrence of such problems in the future.

Discussion items

1. Professor Starkweather in his critique suggests that the way seems to be open for Mr. Hoffman to take the initiative and indicates the approach that should be taken. What is your evaluation of Professor Starkweather's recommended approach?

2. What do you think Mr. Grover should do with regard to the incident that has occurred at Chiefland Memorial Hospital? Why?
3. Should the administrator restrict his activities to problems of an administrative nature as suggested by Dr. Young? Justify your answer.

Suggested reading list

BOOKS

Burack, Elmer H. *Organization Analysis: Theory and Applications.* Hinsdale, Ill.: The Dryden Press, 1975. Chap. 2.

Davis, Keith. *Human Behavior at Work.* 5th ed. New York: McGraw-Hill Book Co., 1977. Chaps. 12, 19.

Flippo, Edwin B., and **Munsinger, Gary M.** *Management.* 4th ed. Boston: Allyn and Bacon, Inc., 1978. Chap. 24.

Hepner, James O., and **Hepner, Donna M.** *The Health Strategy Game.* St. Louis: The C. V. Mosby Co., 1973. Chap. 4.

Hershey, Nathan. *Problems in Hospital Law.* Rockville, Md.: Aspen Systems Corp., 1974. pp. 1–27, 188–204.

Kast, Fremont E., and **Rosenzweig, James E.** *Organizations and Management, A Systems Approach.* 3d ed. New York: McGraw-Hill Book Co., 1979. Chaps. 8, 9, 20.

Koontz, Harold, and **O'Donnell, Cyril.** *Management: A Systems and Contingency Analysis of Managerial Functions.* 6th ed. New York: McGraw-Hill Book Co., 1976. Part 3.

Longnecker, Justin G. *Principles of Management and Organizational Behavior.* 4th ed. Columbus, Ohio: Charles E. Merrill Publishing Co., 1977. Chaps. 11–14.

Shultz, Rockwell, and **Johnson, Alton C.** *Management of Hospitals.* New York: McGraw-Hill Book Co., 1976. Chaps. 4, 5, 8, 9.

Terry, George R. *Principles of Management.* 7th ed. Homewood, Ill.: Richard D. Irwin, Inc., 1977. Chaps. 13–16.

JOURNALS

Benge, Eugene J. "Who Should Do What? Do Your Executives Know?" *Business Management* vol. 33, no. 6 (March 1968):51–56.

Brief, Arthur P., and **Filley, Alan C.** "Selling Proposals For Change." *Business Horizons* vol. 9, no. 2 (April 1976):22–25.

Calhoon, Richard P. "The Most Difficult Person to Work with in Management." *Advanced Management Journal* vol. 32, no. 3 (July 1967):74–78.

Child, John. "Strategies of Control and Organizational Behavior." *Administrative Science Quarterly* vol. 18, no. 1 (March 1973):1–16.

Haire, Mason. "Managing Management Manpower." *Business Horizons* vol. 10, no. 4 (Winter 1967):23–28.

Hand, Herbert H., and **Hollingsworth, A. Thomas.** "Tailoring MBO to Hospitals." *Business Horizons* vol. 18, no. 1 (February 1975):45–52.

Harrison, Frank E., and **Rosenzweig, James E.** "Professional Norms and Organizational Goals." *California Management Review* vol. 14, no. 3 (Spring 1972):38–48.

Howard, Godfrey G. "Anatomy of a Hospital Trustee." *Harvard Business Review* vol. 51, no. 3 (May/June 1973):65–71.

Humphreys, Luther Wade, and **Shrode, William A.** "Decision Making Profile of Female and Male Managers." *MSU Business Topics* vol. 26, no. 4 (Fall 1978):45–51.

Laurent, André. "Managerial Subordinacy: A Neglected Aspect of Organizational Hierarchies." *Academy of Management Review* vol. 3, no. 2 (April 1978):220–30.

Litterer, Joseph A. "Conflict in Organization: A Re-examination." *Academy of Management Journal* vol. 9, no. 3 (September 1966):178–86.

Mendheim, John M. "Dealing With Executive Conflict." *Management Review* vol. 58, no. 7 (July 1969):22–28.

Miller, Floyd G. "Apply Systems Analysis to Hospital Movements." *Journal of Systems Management* vol. 24, no. 10 (October 1973):24–31.

Rice, Linda E., and **Mitchell, Terence R.** "Structural Determinants of Individual Behavior." *Administrative Science Quarterly* vol. 18, no. 1 (March 1973):56–69.

Rizzo, John R.; House, Robert J.; and **Lirtzman, Sidney J.** "Role Conflict and Ambiguity in Complex Organizations." *Administrative Science Quarterly* vol. 15, no. 2 (June 1970):150–63.

8
CONSULTANT'S REPORT

Motivation: theories, projective tests, use of consultants

Incident

THE HARLEE COMPANY, manufacturer of office supplies, decided to establish a branch plant in a large southeastern city. The plant was to be staffed with 16 managers, 34 secretaries and stenographers, and 78 skilled and semiskilled workers. Most of the managers and a few of the skilled workers were to be transferred from other plants. The remaining employees were to be obtained locally.

The position of production manager was one in which staffing was considered to be of utmost importance. Managers of Harlee decided to utilize the services of a management consulting firm for assistance, and such a firm was selected from advertisements listed in the yellow section of the telephone book. The consultants advised that candidates for the position would be administered a projective personality test and given a depth interview.

After much evaluation of personnel records three candidates were sent to the consultants. A digest of three reports, returned to Harlee within two weeks, follows:

D.M.—This candidate appears to believe the average human being has an inherent dislike for work, will avoid responsibility when possible, cannot be trusted, has little ambition, and above all desires security. Thus, D.M. thinks that all persons must be coerced, controlled, directed, and threatened with punishment or rewarded in order to obtain on-the-job efficiency.

J.C.—This candidate appears oversuspicious, possesses delusions of persecution, is beginning to lose contact with reality, and has primitive infantile needs. The prognosis is that J.C. will quite likely become an alcoholic.

F.J.—This candidate believes that all persons are kindly, inherently no-ble, self-sacrificing, well disposed at heart, and that it is possible to influence and modify the behavior of any person by logic and reason. F.J. holds that once the shortcomings of individuals are pointed out to them, they will try to correct them. F.J. is convinced that all workers are or can be made to be happy, content, and dedicated to the goals of the company for which they work.

Critiques

ROBERT T. GOLEMBIEWSKI

Research Professor of
Political Science and
Management
University of Georgia

Let us assume, first, the credibility of the consultant's report. Of course, Harlee's management should know intimately the testing and interview techniques employed by their consultant. The tenuous reliability and validity of most projective techniques, particularly, do not encourage easy acceptance of the report of any consultant, especially one chosen from the classified ads who completes three very specific analyses "within two weeks." In addition, judicial decisions cast serious doubt on the use of any testing techniques whose reliability and validity for the specific job in question have not been established beyond reasonable doubt. Harlee's management should at least be very cautious in making decisions that substantially rest on the projective tests and, even then, only after having been satisfied as to the validation research underlying the tests in relation to the position of production manager. More and more "personnel decisions" end up in the courts nowadays.

The company's purposes and structure, second, will determine the selection of the production manager. Thus, even individuals resembling J.C. have been recruited and trained to handle certain kinds of administrative programs, for example, the tragic mass murder of the Jews during World War II.

Since the Harlee Company no doubt will not provide a congenial home for J.C., the choice lies between D.M. and F.J. Two rudimentary organization charts help make this choice.

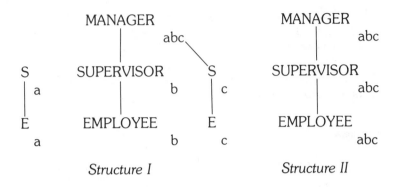

Structure I   Structure II

Many factors suggest that D.M. is well suited as a manager in Structure I. The span of control must be narrow, for only the manager "gets all the way around" the discrete subassembly abc, and he must monitor closely the three separate organization units performing each of the operations. Therefore, only trivial matters can be delegated, which is consistent with D.M.'s beliefs. In addition, supervisors would tend to "kick decisions upstairs," of which D.M. would approve. That the employees perform but a single process or operation and can be closely supervised also suit D.M.'s distrust of people.

Structure II, in contrast, requires a manager like F.J. The span of control can be very wide, and delegation can be substantial, since each supervisor controls an entire discrete subassembly. The style of supervision, consequently, can be general. Indeed, Structure II assumes that trained and motivated employees can be substantially self-controlling, an assumption reinforced by making individuals responsible for some total subassembly (as supervising or performing operations abc versus a or b or c).

The managers at Harlee did not seem impressed with these advantages of Structure II: Decisions are made closer to the action level, and probably more quickly; employees and supervisors receive valuable training; and the implied job enlargement probably will increase satisfaction and output. Notice, to support the point, that Harlee's managers planned on 112 employees and 16 managers. The span of control is seven, within the limits usually prescribed for Structure I. D.M. seems the right person for the structure that Harlee's management has in mind.

HAROLD D. JANES

Professor of Industrial
Relations
University of Alabama

There is abundant empirical research to indicate that positive leaders are "employee-centered" and democratic. They motivate people by increasing their satisfaction and believe that employees will do good work if given the opportunities and incentives. They consult with employees and multiply their abilities through other people. They have a genuine respect for people. On the other hand, they do not go so far as to believe that all people are good people in this best of all possible worlds.

The negative, autocratic, and "production-centered" type of leader attempts to motivate by domination, threats, and fear. This type of leader believes in getting the job done through reprimands and penalties. He or she believes people need to be forced to be cooperative and productive.

Production managers should possess drive and dominance. This dominance, however, should not take the negative form. There is marked agreement among contemporary industrial psychologists that successful production managers are defensive, have a decided preference for the practical over the theoretical, possess a strong self-control, yet lack insight concerning their own personality and motivations.

The merits of positive versus negative management depend upon the time factor under consideration. For immediate results the autocratic, negative approach can produce high productivity, but this is at the expense of incurring low worker morale. For long-range results (over one year) the positive type of approach is necessary.

The selection of any manager is such a responsible undertaking that all facets of the employment procedure should be examined. The digests of D.M., J.C., and F.M., were almost exclusively centered on their personality characteristics—concededly important, but lacking in such fundamental details as:

1. Past managerial successes or failures.

2. Interest patterns.
3. Motivation patterns.
4. Temperament analysis and performance traits.
5. Persuasive ability.
6. Mental adaptability.
7. Practical judgment.
8. Life adjustment.
9. Personal history.

During the 1940s and 1950s D.M. would have been effective in the job of production manager. Today, in the 1980s, the "new breed" of employees would render D.M.'s philosophy practically useless. Further, if Harlee Co. were not unionized, a management using D.M.'s philosophy and methods would almost guarantee unionization.

The Harlee Company would be well advised to take a renewed look for additional candidates. Neither D.M., J.C., nor F.J. appear to fit accepted qualifications for a production manager. Harlee officials should also examine the professional qualifications of their "telephone book" consultants. The digest reports on the three candidates are incomplete and inconclusive. These reports have a transparency that indicates a superficial appraisal on the part of the consultants.

Discussion items:

1. Which of the three candidates do you prefer? Justify your response.

2. How are the concepts of Douglas McGregor related to the decision that officials of the Harlee Company must now make in the selection of a production manager?

3. What would you recommend as the procedure that a company such as Harlee adopt for selection of their top managers?

Suggested reading list

BOOKS

Carroll, Stephen J., and **Tosi, Henry L.** *Organizational Behavior.* Chicago: St. Clair Press, 1977. Chap. 5.

Davis, Keith. *Human Behavior at Work.* 5th ed. New York: McGraw-Hill Book Co., 1977. Part 1.

Flippo, Edwin B., and **Munsinger, Gary M.** *Management.* 4th ed. Boston: Allyn and Bacon, Inc., 1978. Chap. 13.

Jucius, Michael J. *Personnel Management.* 9th ed. Homewood, Ill.: Richard D. Irwin, Inc., 1979. Chaps. 3, 8.

Kast, Fremont E., and **Rosenzweig, James E.** *Organizations and Management: A Systems Approach.* 3d ed. New York: McGraw-Hill Book Co., 1979. Chap. 10.

Longnecker, Justin G. *Principles of Management and Organizational Behavior.* 4th ed. Columbus, Ohio: Charles E. Merrill Publishing Co., 1977. Chaps. 19–22.

McCormick, Ernest J., and **Tiffin, Joseph.** *Industrial Psychology.* 6th ed. Englewood Cliffs, N.J.: Prentice Hall, Inc. 1974. Chaps. 5, 7.

McGregor, Douglas. *The Human Side of Enterprise.* New York: McGraw-Hill Book Co., 1960.

Megginson, Leon C. *Personnel and Human Resources Administration.* 3d ed. Homewood, Ill.: Richard D. Irwin, Inc., 1977. Chaps. 9–11.

Reitz, H. Joseph. *Behavior in Organizations.* Homewood, Ill.: Richard D. Irwin, Inc., 1977. Chap. 20.

Terry, George R. *Principles of Management.* 7th ed. Homewood, Ill.: Richard D. Irwin, Inc., 1977. Chaps. 13, 17, 18.

JOURNALS

Coffina, Richard M. "Management Recruitment Is a Two-Way Street." *Personnel Journal* vol. 58, no. 2 (February 1979):86–89.

Dvorak, Donald F. "ABC's of Interviewing an Executive Job Seeker." *Nation's Business* vol. 61, no. 8 (August 1973):59–60.

Gibson, James L. "Organization Theory and the Nature of Man." *Academy of Management Journal* vol. 9, no. 3 (September 1966):233–45.

Hogarth, Robin M., and **Einhorn, Hillel J.** "Optimal Strategies For Personnel Selection when Candidates Can Reject Offers." *Business Journal* vol. 49, no. 4 (October 1976):478–95.

Jauch, Lawrence R. "Systematizing the Selection Decision." *Personnel Journal* vol. 55, no. 11 (November 1976):564–67.

Jeffery, Ray. "Taking the Guesswork Out of Selection." *Personnel Management* vol. 9, no. 10 (October 1977):40, 41.

Kellogg, Marion S. "The Ethics of Employee Appraisal." *Personnel* vol. 42, no. 4 (July/August 1965):33–39.

Lawler, Edward E., III. "For a More Effective Organization—Match the Man to the Job." *Organizational Dynamics* vol. 3, no. 3 (July 1975):19–28.

Maslow, A. H. "A Theory of Human Motivation." *Psychological Review* vol. 50, no. 4 (July 1943):370–96.

Miner, John B. "The Real Crunch in Managerial Manpower." *Harvard Business Review* vol. 51, no. 6 (November/December 1973):146–58.

Sellery, Robert, Jr. "How to Hire an Executive." *Business Horizons* vol. 19, no. 2 (April 1976):26–32.

Shay, Philip W. "Ethics and Professional Practices in Management Consulting." *Advanced Management Journal* vol. 30, no. 1 (January 1965):13–20.

Stanton, Erwin S. "Do Yourself a Favor—Pick the Right Person for the Job." *Supervisory Management* vol. 19, no. 3 (March 1974):7–13.

9

CONTROVERSIAL PRESIDENT

*Executive qualities, grievance
procedures, personnel practices*

Incident

ROBERT STEVENSON, chairman of the board of directors of
Mangham Glass Corporation, had just been visited by several
other directors of the company. The latter were obviously upset
over the recent actions of the company president, Gerald O'Brien.
They demanded that the board consider firing him.

O'Brien, recently appointed to the office, had tried to improve
some management-employee labor relations problems by dealing directly with individuals and small groups as often as possible.
He felt that in this way he could focus the personal concern of
management for employees and let the employees realize that
management considered them human beings rather than
machines. One action of O'Brien had been to negotiate annual
weekly wages of the foremen with each foreman.

For several months, Paul Kelly, one of the night-shift foremen,
had been trying to arrange a late afternoon appointment to see
O'Brien about his wages. He was highly disgruntled, not only
over his failure to see the president, but also over the lack of
discussion about his wage contract prior to its being effected. As a
family man with six dependents, he felt his weekly income should
be higher than that granted him.

Last Wednesday afternoon Paul Kelly stopped by the president's office and tried to see him. O'Brien's secretary refused his
request on the grounds that O'Brien was too busy. Infuriated,
Kelly stormed into the office anyway and confronted the startled
president with demands for a better wage contract. When O'Brien
stood up and told Kelly to get out of his office and go through organization channels if he had complaints, Kelly took a swing at

the president, who in turn struck the foreman and knocked him unconscious.

Critiques

GEORGE J. GORE
Professor of Management
University of Cincinnati

President O'Brien's premise that the personnel problems were due to impersonal management would seem naive. More probably, inconsistencies in management policy and conduct should be suspected. Three areas in need of improvement are: (1) organization channels of communication; (2) wage and salary administration procedures; and (3) personnel selection and training methods.

Foreman Kelly had reason to believe his wages would be personally reviewed by the president prior to the new contract. Certainly, O'Brien's secretary had relayed his repeated requests for an appointment. Was the president evasive because he didn't want to give Kelly a forthright refusal of his request for a better contract? (If the latter's argument rested on the size of his family, he might need a more realistic understanding of the bases for wage increases.)

Or had O'Brien come to realize that presidential duties didn't leave time to fulfill his unwise plan for direct communication with the workers? Since the directors were demanding discharge, rather than wondering how to extricate an outstanding new president, his performance may have been disappointing before the incident. If he had failed to delegate authority properly, he might have become irritable and error prone as he attempted to carry out an excessive work load.

The incident could have been prevented through a systematic determination of wage and salary structures with the aid of job evaluations. This task and specific procedures for periodic review are normally functions of the Personnel Department.

On that fateful afternoon, did Paul Kelly intend to injure the president or merely need to "let off steam"? Did the receptionist treat the outraged foreman with tact? And, if the president had received his intruder with understanding, would the incident have occurred at all? Certainly, Kelly was wrong; he should be discharged for violent behavior, and the other employees must understand the justification for this. However, since the president hadn't been struck, one might wonder why he didn't try to summon help or restrain the man rather than knock him unconscious. Was the president angry or just trying to defend himself?

An executive is a decision maker and must be able to maintain emotional stability under pressure. Failure in this case has clearly damaged employee relations. Therefore, even though recently hired, his actions are grounds for discharge.

The directors should reexamine their selection methods. A candidate's training, experience, and personality can be appraised through biographical data, observations, and testing. Whether he was promoted from within or brought in from outside, O'Brien's emotional immaturity and inadequacy for office might have been revealed prior to the appointment.

A management training program including the foreman level could be helpful at Mangham Glass Corporation. A knowledge of such things as job descriptions, organization charts, and organizational behavior could have prevented this crisis.

JOHN H. JAMES
*Associate Professor of
Management
University of Florida*

The day President O'Brien established the policy of dealing "personally" with individuals and small groups instead of dealing "organizationally" with them, he set a course toward potential disaster. Every manager, and especially those at or near the top of organizations, may be most effective by using the organization structure and its resources—not by attempting to do everything personally. In a "one-man" organization, the effectiveness of both the "one man" and the organization are likely to be unsatisfactory in significant respects. Mr. O'Brien's months-long delay in meeting with Kelly may well indicate that he had stretched his time, energy, and emotional stability to a near breaking point by attempting to deal personally with too many details of the firm's operation.

The knockout punch is symptomatic of, rather than central to, the essential fact that Mr. O'Brien's efforts to solve the management-employee-relations problems of the firm have apparently escalated the difficulties. The dramatic fact that Mr. O'Brien delivered a knockout punch to foreman Kelly is probably defensible, as an isolated episode, on grounds that it was an accident or that it was done in self-defense—unless, of course, Mr. O'Brien was a trained boxer or unless he was a larger and stronger man than Kelly. In any case, the blow was provoked. But the indefensible aspect of the situation is that Mr. O'Brien, as president, established procedures, made decisions, and took actions that generated the unfortunate Kelly confrontation.

If Mr. O'Brien had taken any one of the following actions, along with announcing an "open door" policy, he would have improved the management-employee relations in the company and probably would have avoided the critical incident with Kelly.

Mr. O'Brien could have installed a grievance procedure for use by the foremen that required that a grievance be submitted in writing to the president prior to a meeting at which the grievance would be discussed. The merits of this procedure include assuring the foremen that their complaints would be reviewed and that a meeting with the president would be scheduled.

The president could have opened channels of communication more effectively than he did. Clearly he should have sent some responsive signal to Kelly during the several months that Kelly was trying to arrange an appointment. This message could have been communicated by means of the chain of command, through the inter-office mail, or by his secretary if Mr. O'Brien had chosen not to see Kelly personally.

Mr. O'Brien could have visited Kelly at his department during the night shift and thereby indicated his concern for Kelly's situation and his willingness to go out of his way to see Kelly. (Of course if Kelly had earned a reputation as a hothead and a brawler, this would not have been advisable.)

The board of directors now must carefully review Mr. O'Brien's general qualifications as a manager and determine if he is to be retained or removed from the president's post. They must decide whether O'Brien was an innocent victim of Kelly's assault or a victim of his own managerial incompetence. In arriving at their decision the board should give primary consideration to the firm's best interests and act accordingly.

Discussion items

1. Do you think that the board of directors of Mangham Glass Corporation should terminate the employment of Mr. O'Brien? Defend your answer.

2. What, in your opinion, created the situation that led to the confrontation between Mr. O'Brien and Mr. Kelly? What can be done to assure that such confrontations will not occur again?

3. What is your evaluation of Mr. O'Brien's implied "open-door" policy of dealing directly with individuals and small groups?

Suggested reading list

BOOKS

Carroll, Stephen J., and **Tosi, Henry L.** *Organizational Behavior.* Chicago: St. Clair Press, 1977. Chaps. 1, 2.

Davis, Keith. *Human Behavior at Work.* 5th ed. New York: McGraw-Hill Book Co., 1977. Chap. 11.

Donnelly, James H.; Gibson, James L.; and **Ivancevich, John M.** *Fundamentals of Management.* 3d ed. Dallas, Tex.: Business Publications, Inc., 1978. Chaps. 7, 13.

Jucius, Michael J. *Personnel Management.* 9th ed. Homewood, Ill.: Richard D. Irwin, Inc., 1979. Chaps. 15, 26, 27.

Koontz, Harold, and **O'Donnell, Cyril.** *Management: A Systems and Contingency Analysis of Managerial Functions.* 6th ed. New York: McGraw-Hill Book Co., 1976. Part 4.

Longnecker, Justin G. *Principles of Management and Organizational Behavior.* 4th ed. Columbus, Ohio: Charles E. Merrill Publishing Co., 1977. Chap. 19.

McCormick, Ernest J., and **Tiffin, Joseph.** *Industrial Psychology.* 6th ed. Englewood Cliffs, N.J.: Prentice Hall, Inc., 1974. Chaps. 12, 13.

McGregor, Douglas. *The Professional Manager.* New York: McGraw-Hill Book Co., 1967.

Megginson, Leon C. *Personnel and Human Resources Administration.* 3d ed. Homewood, Ill.: Richard D. Irwin, Inc., 1977. Chaps. 16–20.

Miner, John B. *The Management Process.* 2d ed. New York: Macmillan Publishing Co., Inc., 1978. Chaps. 22, 23.

Terry, George R. *Principles of Management.* 7th ed. Homewood, Ill.: Richard D. Irwin, Inc., 1977. Part 1.

JOURNALS

Bailey, Joseph. "Cues for Success in the President's Job." *Harvard Business Review* vol. 45, no. 3 (May/June 1967):97–104.

Conant, James C. "The Performance Appraisal." *Business Horizons* vol. 16, no. 3 (June 1973):73–78.

Cummings, L. L., and **Berger, Chris J.** "Organization Structure: How Does It Influence Attitudes and Performance?" *Organizational Dynamics* vol. 5, no. 2 (Autumn 1976):34–49.

Drucker, Peter F. "How the Effective Executive Does It." *Fortune* vol. 75, no. 2 (February 1967):140–43.

Fiedler, Fred E. "Engineer the Job to Fit the Manager." *Harvard Business Review* vol. 43, no. 5 (September/October 1965):115–22.

Fleishman, Edwin A., and **Peters, David R.** "Interpersonal Values, Leadership Attitudes, and Managerial 'Success.' " *Personnel Psychology* vol. 15, no. 2 (Summer 1962):127–43.

Gilman, Glenn. "The Managerial Profile." *Business Horizons* vol. 8, no. 2 (Summer 1965):31–44.

Howe, William C. "Appraisal Systems Measure On-the-Job Effectiveness." *Administrative Management* vol. 38, no. 5 (May 1977):26–29.

Jennings, Eugene E. "Mental Failure: Executive Crisis." *Management of Personnel Quarterly* vol. 4, no. 2 (Summer 1965):7–17.

Levinson, Harry. "The Abrasive Personality." *Harvard Business Review* vol. 56, no. 3 (May/June 1978):86–94.

———. "Who Is to Blame for Maladaptive Managers?" *Harvard Business Review* vol. 43, no. 6 (November/December 1965):143–58.

McMurry, Robert N. "Power and the Ambitious Executive." *Harvard Business Review* vol. 51, no. 6 (November/December 1973):140–45.

Rago, James J., Jr. "Executive Behavioral Cages." *Business Horizons* vol. 16, no. 1 (February 1973):29–36.

Tannenbaum, Robert, and **Schmidt, Warren H.** "How to Choose a Leadership Pattern." *Harvard Business Review* vol. 51, no. 3 (May/June 1973):162–80.

Todd, John. "Management Control Systems: A Key Link between Strategy, Structure and Employee Performance." *Organizational Dynamics* vol. 5, no. 4 (Spring 1977):65–78.

10

DECISION BY THE GROUP

Group decision making: democratic leadership, group participation

Incident

JOHN STEVENS, plant manager of the Fairlee Plant of Lockstead Corporation, attended the advanced management seminar conducted at a large midwestern university. The seminar, of four weeks' duration, was largely devoted to the topic of executive decision making.

Professor Mennon, of the university staff, particularly impressed John Stevens with his lectures on group discussion and group decision making. On the basis of research and experience, Professor Mennon was convinced that employees, if given the opportunity, could meet together, intelligently consider, and then formulate quality decisions that would be enthusiastically accepted.

Returning to his plant at the conclusion of the seminar, Mr. Stevens decided to practice some of the principles he had learned. He called together the 25 employees of Department B and told them that production standards established several years previously were now too low in view of the recent installation of automated equipment. He gave the workers the opportunity to discuss the mitigating circumstances and to decide among themselves, as a group, what their standards should be. Mr. Stevens, on leaving the room, believed that the workers would doubtlessly establish much higher standards than he himself would have dared propose.

After an hour of discussion the group summoned Mr. Stevens and notified him that, contrary to his opinion, their group decision was that the standards were already too high, and since they had been given the authority to establish their own standards, they were making a reduction of 10 percent. These standards, Mr. Stevens knew, were far too low to provide a fair profit on the owner's investment. Yet it was clear that his refusal to accept the group decision would be disastrous. Before taking a course of action, Mr. Stevens called Professor Mennon at the university for his opinion.

Critiques

J. D. FORBES
Professor of Business
History
University of Virginia

Manager Stevens told the employees that they had the authority to set standards. It would bring the company's good faith into question to override the group decision. But the manager should strongly protest the uninformed vote. His protest should take the form of a quiet presentation of the accounting picture to show that the employees themselves would suffer through the company's unprofitability if their decision went into effect. But if he is unable to get the vote changed, the Fairlee Plant of Lockstead must abide by the decision of the employees of Department B to lower production quality standards by 10 percent.

The weakness of the original proposal to introduce group decision making was that it allowed individuals to participate in a decision for which they would bear no subsequent responsibility. To have expected an unselfish decision was naive to a degree.

The employees in question had apparently received no instruction in the basic economics of management, let alone the art of decision making, but even if they had, it is doubtful whether the result would have been different.

Group decision making can have a place in employee relations, but it must be limited to issues in which the impact of the success or failure of the decision falls directly and fairly soon upon those who make it.

Mr. Stevens has the option of firing Professor Mennon either before or after hearing his opinion. It is to be earnestly hoped that Mr. Stevens will not become irrevocably soured on academicians as the result of this painful experience.

HENRY CLAY SMITH
Professor of Psychology
Michigan State University

Stevens is in a mess. How did he get there? How could he have avoided it? What should he do now?

I agree with Professor Mennon that intelligent group participation has enormous potentialities for increasing the effectiveness of company performance. Group participation is a natural by-product of a managerial philosophy, however—not a gimmick for manipulating employees. Stevens saw it as a gimmick. His use of it violated the most basic principle involved in effective group participation: The manager and the group must see that they have a common goal to work toward. Otherwise, as in this case, group participation and group decision making will result in decisions that help the group and harm the manager. The development of common goals is the outgrowth of long experience in which both sides learn to trust each other. The group was, in this case, highly and rightly suspicious of Stevens' intentions.

He could have avoided the situation by consulting with Professor Mennon *first*. He could have avoided the situation by trying his ideas out on a smaller group and on a smaller and less explosive problem. And he could have avoided the problem by talking informally with his supervisors and members of the group about his idea.

Now, unless he wishes to discard any possibility of using the power of group decision in the future, he must stick to his promise. He might well, however, use the situation as a bad start toward something better. He can tell the group where he got the idea, why he decided to try it out, what he thought would happen, and how he feels about the outcome. He should stress that he would stick to his promise if the group felt he should, but that he would like to discuss the matter at greater length to see if it were possible to work out a solution that was mutually satisfactory to both and that might be even more satisfactory to the group. Why did the group feel that the standards were too high? Was there any feasible way of rewarding the group adequately for increasing productivity? Would it be better to install the promised change in standards while alternatives were being discussed or not? Even if the group were adamant, Stevens would not have lost all. He would have learned a valuable lesson in how to do it better next time.

GEORGE R. TERRY
Late Distinguished Professor
of Business Administration
Ball State University

John Stevens should call another meeting with the production employees of Department B. In his request for this meeting he should indicate that there is additional and pertinent information concerning the subject of production standards and he wishes to offer it to the group. Next, he should get together all data dealing with the company's production standards and fair profits on the owner's investment, continuity of the enterprise, and other significant and applicable data. Preferably the additional data should be in a visual form to increase their effectiveness. Also, it is advisable for John Stevens to talk informally with leaders of Department B employees in order to disclose why the group recommended lower production standards. This information can be used by John Stevens to shape his presentation at the forthcoming meeting.

The best approach for John Stevens to follow at the meeting is:

1. Thank each member for his or her interest and past participation.

2. Advise that additional information, vital to the modification of present production standards, will be presented, this to be followed by a group discussion.

3. Present the additional information in a forthright manner.

4. Remain with the group and join in the discussion from which will evolve the basis for the decision regarding the production standards to be adopted.

The emphasis of the meeting might well be the determination of direct labor cost goals, why such goals are needed, and assistance the group members can make in establishing and achieving these goals by means of open and honest discussion and participation.

Could this problem faced by John Stevens have been avoided? Yes, I believe so. Had John Stevens *explained why* production standards are too low and not confined his initial remarks to *telling* the employees that the standards are too low, the results of the conference would certainly have been more effective. Furthermore, he should have remained with the group and discussed the subject of production standards. He failed to establish two-way communication, to exchange ideas, to air differences of opinion, and to provide reasons why certain actions could or could not be followed. Had he remained with the group, John Stevens could have stated that he has been thinking about the problem of production standards and, in his opinion, such and such should be done and then ask the group members what they think about following the approach he has outlined. The ensuing discussion will shape a suggested course of action to follow and represent the group's opinions as well as those of John Stevens as to what should be done.

It is poor practice for a manager to abdicate as John Stevens did in this incident. An important part of a manager's job is to provide effective leadership, "to show the way" by offering a plan, giving reasons for the plan, and taking into account suggestions offered by the members who will be affected by the plan. By this approach the manager's ideas, the group's wishes, and the needs of the enterprise can be blended into an effective program.

It might be that the employees are correct—that standards should be reduced. For example, errors in calculating the standards are possible. The employees must be given complete opportunity to present their reasons for recommending that the production standards be reduced.

Both facts and experience are important in determining the level of production standards adopted. John Stevens should abstain from forcing any decision. It may take several weeks or months for events to demonstrate what standards should be established, for they will be influenced, among other things, by the verification of employee major beliefs, the correctness of John Stevens's statements, the extent of modifications required, and the full comprehension of the situation by the employees.

It should be observed that the subject of raising production standards, in itself, is not a popular subject among employees. One must be quite naive to believe that an employee will accept an increase in production standards without some explanation of the reason it is requested or required. The issue in this incident could be better identified as "How can the enterprise survive?" or "How to increase our production output?" or "How to regain a strong competitive position for our company?"

One might also raise the question whether John Stevens was adequately in touch with the attitudes and beliefs of Department B employees toward their work, especially production standards. It does not appear that he is. Better communication, improved supervision, and effective leadership appear to be definitely in order.

Discussion items

1. What is the correct course of action for John Stevens to adopt? Why? What would have been the correct procedure for him to follow prior to, during, and subsequent to calling the 25 employees together?

2. Do you agree or disagree with Professor Forbes that it is "naive to a degree" to expect employees to make unselfish decisions? Why?

3. Professor Terry indicates in his critique that better communication, improved supervision, and effective leadership appear to be in order at Lockstead Corporation. On what basis do you think he makes this analysis? How can it be achieved?

Suggested reading list

BOOKS

Carroll, Stephen J., and **Tosi, Henry L.** *Organizational Behavior,* Chicago: St. Clair Press, 1977. Chap. 12.

Davis, Keith. *Human Behavior at Work.* 5th ed. New York: McGraw-Hill Book Co., 1977. Chap. 9.

Donnelly, James H.; Gibson, James L.; and Ivancevich, John M. *Fundamentals of Management,* 3d ed. Dallas, Tex.: Business Publications, Inc., 1978. Chap. 9.

Jucius, Michael J. *Personnel Management.* 9th ed. Homewood, Ill.: Richard D. Irwin, Inc., 1979. Chap. 3.

Koontz, Harold and **O'Donnell, Cyril.** *Management: A Systems and Contingency Analysis of Managerial Functions.* 6th ed. New York: McGraw-Hill Book Co., 1976. Chaps. 9, 17.

Longnecker, Justin G. *Principles of Management and Organizational Behavior.* 4th ed. Columbus, Ohio: Charles E. Merrill Publishing Co., 1977. Chaps. 8, 15.

McCormick, Ernest J., and **Tiffin, Joseph.** *Industrial Psychology.* 6th ed. Englewood Cliffs, N.J.: Prentice Hall, Inc., 1974. Chap. 14.

Megginson, Leon C. *Personnel and Human Resources Administration.* 3d ed. Homewood, Ill.: Richard D. Irwin, Inc., 1977. Chap. 15.

Miner, John G. *The Management Process.* 2d ed. New York: Macmillan Publishing Co., Inc., 1978. Chaps. 24, 25.

Reitz, H. Joseph. *Behavior in Organizations.* Homewood, Ill.: Richard D. Irwin, Inc., 1977. Chap. 15.

Terry, George R. *Principles of Management.* 7th ed. Homewood, Ill.: Richard D. Irwin, Inc., 1977. Chaps. 6, 7.

JOURNALS

Cummings, Thomas G. "Self-Regulating Work Group: A Socio-Technical Synthesis." *Academy of Management Review* vol. 3, no. 3 (July 1978):625–34.

Darr, John W. "Motivation and Morale: Two Keys to Participation." *Personnel Journal* vol. 47, no. 6 (June 1968):388–97.

Davis, Keith. "The Case for Participative Management." *Business Horizons* vol. 6, no. 3 (Fall 1963):55–60.

Donnelly, John F. "Participative Management at Work." *Harvard Business Review* vol. 55, no. 1 (January/February 1977):117–27.

Gray, Edmund R. "The Non-Linear Systems Experience: A Requiem." *Business Horizons* vol. 21, no. 1 (February 1978):31–36.

Hollander, Edwin P. "Leadership Role." *Administrative Science Quarterly* vol. 16, no. 1 (March 1971):1–5.

Lederer, Victor. "Decision Making: Should Employees Get in on the Act?" *Administrative Management* vol. 40, no. 9 (September 1978):51–62.

Locke, Edwin A. "The Ubiquity of the Technique of Goal Setting in Theories of and Approaches to Employee Motivation." *Academy of Management Review* vol. 3, no. 3 (July 1978):594–601.

Malone, Erwin L. "The Non-Linear Systems Experiment in Participative Management." *Journal of Business* vol. 48, no. 1 (January 1975):52–64.

Patchen, Martin. "Participation in Decision-Making and Motivation: What is the Relation?" *Personnel Administration* vol. 27, no. 6 (November/December 1964):24–31.

Rosenfeld, Joel M., and **Smith, Matthew, J.** "Participative Management: An Overview." *Personnel Journal* vol. 46, no. 2 (February 1967):101–04.

Rubenstein, Sidney. "Participative Problem Solving: How to Increase Organizational Effectiveness." *Personnel* vol. 54, no. 1 (January/February 1977):30–39.

Solem, Allen R. "Almost Anything I Can Do, We Can Do Better." *Personnel Administration* vol. 28, no. 6 (November/December 1965):6–16.

———. "Group Methods in Management." *Personnel Administration* vol. 27, no. 1 (January/February 1964):20–26.

Uris, Auren. "Can Employees Manage Themselves?" *Advanced Management Journal* vol. 36, no. 2 (April 1971):20–25.

11

DECISION FOR THE BOARD

Authority-responsibility: sharing responsibility,
responsibility for actions of subordinates,
job of the board of directors

Incident

THE MOTTON ELECTRONICS FIRM was widely respected in the industry as being fair, dependable, and progressive. Cy Bennett, original founder of the company, was chairman of the board and chief stockholder. One of the progressive practices of the company was to employ professional managers as members of top management. None of the top management group served as board members, but each had been carefully selected and received an excellent salary for performing his or her management job.

One month ago, William Bennett, board member and brother of the founder, reported to the board that he had facts to prove that Russell Hale, director of purchases for the company, was involved in giving preferred treatment to certain vendors and, in turn, was receiving merchandise and money for these favors. William Bennett recommended that the chairman substantiate the charges, and if found to be true as he maintained, the board should meet again to condemn formally such practices and to fire Russell Hale. The board agreed to the recommendation, and one week later Cy Bennett reported to the board that his brother's accusations had been true. The board formally condemned such purchasing practices and, by a vote of eight to nothing, fired Russell Hale. Immediately following this action, William Bennett moved that the company president be fired also. It was his opinion that the company president was responsible for any and all acts of employees on the job, and such administrative negligence should not be tolerated. After additional discussion a secret vote was taken, and the result was as follows:

                    To fire   . . . . four votes
                    To reprimand but not to fire . . four votes

   Under the by-laws of the board of directors, any tie vote was to
be broken by the chairman casting a vote.

   Cy Bennett proposed that the board take a 15-minute break
while he pondered his decision.

Critiques

ROBERT FREEDMAN, JR.
Professor of Economics
Colgate University

   What is at stake here is a theory of organization with far-reach-
ing implications for business practices in large-scale organizations.
To assume, as William Bennett does, that the president has failed
because his subordinate was untrustworthy implies a rather old-
fashioned and narrow view of the role of business leadership.
The theory implied is that an organization is simply an extension
of the executive without autonomy of any sort and, ultimately,
without any flexibility. According to the view I impute to William
Bennett, the president's job is to set up a perfectly frictionless
chain of command sensitively tuned to his wave length. Unam-
biguous orders are to be perfectly and almost instantaneously
executed by a properly designed and supervised bureaucracy. By
this standard Mr. Hale's failure was the president's.

   More recent organization theory recognizes the practical difficulties of controlling large organizations from the top in this way.
To provide subordinates with a degree of autonomy has advantages. It provides the flexibility often lacking in tightly run
bureaucracies. Also it makes possible the recruitment of good
employees. The president who has done a good job is one who
has created an organization that is both responsible to leadership
and flexible. Good leadership combines autonomy and control in
the right proportions.

   Presidents who organize their staffs this way take a calculated
risk. They must find employees whose judgment and integrity are

beyond question. Good subordinates free an executive from excessive supervision for higher level decision making. But a president so freed is likely to be less able to prevent incidents such as the one under discussion here and is in that sense "in the hands" of subordinates.

Errors of this sort are an unavoidable consequence of this newer theory of organization and are to be expected. Before accepting William Bennett's implied conclusion that the president is incompetent, I would want to know about a wider range of outcomes. It is possible that the error of hiring Mr. Hale, serious as it seemed, has been more than compensated by the existence of an otherwise well-ordered organization. On the slim evidence provided, I would be most reluctant to forego the services of a man who might otherwise be an excellent executive.

MICHAEL J. JUCIUS
Professor of Management
University of Arizona

This case raises a number of issues to which attention must be directed before Cy Bennett casts his deciding vote or asks the board to review the case again. These issues are as follows: How "responsible" is an executive for the acts of subordinates? Did the president use reasonable care in supervising subordinates? And what policies had the board established in regard to ethical practices?

Taking up the first of these issues, it is nonsense to assume that an executive is responsible for all of the acts of his subordinates while on company business. If he really were, no sensible person would accept certain positions of leadership. Otherwise he would be obligating himself in one way or another for the errors, weaknesses, and foibles that are inherent in the best of human beings. To vote against the president on the basis of such an over-all rule would be an illogical and unfair action.

This takes us then to the next issue—was the president using reasonable care in supervising his subordinates? Now we come to a more intelligent basis for reaching a decision. A man who accepts a "responsible" position should use care, reasonable, proper, and technically equated to that position. No less should we expect of him, no more can we ask. In the present incident, we are faced with a question of facts—which are unavailable—to determine if competent leadership was exercised. If the president used care pertinent to his position, he should not be condemned to discharge. If he did not, he stands on the brink of disaster, unless the final issue has some forgiving feature.

Now we come to the board of directors. Does it come to court with clean hands? Has it established, promulgated, and expected ethical behavior? Has it lived up to its own "good" policies, if the answer to the foregoing questions is yes?

If there are negative answers to the foregoing, then the board had better "resign" after it discharges the president.

But if the board has acted correctly in planning and promulgating policies, then it can in good conscience discharge the president if he did not reasonably and professionally execute the duties of his office.

In summary, to judge any executive or person at any level in the organization requires that the "law" which presumably has been violated must be fair, it must be known, the judge must be above suspicion, and the facts ascertained if justice is to be done.

Discussion items

1. How responsible is an executive for the action of subordinates? Justify your position.

2. What is legally or ethically wrong with giving preferred treatment to selected vendors and receiving favors of merchandise and money in return?

3. Draft a policy statement of the board's expectations regarding (a) ethical behavior and (b) the responsibility of superiors for the ethical behavior of their subordinates.

Suggested reading list

BOOKS

Carroll, Stephen J., and **Tosi, Henry L.** *Organizational Behavior.* Chicago: St. Clair Press, 1977. Chap. 16.

Davis, Keith. *Human Behavior at Work.* 5th ed. New York: McGraw-Hill Book Co., 1977. Part 3.

Donnelly, James H.; Gibson, James L.; and **Ivancevich, John M.** *Fundamentals of Management.* 3d ed. Dallas, Tex.: Business Publications, Inc., 1978. Chap. 5.

Filley, Alan C.; House, Robert J.; and **Kerr, Steven.** *Managerial Process and Organizational Behavior.* 2d ed. Glenview, Ill.: Scott, Foresman and Co., 1976. Chap. 9.

Flippo, Edwin B., and **Munsinger, Gary M.** *Management.* 4th ed. Boston: Allyn and Bacon, Inc., 1978. Chaps. 8, 9.

Jucius, Michael J. *Personnel Management.* 9th ed. Homewood, Ill.: Richard D. Irwin, Inc., 1979. Chap. 27.

Kast, Fremont E., and **Rosenzweig, James E.** *Organizations and Management: A Systems Approach.* 3d ed. New York: McGraw-Hill Book Co., 1979. Chaps. 6, 7.

Koontz, Harold, and **O'Donnell, Cyril.** *Management: A Systems and Contingency Analysis of Managerial Functions.* 6th ed. New York: McGraw-Hill Book Co., 1976. Part 3.

Longnecker, Justin G. *Principles of Management and Organizational Behavior.* 4th ed. Columbus, Ohio: Charles E. Merrill Publishing Co., 1977. Chap. 13.

Miner, John B. *The Management Process.* 2d ed. New York: Macmillan Publishing Co., Inc., 1978. Chaps. 14–19.

Reitz, H. Joseph. *Behavior in Organizations.* Homewood, Ill.: Richard D. Irwin, Inc., 1977.

Terry, George R. *Principles of Management.* 7th ed. Homewood, Ill.: Richard D. Irwin, Inc., 1977. Chaps. 13, 14.

JOURNALS

Bailey, Joseph. "Clues for Success in the President's Job." *Harvard Business Review* vol. 45, no. 3 (May/June 1967):97–104.

Boulton, William R. "The Evolving Board: A Look at the Board's Changing Roles and Information Needs." *Academy of Management Review* vol. 3, no. 4 (October 1978):827–36.

Donnelley, Robert G. "The Family Business." *Harvard Business Review* vol. 42, no. 4 (July/August 1964): 93–105.

Drucker, Peter F. "The Effective Decision." *Harvard Business Review* vol. 45, no. 1 (January/February 1967):92–98.

Gill, Deirdre. "Towards More Open Performance Appraisal." *Personnel Management* vol. 9, no. 12 (December 1977):31–33,ff.

Hamilton, T. M. "Clarifying Responsibility Relationships." *California Management Review* vol. 10, no. 3 (Spring 1968):41–52.

Jindal, Gopi R., and **Sandberg, Carl H.** "What it Costs to Hire a Professional." *Research Management* vol. 21, no. 4 (July 1978):26–28.

Koprowski, Eugene J. "Toward Innovative Leadership." *Business Horizons* vol. 10, no. 4 (Winter 1967):79–88.

Lauenstein, Milton C. "Classroom to Boardroom: What You Learned May Not Help You." *Business Horizons* vol. 21, no. 6 (December 1978):74–81.

McNamar, Richard T. "Building A Better Executive Team." *California Management Review* vol. 16, no. 2 (Winter 1973):59–70.

Mace, Myles L. "The Board and the New CEO." *Harvard Business Review* vol. 55, no. 2 (March/April 1977):16–20 ff.

Mueller, Robert K. "Wider Horizons for the Corporate Board." *Management Review* vol. 63, no. 1 (January 1974):4–12.

Urwick, Lyndall. "The Responsibility You Can't Escape." *Supervisory Management* vol. 6, no. 6 (June 1961):11–13.

12

DELINQUENT SUPERVISOR

Motivating supervisors: nepotism, apathy, discharge, organization problems

Incident

CHARLES WATSON, one of five supervisors in the machine accounting department of the Western Power Company and cousin to the vice president and personnel director, had shown signs of indifference and unconcern about his position for about nine months. Ms. Rogers, manager of the machine accounting department, found Watson absent from his duties within the department on two occasions. Rogers later learned through the grapevine that Watson had been wandering about, reading a newspaper, and talking to employees in other departments.

Ms. Rogers, after Watson's third unauthorized absence from his department, called him into her office and talked to him about his general attitude toward his job. She reminded him of his responsibilities to the company as an employee in a supervisory capacity. Watson apologized for his actions and promised that he would not be lax in his duties again.

Ms. Rogers, still concerned with Watson's attitude, discussed the situation with Mr. Broadman, vice president and personnel director. The next day Mr. Broadman called Watson to his office and talked to him on a very personal basis about his indifference toward his job. He reminded Watson that his being a relative made it uncomfortable for all concerned. A meeting of minds seemed to have taken place, for Watson's performance became that of a model supervisor.

About two months later Ms. Rogers had cause to visit the company's printing department. There she found Watson relaxed in a chair, working a crossword puzzle, when he should have been tending to his supervisory duties. Ms. Rogers immediately fired Watson.

The next morning Mr. Broadman called Ms. Rogers to his office and asked her why she fired an employee without going through channels and talking with higher management first. He suggested that Ms. Rogers reconsider Watson's dismissal since it set a precedent that other department managers might wish to follow.

Critiques

QUINN G. McKAY
Tandy Chair of American
Enterprise Management
Texas Christian University

In this incident there appears to be three key issues involved and also two subsidiary issues that may be explored, although there is not enough information to really come to grips with the latter two issues.

First of all, the administrative problem of designating responsibility for hiring and firing of employees is certainly unclear in this case. It seems very unlikely that Ms. Rogers would deliberately fire someone if she honestly felt she did not have the authority to do so. Mr. Broadman feels that the proper procedure in terms of firing personnel is to consult the personnel director first. These two different understandings of who has authority and responsibility to dismiss employees makes it rather conclusive that in this company there has been no clear policy outlining the extent of the department manager's responsibilities.

While there is a problem here of whether Ms. Rogers should reconsider the dismissal of Mr. Watson, it seems that this is merely a symptom of the basic problem concerning the necessity of outlining responsibilities and authority clearly. Actually, if I were Ms. Rogers, I believe it would be unwise to reconsider Mr. Watson's dismissal. I think the lesson this would teach the other employees would be that in this company it pays to have relatives at the top. If I were Ms. Rogers, I would recommend to Mr. Broadman that if he felt that Mr. Watson should be retained in this company that he be rehired in some other department and then ask for a clearer policy on authority for hiring and firing.

The second issue worth investigating is the hiring policy specifically concerning nepotism or hiring of family relations. While I am not ready to take a stand on whether relatives should be hired or not in a company, I believe the pros and cons should be thoroughly explored. I am sure in some cases it would be most appropriate to include family members in a business concern. Maybe the size of a company gives a key as to the hiring of relatives or not. This incident gives a good springboard into the ramifications of a personnel policy concerning the hiring of relatives.

The third issue deals with the concerns of the procedure for how Mr. Watson was dismissed, especially in light of the most recent developments of frequent lawsuits filed by employees who have either been disciplined or fired on the basis of discrimination. Supervisors must be more careful about their documentation on firing people. The incident does not indicate exactly how it was handled except that verbal discussions were held. In today's legal environment, the supervisor would be much wiser after each reprimand to write it down, sign it, have the employee sign it, if possible, as a warning, and then place it in the employee's folder. This kind of written documentation is often useful in warding off legal cases, and where legal cases arise, it puts management on a much more solid footing in defending its position.

The fourth issue is the possibility of exploring Ms. Rogers's activities in connection with assisting Mr. Watson. By this I mean has Ms. Rogers really done all that she should be expected to do as a superior to get Mr. Watson to perform responsibly, or has she just merely rebuked him periodically in the form of a reprimand? A significant part of a supervisor's responsibility is to develop subordinates, and it should be investigated whether Ms. Rogers has lived up to her responsibility in this regard. Again, sufficient information is not given to explore this fully, but at least the point should be raised.

Finally, the question arises in my mind: How do you measure a supervisor's performance? Again, enough information is not available, but I would surely be concerned with whether Mr. Watson's department has been falling down in terms of production or whether it is maintaining its production and Ms. Rogers is just disturbed about seeing one of her supervisors reading a newspaper on the job. In other words, is Ms. Rogers more concerned with the appearance of being a good supervisor, or is she really aware of the department's production? This, of course, opens the door to a discussion of the difficult area of measuring performance in the echelons of supervision.

WILLIAM A. PRESHING

Director of Institutional
Research and Planning
University of Alberta

While Ms. Rogers's dismissal of Mr. Watson is understandable, she is at fault in two respects. For one, she has neglected to ascertain why Mr. Watson was in the print shop. Was the latter waiting for a job to be completed or was he merely killing time? More importantly, she has fired Mr. Watson without specific advance warning, since no mention has been made of possible dismissal in the early part of the case.

A basic need is the reformulation of policy on grievance and dismissal. Mr. Broadman implies that there is a policy to govern these situations when he argues that Mr. Watson should be re-hired to prevent the establishment of a precedent. As well, policy must be established on nepotism within the organization. Here, this problem has been heightened by Ms. Rogers's earlier approach to Mr. Watson and heavily underlined by Mr. Broadman's very personalized appeal to Mr. Watson.

Mr. Broadman's influence in the organization is creating difficulties. In a staff position he is actually exerting line pressure due to his position as vice president of the company. There is little that Ms. Rogers can do to overcome this problem, but recognition of the position could make the situation liveable.

What can Ms. Rogers do at this particular point? Ms. Rogers must fight for her rights as manager of the machine accounting department. Though partially at fault, if she backs down at this stage the effect on her status will be such that she might well have to leave the company. Rehiring Mr. Watson could weaken her authority to such an extent that her position would become only marginal. However, recognition of Ms. Rogers's fight to establish her authority creates very real problems for her. Conceivably, she could lose her position and must be prepared to make this sacrifice. But, it is imperative that she fight for her right to control; if nothing else, her fight may help clarify the question of personnel policy.

Discussion items

1. What are your views regarding the "key issues" that Professor McKay discusses in his critique?

2. Was it a mistake for Mr. Broadman to talk to Watson as he did, on a personal basis, pointing out the difficulties that might arise from their being relatives? Justify your response.

3. Discuss the principle that states authority should be commensurate with responsibility. How does that principle relate to this incident?

Suggested reading list

BOOKS

Carroll, Stephen J., and **Tosi, Henry L.** *Organizational Behavior.* Chicago: St. Clair Press, 1977. Chap. 5.

Davis, Keith. *Human Behavior at Work.* 5th ed. New York: McGraw-Hill Book Co., 1977. Chaps. 7, 8.

Flippo, Edwin B., and **Munsinger, Gary M.** *Management.* 4th ed. Boston: Allyn and Bacon, Inc., 1978. Chaps. 13, 14.

Hicks, Herbert G., and **Gullett, C. Ray.** *The Management of Organizations.* 3d ed. New York: McGraw-Hill Book Co., 1976. Chaps. 21–24.

Koontz, Harold, and **O'Donnell, Cyril.** *Management: A Systems and Contingency Analysis of Managerial Functions.* 6th ed. New York: McGraw-Hill Book Co., 1976. Chaps. 10, 16.

Longnecker, Justin G. *Principles of Management and Organizational Behavior.* 4th ed. Columbus, Ohio: Charles E. Merrill Publishing Co., 1977. Chaps. 20–23.

Luthans, Fred. *Introduction to Management.* New York: McGraw-Hill Book Co., 1976. Chap. 13.

McCormick, Ernest J., and **Tiffin, Joseph.** *Industrial Psychology.* 6th ed. Englewood Cliffs, N.J.: Prentice Hall, Inc., 1974. Chap. 12.

Miner, John B. *The Management Process.* 2d ed. New York: Macmillan Publishing Co., Inc., 1978. Chaps. 20–23.

Terry, George R. *Principles of Management.* 7th ed. Homewood, Ill.: Richard D. Irwin, Inc., 1977. Chaps. 19–22.

JOURNALS

Behling, Orlando, and **Shapiro, Mitchell B.** "Motivation Theory: Source of Solution or Part of Problem?" *Business Horizons* vol. 17, no. 1 (February 1974):59–66.

Bittle, Lestor R. "Improving Supervisory Time Management." *Training and Development Journal* vol. 31, no. 9 (September 1977):25–31.

Conner, Samuel R., and **Fielden, John S.** "Rx for Managerial 'Shelf Sitters.' " *Harvard Business Review* vol. 51, no. 6 (November/December 1973):113–20.

Delong, Thomas. "What do Middle Managers Really Want From First Level Supervisors?" *Supervisory Management* vol. 22, no. 9 (September 1977):8–12.

Ewing, David W. "Is Nepotism So Bad?" *Harvard Business Review* vol. 43, no. 1 (January/February 1965):22–40, 156–60.

Fisher, John E. "Playing Favorite in Large Organizations." *Business Horizons* vol. 20, no. 3 (June 1977):68–74.

Gottfried, I. S., and **Dunn, J. D.** "Management to Manage Your Working Day." *Administrative Management* vol. 30, no. 1 (January 1969):38–40.

Hegarty, W. Harvey. "Supervisors' Reactions to Subordinates Appraisals." *Personnel* vol. 50, no. 6 (November/December 1973):30–35.

Kirkpatrick, Donald L. "How to Plan and Implement a Supervisory Training Program." *Training and Development Journal* vol. 32, no. 4 (April 1978):8–13.

Lawler, Edmund J., and **Bacharach, Samuel B.** "Power Dependence on Individual Bargaining: The Expected Utility of Influence." *Industrial and Labor Relations Review* vol. 32, no. 2 (January 1979):196–204.

Preshing, William A. "Participative Management Motivates." *Journal of Systems Management* vol. 28, no. 3 (March 1972):28–31.

Roethlisberger, F. J. "The Foreman: Master and Victim of Double Talk." *Harvard Business Review* vol. 43, no. 5 (September/October 1965):22–37, 178–84.

Schwyhart, Winston R., and **Smith, Patricia Cain.** "Factors in Job Involvement of Middle Managers." *Journal of Applied Psychology* vol. 56, no. 3 (June 1972):227–33.

Svenson, Arthur L. "Moratorium on Motivation." *Advanced Management Journal* vol. 36, no. 2 (April 1971):26–31.

Truell, George. "Where Have All the Achievers Gone?" *Personnel* vol. 50, no. 6 (November/December 1973):36–40.

13

DETERMINED LIFEGUARDS

Motivation, compensation, upward communication, group action

Incident

THE ATLANTIC COUNTY DIVISION OF BEACH SAFETY employs 100 trained lifeguards during the summer months on the county's ocean beaches. The lifeguard corps is mainly comprised of young college-age males and females who have completed specific courses in swimming, water safety, and lifesaving, and who are strong swimmers. Officials in the Division of Beach Safety have been proud of the beach patrol, and justifiably so, as it was ranked second in the nation on the quality of its job performance.

Last summer, however, the lifeguards exhibited an obvious lack of motivation and voiced complaints about the terms of their employment and working conditions, but continued to work effectively. Their discontent centered upon the issue of adequate wages. Compared with other ocean lifeguards, they were receiving one to three dollars less per hour. Compared with other Atlantic County employees, the lifeguards were the lowest on the pay scale. Entry-level secretaries, for example, received higher pay than the lifeguards.

In their effort to achieve a reasonable resolution of their low pay problem, the lifeguards met with their immediate supervisors and were told, "We can do nothing about your low pay. The Division of Beach Safety sets your wage rates, not us. We have many applicants for lifeguard jobs, and jobs are scarce in the summer. You are lucky to have your jobs. Don't rock the boat; but, if you still want to try and do something about your pay, see the head of the Division of Beach Safety or the head of the Department of Public Safety." (Refer to organization chart, Figure 1.)

After appropriate appointments had been arranged, the head officials of beach safety and public safety, accompanied by staff members, came to a meeting of the lifeguards at the main lifeguard station. In reply to demands for increased pay, Sally Wingate, head of the Department of Public Safety, stated in an easy manner, "There's nothing I can do to alter the adopted budget. Remember that volunteer lifeguards originally did your jobs. Being a lifeguard puts you where the action is and it doesn't hurt your tan, either! After all, we do pay minimum wages. You'll have to see the county administrator about any budget changes." Subsequently, a meeting with the county administrator was arranged for the following week. After hearing the lifeguards' request for increased pay and their reasons, he responded, "The county budget process is complete for this year. I assure you that we considered all budget requests fairly. Unfortunately, we are constrained by the tax dollars available." When asked about the raises included in the budget for other county employees, the administrator retorted, "Yes, sufficient funds were available to support raises for most other employees. Lifeguard 'work' can't be easily compared with the jobs of other county employees. It's different. I repeat, the budget has been finalized and approved by the county commissioners after a lot of hard work by us all. It's a tight budget with no uncommitted funds. It is set! Now, I'm ready for a swim and a little sun while I'm over here at the beach. Have a good summer."

Events moved swiftly. Feeling frustrated, rebuffed and unappreciated even though their daily work involved life-and-death situations, the lifeguards sought legal advice. Learning that they could strike without breaking the state law (because they were not unionized), the lifeguards decided to "go public" with their grievance. They decided to strike on Saturday of the Fourth-of-July weekend, the busiest of the year. They informed area newspapers and television and radio stations of their intentions.

On the designated strike day, all lifeguards showed up at the main lifeguard station and more than 75 percent of them declared support for the strike. The striking lifeguards remained in front of the main station, refusing to go to appropriate guard stations along the beach. People began to fill the beaches and the water. The probability of accidental injury and drowning increased steadily along the crowded, unguarded ocean shore. As the danger mounted, the supervisors contacted county officials who wondered how best to proceed.

FIGURE 1
COUNTY GOVERNMENT
ORGANIZATION

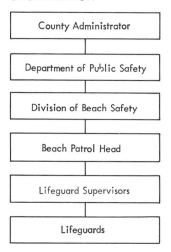

Critiques

DOROTHY N. HARLOW
Professor of Management
University of South Florida

One way to approach this incident is to answer three questions: (1) Why were the lifeguards reacting the way they were? (2) How can management's response be explained? and (3) What options exist for easing the tension in the immediate time period and for a more permanent solution? A framework useful here is the modified Lewin behavioral equation, $B = f(P, E, L)$, where the behavior (B) of interest, whether functional or dysfunctional, is a result of the kinds of people (P) in the situation, the uniqueness of the environment (E) where the interaction takes place, and the impact of the informal leaders or managers (L).

The behavior (B) of interest in this incident is the dissatisfaction with pay which culminates in a lifeguard strike or refusal to work during the busiest period of the summer season—Fourth-of-July weekend.

The people (P) of the equation are the lifeguards of Atlantic County. There are 100 of these well-trained young people, both men and women who work full time but seasonal, in the summer months. This is an effective group, ranked second nationally "on the quality of its job performance."

The environment (E) can be broken down into the kind of job being done as well as where it is performed, or its location. A skill level is required of these lifeguards as well as specified training because they must have "completed specific courses in swimming, water safety, and lifesaving, and be strong swimmers." Thus it is possible these people take their jobs seriously; they may see themselves as "professionals" rather than craftspeople or clericals because they are on the job to prevent loss of life. Their responsibilities somewhat resemble firefighters and police officers; two categories of public employees who are often underpaid. In fact, choosing the Fourth of July for their walkout is reminiscent of New Orleans police striking during Mardi Gras (1979).

These lifeguards are assigned to the ocean beach rather than a swimming pool. One difference between the two is that people often go to the beach in family groups for picnics and sunbathing and perhaps spend more time on the beach than in the water. But if a person got into trouble, it would probably take a stronger swimmer to reach them than it would if the same incident occurred in a pool where the water is clear, the area more concentrated, more assistance is available, and so forth.

By any comparison provided in the incident, these employees are underpaid: one to three dollars less per hour than beach lifeguards in other cities and the lowest paid county employees. While money seems to be valued for different reasons, a good possibility exists that these lifeguards see their low pay as an index of how little valued they are both as individuals and collectively as a group.

These lifeguards are assigned to the beach, which on any yardstick of occupational glamour must rank close to airline flight attendants and ski instructors (snow). Their immediate supervisors undoubtedly know differently, but managers more distant such as Sally Wingate, the county administrator, and the county commissioners seem to feel that lifeguards "play" rather than "work." Wingate even reminds them that historically lifeguards were volunteers—that people would do the job for "nothing," and after all they are now getting at least minimum wage. And it is a fact that under certain conditions the county actually could pay less than minimum wage.

That the lifeguards value their jobs more highly than does management—that the two groups "see" things differently—can be explained in part because of perception. People tend to find in a situation what they look for, they remember what is important to them, and so on. But it is important for management to recognize that people respond to their perceptions even if these are at variance with objective reality. Thus if county management continues to view lifeguards as "playing" rather than "working," one could predict little effort expended to push a raise request through future budget hearings. Management's philosophy and behavior are parts of the leadership factor (L) of the behavioral equation. Their perception of the kind of work lifeguards do, as just discussed, is an illustration of the potential impact leadership has for influencing employee behavior. Wingate, for example, evidently does not take seriously the efforts of these employees when she says "being a lifeguard puts you where the action is and it doesn't hurt your tan, either!" The county administrator insists that "lifeguard 'work' can't be easily compared with the jobs of other county employees. It's different."

The disgruntled employees followed the line of formal authority starting with their immediate supervisor and successively met with each higher level administrator. Each one disowns any responsibility for wage increases and insists that all of the limited tax revenue has already been earmarked for another year. "There is nothing I can do." With a common cause and the enemy now identified, what has become a cohesive group decides to "go public." The Fourth-of-July weekend is shrewdly selected for the strike. The incident concludes with county officials wondering what to do. While no level of management felt any responsibility for getting the lifeguards raises, they must now answer to the public about why there are no lifeguards on duty.

Problem Statement: How can management insure that the 75 lifeguards go to their work stations before someone gets hurt? *Alternative 1:* Do nothing and hope those who went out on strike will respond to professional pressure, both from their 25 colleagues who continue to work and their own professional conscience. The pressure to go to their stations should amplify as the number of beach patrons increases and possible danger mounts. Certainly one of the disadvantages to this approach is that management itself would be taking no steps of its own to terminate this negative behavior and would be leaving everything to chance. Neither does this alternative provide any strokes (in TA language) for the bruised ego of these employees who are not getting paid what they believe they are worth. From their perspective, for example, they probably feel they have more skills and training and perform a more important job than do beginning secretaries. *Alternative 2:* Rejecting the "do nothing and wait and see" possibility, management should be encouraged to take a course of action that resembles the following. This plan deals with the immediate crisis and provides for a possible long-term solution.

Short Run: The county commissioners, or county administrator, could contact the appropriate departments in the county to have these two things accomplished as quickly as possible: *(a)* Signs, probably easily available for all off-duty swimming hours, such as "Swim at own risk—lifeguard not on duty," should be put up along the beach. Close three fourths of the beach immediately, and send the 25 nonstriking lifeguards to the remaining and still open strip of beach. *(b)* Provide a news release to newspapers and radio and television stations describing the situation at the beach and ask the public to change their plans for beach picnics and to go instead to county and city parks.

Long Run: On the first working day after the long weekend, the county commissioners are encouraged to develop a plan that establishes a beach useage charge and the revenue used to subsidize limited tax dollars—which this year are now nonexistent. If the commissioners, for example, decide on an increase of one dollar an hour, the calculations would be: 100(number of employees) $\times$ 40 hours in work week $\times$ \$1 increase $\times$ 8 (number of weeks after July 4th estimated remaining in the swimming season) = $32,000. This would be the additional monies needed for a one dollar increase. The commissioners would then be following the wage pattern for ocean lifeguards in other cities. The new charge to beach patrons could be the average fee achieved by dividing the $32,000 (plus any additional implementing cost such as turnstyles and turnstyle operator wages) by an estimate of expected users which could be based on historical records.

Implementation Plan: The above recommendation is but an example of several possibilities that could encourage county management to think of other immediate revenue-generating ideas that would be independent of an already totally allocated tax-based budget. Lifeguard salaries for the next year could be included in the regular budget process. To implement the above proposal, the total group of lifeguards could receive the announcement at a meeting that would be called after the county commissioners approved the recommendation. Other noncost or low-cost recognitions ideas could be solicited from the employees themselves; even the now-trite "Lifeguard of the Week" award might help.

FRED LUTHANS
*Regents Professor of
Management
University of Nebraska*

This incident has several interesting aspects for motivation and human-resource management. First of all it should be recognized that there definitely is a problem here. A great majority of the lifeguards feel they are underpaid and have become so frustrated that they are willing to go on strike with the risk of someone drowning. How did they get to this point? Is pay really that important to them? How did the various levels of supervision handle the lifeguards' grievances? These are some of the obvious questions that are raised by the incident.

Employee motivation problems such as the one depicted in the incident can be analyzed from an internal or external perspective. From an internal approach it is obvious that the lifeguards' expectancies for equitable pay are not being met. This imbalance between their perceived equitable reward for their performance and their actual reward has led to considerable dissatisfaction. The solution for management is to either change the lifeguards' perceptions of equitable pay or to increase the actual pay to bring it in line with their current perceptions. The supervisors' attempts at doing this have failed. Supervisors tried to convince the lifeguards: "You are lucky to have your job" or "Being a lifeguard puts you where the action is and it doesn't hurt your tan, either" and they said that since the budget was set there was no way that wages could be increased. In other words, by taking an internal approach it can be readily explained what is going on here, but very few, if any, solutions to the problem are offered.

An external approach would concentrate on the environmental contingencies that affect the observable behaviors that are occurring in this incident. Instead of trying to analyze unobservable expectancies, perceptions, attitudes, and satisfactions of more importance would be the antecedents and, especially, consequences of observable behaviors. The consequence of the apparently good performance of the lifeguards is their supervisor telling them they are lucky to have a job and there is no way they are going to get more money. In other words, the supervisors seem to be punishing their employees for their good performance. The supervisors' words and refusal to do anything is a punishing consequence for the lifeguards' desirable performance behaviors. This will result in a decrease in performance and eventually led to them walking off the job. Obviously pay is an important consequence for these young people, but it is not the only possible reward for their efforts. The supervisors could have had a more sympathetic reaction and be more concerned with the lifeguards' request for more pay. The supervisors could have pointed out other contingent consequences of their good performance besides the pay. They may be able to appeal to the lifeguards' fine record in saving lives or provide alternative rewards such as more free time, days off, or choice of assignment/location. The supervisors could also provide specific feedback concerning their job performance (for example, absenteeism, tardiness, staying at assigned positions, compliments/complaints from patrons, saving swimmers, following procedures, socializing on the job, and so forth) and contingent recognition and attention for progress or attainment of mutually determined goals. In other words, the supervisors could have handled the guards much differently. They could have possibly prevented the problem by providing more nonfinancial rewards for effective job behaviors, and once the problem arose, they could have given a different reaction than they did. Again, it should be emphasized that there is no intention of implying that pay is not important. Pay is very important as to whether the lifeguards stay or leave their jobs now or in the future. In the long run, at least, higher wages will have to be forthcoming. But for day-to-day job behaviors, feedback and social rewards are critical to the effective performance of these lifeguards.

Discussion items

1. Consider and evaluate the options open to the county officials when the lifeguards refused to assume their appropriate guard stations on the beach.

2. As public employees, were the lifeguards justified in jeopardizing the lives of innocent citizens by use of a strike as a means of increasing their own pay? Explain your position.

3. Critique the attitudes and actions of the supervisors and other officials in the county hierarchy.

Suggested reading list

BOOKS

Donnelly, James H.; Gibson, James L.; and Ivancevich, John M. *Fundamentals of Management.* 3d ed. Dallas, Texas: Business Publications, Inc., 1978. Chap. 8.

Flippo, Edwin B., and Munsinger, Gary M. *Management.* 4th ed. Boston: Allyn and Bacon, Inc., 1978. Chaps. 10, 17, 24.

Harlow, Dorothy N., and Hanke, Jean J. *Behavior in Organizations.* Boston: Little, Brown and Co., 1975. Chaps. 2–5.

Jucius, Michael J. *Personnel Management.* 9th ed. Homewood, Ill.: Richard D. Irwin, Inc., 1979. Chaps. 16–18, 24, 26.

Katz, Daniel, and Kahn, Robert. *The Social Psychology of Organizations.* New York: John Wiley and Sons, 1966. Chap. 6.

Koontz, Harold, and **O'Donnell, Cyril.** *Management: A Systems and Contingency Analysis of Managerial Functions.* 6th ed. New York: McGraw-Hill Book Co., 1976. Chaps. 4, 26.

Luthans, Fred. *Organizational Behavior.* 2d ed. New York: McGraw-Hill Book Co., 1977. Part 4.

McCormick, Ernest J., and **Tiffin, Joseph.** *Industrial Psychology.* 6th ed. Englewood Cliffs, N.J.: Prentice Hall, Inc., 1974. Chap. 15.

Megginson, Leon C. *Personnel and Human Resources Administration.* 3d ed. Homewood, Ill.: Richard D. Irwin, Inc., 1977. Chaps. 23–25.

Porter, Lyman W., and **Lawler, Edward E.** *Managerial Attitudes and Performance.* Homewood, Ill.: Richard D. Irwin, Inc., 1968. Chaps. 4–7.

JOURNALS

Bassett, Glenn A., and **Nelson, Harlow.** "Keys to Better Salary Administration." *Personnel* vol. 44, no. 2 (March/April 1967):23–30.

Business Week ed. "Deep Sensing: A Pipeline to Employee Morale." No. 2570 (January 29, 1979): 124–28.

Caldwell, David. "Employee Motivation Under Merit Systems." *Public Personnel Management* vol. 7, no. 6 (January/February 1978):65–71.

Farr, James L.; Vance, Robert J.; and **McIntyre, Robert M.** "Further Examination of the Relationships Between Reward Contingency and Intrinsic Motivation." *Organizational Behavior and Human Performance* vol. 20, no. 1 (October 1977):31–53.

Harrington, C., Jr. "Importance of Communication to the Success of a Salary Administration Program." *Personnel Journal* vol. 14, no. 3 (March 1962):111–14.

Jago, Arthur G., and **Vroom, Victor H.** "Hierarchical Level and Leadership Style." *Organizational Behavior and Human Performance* vol. 18, no. 1 (February 1977):131–45.

King, Corwin P. "Keep Your Communication Climate Healthy." *Personnel Journal* vol. 57, no. 4 (April 1978):204–6.

Klein, Stuart M. "Pay Factors as Predictors to Satisfaction: A Comparison of Reinforcement, Equity and Expectancy." *Academy of Management Journal* vol. 16, no. 4 (December 1973):598–609.

Lawson, Theodore R. "How Much Is a Job Worth?" *Personnel* vol. 43, no. 5 (September/October 1966):16–21.

Mack, Harold. "Some Lessons in Motivation." *Supervisory Management* vol. 21, no. 8 (August 1976):2–7.

Mansfield, Roger. "Bureaucracy and Centralization: An Examination of

Organizational Structure." *Administrative Science Quarterly* vol. 18, no. 4 (December 1973):477–88.

McClelland, David C. "Money as a Motivator: Some Research Insights." *Management Review* vol. 57, no. 2 (February 1968):23–28.

Miner, Mary G. "Pay Policies: Secret or Open? And Why?" *Personnel Journal* vol. 53, no. 2 (February 1974):110–15.

Petrie, Donald J. "How to Explain the Dollars and Sense of Pay Policies." *Personnel* vol. 21, no. 3 (January/February 1976):26–32.

Tannenbaum, Arnold S., and **Kuleck, Walter J., Jr.** "The Effect on Organization Members of Discrepancy Between Perceived and Preferred Reward Implicit in Work." *Human Relations* vol. 31, no. 9 (September 1978):809–21.

14

EFFECTIVE LEADERSHIP

Leadership styles, contingency management, managerial strategies

Incident

DR. SAM PERKINS, a graduate of the Harvard University College of Medicine, was engaged in the private practice of internal medicine for 12 years. Fourteen months ago he was persuaded by the governor to give up his private practice to be director of the Public Health Section of the State Division of Human Services.

After one year as director, Dr. Perkins realized he had made little progress in reducing the considerable inefficiency that exists in the Public Health Section. Morale of the section's 250 employees seemed to be even lower than when he assumed the position. Upon reflection, Dr. Perkins realized his past training and experiences were of a clinical nature with little exposure to techniques of effective leadership. He decided to research literature published on the subject of leadership available to him at a local university.

Dr. Perkins soon realized that management scholars are divided in their opinions regarding the question of "what constitutes effective leadership?" Some feel that leaders are born with certain identifiable personality traits that cause them to be effective. Others feel a leader can learn to be effective by treating subordinates with a personal and considerate approach and by giving particular attention to the subordinate's need for good working conditions. Still others emphasize the importance of developing a style of leadership characterized by either authoritarian, democratic, or laissez-faire approaches. Dr. Perkins was confused further when he learned there is a growing number of scholars who advocate that effective leadership is contingent on the situation, and a proper response to the question of what constitutes effective leadership is that it "depends on the situation."

Dr. Perkins turned to you, the president of a nationally known management consulting firm, for assistance. He has asked that you reconcile for him this seeming lack of congruence so that he can take the steps necessary to become an effective leader. You have agreed to do so.

Critiques

ELMER H. BURACK
Professor and Head of Management
University of Illinois at
Chicago Circle

The fact that Dr. Perkins has turned to somebody, presumably an authority on leadership, may turn out to be a more important leadership fact than any referred to in the incident. Leadership's major challenge invariably involves introducing or managing change—helping people to change, changing situations to remove blockages, or paving the way to new performance levels. But regardless of the circumstances, change is not possible unless the principal involved in this case, Dr. Perkins himself, recognizes the need for change. On the other hand, there are no guarantees that effective changes will take place even if the nature of the situation and involvement of the "leader" is recognized by the leader. The causal factors may lie completely outside of his scope of influence and things may be getting worse because of organizational matters outside of the leader's control. Thus two initial lessons are to be learned here: (1) leader recognizes change has taken place (he is new head), and (2) leader recognizes that problem (may) involve(s) him. No corrections are possible without satisfying these minimal requirements. The next steps raise the question, "can Dr. Perkins acquire the necessary skills" and "does he himself want to change or introduce change(?)." Let's assume the answer to the latter is *yes*. Then the issue and leadership question is "can he acquire the needed skills to become an 'effective' leader?" Research and our observations indicate that he probably can improve sufficiently in the ways he "comes into people" and how he does things to improve his image as seen by the employees. In other words, leadership performance can be improved by those formal leaders who understand leadership situations, express greater understanding of other viewpoints, and can shift approaches as situations vary. For the most part, these types of analytical skills or approaches can be rationalized and people can practice them. Yet high levels of effective leadership as might be described by systematic analyses are probably *not* reachable through these approaches. The famous Management Progress Study at the American Telephone & Telegraph Co. suggested that certain early indicators such as performance in school, independence, and the like may give clues as to these abilities. In the Management Progress Study and subsequent studies, leadership and broader management abilities have been judged through systematic observation of applicants by trained panels of experts plus performance on various "pencil and paper" tests.

Abstracting from these observations, it appears that:

1. Particular managerial or leadership needs emerge from a specific situation involving individuals, groups, work, and organization.
2. Individual change or improvement requires recognition of this need (here, securing needed leadership qualities).
3. People must be able to change, to acquire needed skills and outlooks.
4. Various leadership characteristics can be learned.
5. High levels of leadership effectiveness probably reflect innate talents and abilities.

DENNIS F. RAY
Professor and Head of Management
Mississippi State University

The underlying problem in this incident is a situation that often plagues managers, especially those with a specialized or technical background. This is the lack of a basic understanding of the management function and the lack of basic managerial skills.

In this instance, Dr. Perkins has raised the issue of leadership style as the basic root of his difficulties. Although leadership does play a vital role in managerial effectiveness, it is clearly not the only factor. It will be necessary for Dr. Perkins to examine very carefully his qualifications and his performance in the other areas that would be very important to a manager. One classification of these other areas is the basic functions of management—planning, organizing, staffing, directing, and controlling. Besides leadership skills, a manager's success is also influenced by performances in these other functional areas.

Nevertheless, this particular incident emphasizes the issue of reconciling the various leadership theories which often appear to be inconsistent. The leadership theories that support the personal-traits concept do not effectively delineate (or identify) a basic list of traits. Even after some traits have been identified, it then becomes a question of whether or not these traits really were a part of the individual's makeup at the time of birth or have been acquired through experiences. By the time the individual is in a managerial role, it is almost impossible to separate characteristics that were original traits from those that have been acquired. Whether the traits were present at birth or acquired later, there appears to be some justification for believing that certain traits might contribute to the individual's effectiveness as a leader. Temperament traits could be an example.

The characterizing of leadership as either authoritarian, democratic, or laissez faire is only a classification of leadership styles. The more important issue seems to arise out of the controversy as to which one of these particular leadership styles is the most effective. Research has shown that either of the three listed categories might very well be effective in a particular situation.

The contingency approach to explain effective leadership is likely to be an outgrowth of the controversy over the various theories concerning leadership effectiveness. Many writers on the subject seem to have come to the conclusion that the answer to this leadership dilemma is dependent upon contingencies in the situation. Some of these contingencies would include types of individuals involved (skilled, nonskilled, professional), types of jobs being performed (routine tasks or research and development type activities), or the leadership skills possessed by the manager. These are just a few of the many contingencies that can influence the effectiveness of leadership.

If I were acting as the president of the management consulting firm contacted by Dr. Perkins, I would point out the various considerations that I have just mentioned. I would recommend that he get involved in some evaluation process to assess his own leadership style. In this way Dr. Perkins might very well discover some attitudes that have influenced his leadership effectiveness. He might also develop an understanding of the various other factors that influence his leadership effectiveness. I would also recommend to him that he consider a much broader approach to his problem in that consideration be given to developing his skills in the other functions of management as well. His problems are more likely to be solved when he reaches a higher level of competence in all the management skills.

Discussion items

1. Evaluate the validity of Professor Burack's statement that various leadership characteristics can be learned. Is this compatible with his statement that high levels of leadership effectiveness probably reflect innate talents and abilities?

2. What is the current status of research relating to the question of what constitutes effective leadership?

3. What steps should Dr. Perkins take to become an effective leader?

Suggested reading list

BOOKS

Burack, Elmer H. *Organization Analysis: Theory and Applications.* Hinsdale, Ill.: The Dryden Press, 1975. Chaps. 8, 9.

Carroll, Stephen J., and **Tosi, Henry L.** *Organizational Behavior.* Chicago: St. Clair Press, 1977. Chaps. 1, 8.

Davis, Keith. *Human Behavior at Work.* 5th ed. New York: McGraw-Hill Book Co., 1977. Chaps. 1, 4, 5, 7, 8, 26, 27.

Donnelly, James H.; Gibson, James L.; and **Ivancevich, John M.** *Fundamentals of Management.* 3d ed. Dallas, Tex.: Business Publications, Inc., 1978. Chap. 10.

Duncan, W. Jack. *Organizational Behavior.* Boston: Houghton Mifflin Co., 1978. Chap. 8.

Filley, Alan C.; House, Robert J.; and **Kerr, Steven.** *Managerial Process and Organizational Behavior.* 2d ed. Glenview, Ill.: Scott, Foresman and Co., 1976. Chaps. 11, 12.

Flippo, Edwin B., and **Munsinger, Gary M.** *Management.* 4th ed. Boston: Allyn and Bacon, Inc., 1978. Chaps. 1, 2, 15.

Kast, Fremont E., and **Rosenzweig, James. E.** *Organizations and Management: A Systems Approach.* 3d ed. New York: McGraw-Hill Book Co., 1979. Chap. 19.

Koontz, Harold, and **O'Donnell, Cyril.** *Management: A Systems and Contingency Analysis of Managerial Functions.* 6th ed. New York: McGraw-Hill Book Co., 1976. Chap. 25.

Reitz, H. Joseph. *Behavior in Organizations.* Homewood, Ill.: Richard D. Irwin, Inc., 1977. Chap. 20.

Terry, George R. *Principles of Management.* 7th ed. Homewood, Ill.: Richard D. Irwin, Inc., 1977. Chaps. 2, 19.

JOURNALS

Buckholz, Roger A. "The Work Ethic Reconsidered." *Industrial and Labor Relations Review* vol. 31, no. 4 (July 1978):450–59.

Dimarco, Nicholas J., and **Huehl, Charles R.** "Winning Moves in Motivating Junior Staff." *Advanced Management Journal* vol. 40, no. 4 (Fall 1975): 12–22.

Frew, David R. "Leadership and Followership." *Personnel Journal* vol. 56, no. 2 (February 1977):90–97.

Green, Stephen G., and **Nebeker, Delber M.** "The Effects of Situational Factors and Leadership Style on Leader Behavior." *Organizational Behavior and Human Performance* vol. 19, no. 2 (August 1977):368–77.

Hill, Thomas E., and **Schmitt, Neal.** "Individual Differences in Leadership Decision-Making." *Organizational Behavior and Human Performance* vol. 19, no. 2 (August 1977):353–67.

Hunt, J. G.; Osborn, R. N.; and **Schuler, R. S.** "Relations of Discretionary and Non-Discretionary Leadership to Performance and Satisfaction in a Complex Organization." *Human Relations* vol. 31, no. 6 (June 1978):507–23.

Johnston, Robert W. "Seven Steps to Whole Organization Development." *Training and Development Journal* vol. 33, no. 1 (January 1979):12–25.

Kotter, John P. "Power, Success and Organizational Effectiveness." *Organizational Dynamics* vol. 26, no. 40 (Winter 1978):26–40.

Kuell, Charles R. "Leader Effectiveness in Committee-Like Groups." *Business Journal* vol. 50, no. 2 (April 1977):223–25.

Reimann, Bernard C., and **Negandhi, Arant.** "Strategies of Administrative Control and Organizational Effectiveness." *Human Relations* vol. 28, no. 5 (July 1975):475–85.

Schriesheim, Chester A.; Tolliver, James M.; and **Behling, Orlando C.** "Leadership Theory: Some Implications for Managers. "*MSU Business Topics* vol. 26, no. 3 (Summer 1978):34–40.

Walters, Toy W. "Games Managers Play." *Training and Development Journal* vol. 31, no. 9 (September 1977):12–18.

Welte, Carl E. "Management and Leadership: Concepts With an Important Difference." *Personnel Journal* vol. 57, no. 11 (November 1978):630–32.

Zaleznik, Abraham. "Managers and Leaders: Are They Different?" *Harvard Business Review* vol. 55, no. 3 (May/June 1977):67–78.

15

EMPLOYEE COMPLAINT

Management's responsibility to owners and employees, alcoholism, compensation claims

Incident

JAMES SIKES, A RECENT GRADUATE of a New England university with a major in Marketing, applied for a sales position with a firm producing fabricated aluminum. In offering Sikes the position the sales manager made it clear that an essential feature of the job involved entertaining purchasing agents and that a certain amount of social drinking was necessary. Sikes assured the sales manager that he was a moderate imbiber with no moral or religious prejudices against drinking.

During the following three years James Sikes became a successful salesman and on two occasions received an award for being top salesman of the month. He found, however, that he was encountering a problem resulting from the necessity of entertaining customers at least two or three times a week. The problem was that he felt he was becoming an alcoholic, since he had recently been overindulging when not entertaining customers. The problem became progressively worse until he found himself in a constantly inebriated condition and unable to conduct business.

Sikes was sent at company expense to an alcoholic rehabilitation center, from which he was discharged after six weeks of rest and recuperation. Sikes had returned to his duties only two weeks when he was arrested in a local night club and charged with drunkenness and assault. The victim of his assault was a customer whom he had taken to the club to discuss a sale.

Company officials took an extremely dim view of the incident and fired Sikes. Shortly thereafter an attorney representing Sikes informed the president of the company, Mr. Joyce, that Sikes intended to bring legal action against the company. Sikes felt the company was liable since his alcoholism was a result of his employment. He contended that drinking was a requirement of his job, and therefore alcoholism represented an occupational hazard. Mr. Joyce appointed a committee to recommend a course of action.

Critiques

WALTER T. GREANEY, JR.
Professor and Chairman of
Management
Boston College

Two issues are involved in the Sikes case. First, has the employer any legal liability to this employee? Second, what policy can be adopted in the future for the benefit of the company and its sales force?

Legal responsibility grounded on the allegation of an occupational hazard can be easily defended by the firm. Sikes had been informed of the demands of his position. Moreover, it is common knowledge that social drinking is often a useful adjunct to the talents of salesmen. The payment for the rehabilitation period was a voluntary act from which an admission of legal responsibility cannot be inferred. Sikes had an obligation to limit his drinking to a reasonable amount. As alternatives he might have attempted to handle his work without drinking or to make provision that he quietly be served a soft drink. He has not done anything on his own to help himself. An organization such as Alcoholics Anonymous might have been very helpful.

Sikes does not appear to have the strength of character required to perform his job. All sales effort is not tied to social drinking and he should seek more suitable employment. He is a recent university graduate and undoubtedly could quickly get another job. After a short training period he should be a success. Sales ability is an individualistic talent which is not weakened by a change of employers.

The firm must look beyond the particular problem that it has with Sikes. To offer him a different type of job in the company might add frustration to his present difficulties and cause another problem for the firm. To seek a legal victory as the final solution would be a bootless goal. The firm must try to avoid such problems in the future. To this end its hiring policy should require extensive investigation of a potential salesman's adjustment to the course of his life. This would involve his family situation and his work and school histories with special emphasis on his adjustment to stress situations. On the particular aspects of alcoholism the firm can contact a large eastern university which has been conducting research on this problem in order to set up procedures for prehiring or early discovery and for periodic checks.

KARL O. MANN
*Professor of Industrial
Relations
Rider College*

The discharge of an employee has frequently been compared to capital punishment. It is the most severe form of disciplinary action and, as such, should be used only in extreme situations where the facts fully justify this penalty. Under the circumstances described in this case, the legal liability of the company with respect to James Sikes can be decided only by the courts. However, from a personnel management point of view, which seeks to improve employer-employee relations, company officials should not have fired Sikes when they learned that he had been arrested in a local night club and charged with drunkenness and assault.

It cannot be assumed that the basic cause of Sikes' alcoholism was the social drinking required by his job, although this drinking was probably a contributing and precipitating factor. Psychological research indicates that alcoholism is often associated with such factors as insecurity, personal problems, inability to cope with the environment, and lack of self-discipline. However, the company neither knew nor made an effort to find out what factors other than the job were related to Sikes becoming an alcoholic. His six weeks at an alcoholic rehabilitation center may have been sufficient to permit him to recover from his inebriated condition, but could not be expected to determine and eliminate the basic cause of his alcoholism. Yet, the company allowed Sikes to return to work without requiring further treatment and without giving him a warning. In fact, he was permitted to continue in his old job, requiring social drinking, although it is generally recognized that the arresting of alcoholism demands total abstention from alcohol and even a single drink may precipitate a return to this condition. Therefore, the company was to some extent responsible for the incident at the night club and should not have fired Sikes.

This incident might have been avoided if company officials had taken preventive action. For example, Sikes could have been required to submit to further treatment after returning from the alcoholic rehabilitation center. In addition, he could have been transferred to a job that did not require drinking. And he could have been warned that, in the future, certain offenses would result in specified penalties.

A fundamental reason for the failure of the company to act along these lines was that neither a sound disciplinary policy nor an effective policy dealing with alcoholism had been established. Consequently, the formulation of such policies should be the primary task of the committee appointed by Mr. Joyce. These policies would help to prevent similar incidents in the future and, at the same time, would permit Mr. Joyce to review the discharge of James Sikes.

Discussion items

1. What would you like to see the committee appointed by Mr. Joyce recommend in the case of James Sikes? Why?

2. Was the company justified in sending Sikes to an alcoholic rehabilitation center at its expense? Where would you draw the line?

3. What policies should be established with regard to employee alcoholism?

Suggested reading list

BOOKS

Carroll, Stephen J., and **Tosi, Henry L.** *Organizational Behavior.* Chicago: St. Clair Press, 1977. Chap. 14.

Davis, Keith. *Human Behavior at Work.* 5th ed. New York: McGraw-Hill Book Co., 1977. Chaps. 15, 23, 16.

Donnelly, James H.; Gibson, James L.; and **Ivancevich, John M.** *Fundamentals of Management.* 3d ed. Dallas, Tex.: Business Publications, Inc., 1978. Chap 17.

Filley, Alan C.; House, Robert J.; and **Kerr, Steven.** *Managerial Process and Organizational Behavior.* 2d ed. Glenview, Ill.: Scott, Foresman and Co., 1976. Chaps. 4, 6, 7.

Jucius, Michael J. *Personnel Management.* 9th ed. Homewood, Ill.: Richard D. Irwin, Inc., 1979. Chaps. 19–22.

Kast, Fremont E., and **Rosenzweig, James E.** *Organizations and Management: A Systems Approach.* 3d ed. New York: McGraw-Hill Book Co., 1979. Chaps. 6, 7.

Koontz, Harold, and **O'Donnell, Cyril.** *Management: A Systems and Contingency Analysis of Managerial Functions.* 6th ed. New York: McGraw-Hill Book Co., 1976. Part 1.

Longnecker, Justin G. *Principles of Management and Organizational Behavior.* 4th ed. Columbus, Ohio: Charles E. Merrill Publishing Co., 1977. Chap. 20.

Megginson, Leon C. *Personnel and Human Resources Administration.* 3d ed. Homewood, Ill.: Richard D. Irwin, Inc., 1977. Chap. 23.

Miner, John B. *The Management Process.* 2d ed. New York: Macmillan Publishing Co., Inc., 1978. Chap. 30.

Terry, George R. *Principles of Management.* 7th ed. Homewood, Ill.: Richard D. Irwin, Inc., 1977. Chaps. 3, 14, 19.

JOURNALS

Aikin, Olga. "Dismissal for Ill Health." *Personnel Management* vol. 9, no. 7 (July 1977):42.

Buchanan, Heydon. "How Companies Are Dealing with Alcoholism." *Personnel* vol. 43, no. 6 (November/December 1966):19–26.

Doyle, Christine. "Work and Mental Stress." *The Labour Gazette* vol. 72 (January 1972):18–24.

Dutton, Richard E. "Industry's $2-Billion Headache—The Problem Drinker." *Personnel Journal* vol. 44, no. 6 (June 1965):303–6.

Gomberg, Edith S. "Women, Work and Alcohol: A Disturbing Trend." *Supervisory Management* vol. 22, no. 12 (December 1977):16–20.

Hanson, Marlys C. "Career Development Responsibility of Managers." *Personnel Journal* vol. 56, no. 9 (September 1977):443–45.

Kane, Kervin W. "The Corporate Responsibility in the Area of Alcoholism." *Personnel Journal* vol. 54, no. 7 (July 1975):380–84.

Klein, Stanley J. "Negligent Design Can Land You in Court." *Management Review* vol. 61, no. 2 (February 1972):50–52.

Lorig, Arthur W. "Where Do Corporate Responsibilities Really Lie?" *Business Horizons* vol. 10, no. 1 (Spring 1967):51–54.

Presnall, Lewis F., and **Hersey, Robert.** "How Should We Deal with the Alcoholic Employee?" *Personnel Administration* vol. 25, no. 1 (January/February 1962):55–57.

Tansik, David A. "Influences of Organizational Goal Structures upon Participant Evaluations." *Academy of Management Journal* vol. 16, no. 2 (June 1973):265–76.

Taylor, John F. "Is the Corporation above the Law?" *Harvard Business Review* vol. 43, no. 2 (March/April 1965):119–30.

Wilson, Joseph C. "Social Responsibility of the Businessman." *Personnel* vol. 43, no. 1 (January/February 1966):17–25.

Zepke, Brent E. "What the Supervisor Should Know about Employer Liability for Intoxicated Employees." *Supervisory Management* vol. 22, no. 7 (July 1977):32–39.

FRANK P. NUMER
*Professor of Business
Administration
Robert Morris College in
Pittsburgh*

These false reports constitute fraudulent conduct—downright dishonesty—on the part of the Blue Ridge Furniture Company sales personnel. *They should be summarily dismissed.* Perhaps a rash decision, but in lieu of Watergate, bribery scandals in high places, and a generally low regard for top officials by the American public, strong action is required. The salespeople represent the company and in many cases are the only direct contacts between the company and the customers. What a tarnished image these unethical salespeople present!

Mr. Baxter did not wish to cripple the sales program by a wholesale dismissal, but he must look to the long-range sales program as well as the immediacy of the present. It will be to Mr. Baxter's advantage to recruit new sales personnel at once and start anew. He must have a first-rate sales team in order to succeed, and the first-rate qualities would include loyalty and integrity.

This deplorable situation could have been avoided, however, if the company had instituted a more alert followup sales program on the prospective accounts. The sending of a "welcome aboard" letter together with printed sales promotion literature would be a means of such control. Further, the cost department, through a ferreting-out technique could have established the trend of such fraudulent conduct on the part of the salespeople, although the basic lack of supervisory follow-up must be placed on the shoulders of the sales manager, Mr. Baxter. His delay of six months before instituting a follow-up program indicates a certain question of degree of judgment on his part. The fact that all of the salespeople participated in this devious scheme indicates the laxity of the company management in its control procedures.

In the future, all prospective accounts submitted by the sales personnel should be sent specific sales literature with a direct reference to the name of the salesperson who had submitted the account. The follow-up cycle should be reduced to either 30 days or perhaps 90 days at the most. Since "honesty is the best policy," it must be vividly demonstrated to the sales personnel of the Blue Ridge Company through immediate wholesale dismissals.

Discussion items

1. If you were Mr. Baxter, what would you decide to do about the false reports? Why?

2. What actions could have been taken to prevent the occurrence of this incident? What actions should be taken to prevent a reoccurrence?

3. Professor Numer thinks that immediate wholesale dismissals will vividly demonstrate that "honesty is the best policy." Is this an example of the "end justifying the means"? Comment.

Suggested reading list

BOOKS

Carroll, Stephen J., and **Tosi, Henry L.** *Organizational Behavior.* Chicago: St. Clair Press, 1977. Chap. 17.

Davis, Keith. *Human Behavior at Work.* 5th ed. New York: McGraw-Hill Book Co., 1977. Chaps. 24–26.

Duncan, W. Jack. *Organizational Behavior.* Boston: Houghton Mifflin Co., 1978. Chap. 7.

Jucius, Michael J. *Personnel Management.* 9th ed. Homewood, Ill.: Richard D. Irwin, Inc., 1979. Chaps. 1–5, 16–19.

Kast, Fremont E., and **Rosenzweig, James E.** *Organizations and Management: A Systems Approach.* 3d ed. New York: McGraw-Hill Book Co., 1979. Chap. 18.

Koontz, Harold, and **O'Donnell, Cyril.** *Management: A Systems and Contingency Analysis of Managerial Functions.* 6th ed. New York: McGraw-Hill Book Co., 1976. Chaps. 12–14, 27–30.

Longnecker, Justin G. *Principles of Management and Organizational Behavior.* 4th ed. Columbus, Ohio: Charles E. Merrill Publishing Co., 1977. Chaps. 24–26.

McCormick, Ernest J., and **Tiffin, Joseph.** *Industrial Psychology.* 6th ed. Englewood Cliffs, N.J.: Prentice-Hall, Inc., 1974. Chaps. 2, 3, 20.

Miner, John B. *The Management Process.* 2d ed. New York: Macmillan Publishing Co., Inc., 1978. Chaps. 20, 21.

Terry, George R. *Principles of Management.* 7th ed. Homewood, Ill.: Richard D. Irwin, Inc., 1977. Chaps. 22–24.

JOURNALS

Bromage, Mary C. "Bridging the Corporate Communications Gap." *Advanced Management Journal* vol. 41, no. 1 (Winter 1976):44–51.

Business Week ed. "More Pressure to Prosecute Executive Crime." No. 2565 (December 18, 1978):104–9.

Caruth, Donald L. "Basic Psychology for a Systems Change." *Journal of Systems Management* vol. 25, no. 2 (February 1974):10–14.

Davis, Keith. "Steps toward a More Flexible Disciplinary Policy." *Personnel* vol. 38, no. 3 (May/June 1961):52–56.

Howard, Daniel D. "What To Do when Salesmen Run Out of Steam." *Management Review* vol. 56, no. 9 (September 1967):4–11.

Jones, Dean C. "Employee Theft in Organization." *Advanced Management Journal* vol. 37, no. 3 (July 1972):59.

Kotter, John Potter. "The Psychological Contract: Managing the Join-up Process." *California Management Review* vol. 15, no. 3 (Spring 1973):91–99.

Lindo, David K. "How to Manage Your Far Away Staff." *Administrative Management* vol. 39, no. 5 (May 1978):28–30.

Livingstone, John L. "Management Controls and Organizational Performance." *Personnel Administration* vol. 28, no. 1 (January/February 1965):37–43.

McGregor, Douglas. "Do Management Control Systems Achieve Their Purpose?" *Management Review* vol. 56, no. 2 (February 1967):5–18.

McMahon, J. Timothy, and **Perrit, G. W.** "Toward a Contingency Theory of Organizational Control." *Academy of Management Journal* vol. 16, no. 4 (December 1973):624–35.

O'Reilly, Charles A., III. "The Intentional Distortion of Information in Organizational Communication: A Laboratory and Field Investigation." *Human Relations* vol. 31, no. 2 (February 1978):173–93.

Schiffer, Richard L. "Some Guideposts for Administering Discipline." *Personnel* vol. 38, no. 1 (January/February 1961):32–38.

Vancil, R. F. "What Kind of Management Control Do You Need?" *Harvard Business Review* vol. 51, no. 2 (March/April 1973):75–86.

17

FIRED FOR MOONLIGHTING

Objectives and policies, personal value structure, ethical considerations, responding to provocation

Incident

FIVE KEY EMPLOYEES of General Electronic's Brasstown plant, which employs about 1,300 persons producing and assembling printed circuit boards for computers and military equipment, were fired in late January, after company officials discovered they were starting their own business. A spokesman for the company said it learned of the group's activities on Tuesday of last week and took action to terminate their employment on Thursday.

"Company policy does not allow employees to be involved in business that could be in conflict or competition with General Electronic," said Mark Stone, manager of central operations and acting vice president for operations. He added that many of General Electronic's employees have part-time jobs on the side, "but these five people did not ask us or do this in the open. They chartered their company more than three months ago under the name of Advanced Board Circuitries, Inc., with Dale Garfield as president and the other four persons as either officers or founders of the new company."

Upon being interviewed, Dale Garfield, a six-year employee who had formerly been unit manager over engineering and production of printed circuit boards at General Electronic, said it was "self-preservation" that kept them from revealing their plans to General Electronic while working weekends and evenings on the building that houses their embryonic company and while installing equipment. He said it was "challenge" as much as anything that had provided the drive to start their own company. "We have no animosity toward General Electronic whatsoever. Every company has the prerogative to manage as it sees fit. We have no ax to grind," he stated emphatically. Garfield said his group even hoped to have a working relationship with General Electronic, possibly supplying circuit boards to the plant's assembly lines. If this worked out, the new company would be more of a supplier than a competitor to General Electronic, he believed.

Mr. Stone was careful to point out that "there is nothing illegal here as far as we know and, as far as we can determine, no business was siphoned off from General Electronic. It is", added Stone, "an unpleasant situation."

Garfield said, "We sweated blood to make that Brasstown plant one of the best in the country. But we, too, have a desire to have the best circuit board shop in the country. Maybe not the biggest, but the best."

There was no indication from Stone of any dissatisfaction with the on-the-job performance of any of the five people who had been fired. Indeed, they were viewed as key employees by the company.

On the charter of Advanced Board Circuitries, Inc., a Brasstown attorney was listed as resident agent. When contacted and asked about the firing of the people for moonlighting, he said that he had advised the group of former General Electronic employees "to make no statements concerning either their position or General Electronic's position."

Critiques

BERNARD J. BIENVENU

Professor and Head, Management
and Administrative Studies
University of Southwestern
Louisiana

The wisdom of the summary dismissal of five key employees of the General Electronic's Brasstown plant can be seriously questioned and could be symptomatic of basic management philosophy that leaves much room for disagreement. It does not appear that the decision and its possible implications were well thought out. In fact, the dismissal on Thursday after finding out about the "moonlighting" on Tuesday indicates rather hasty action. This kind of action is usually more emotional than logical and more likely to be damaging than beneficial to the organization. The action also raises the question of the right of an organization to determine the conduct of its employees on a 24-hour-a-day basis. Most certainly the employees of any organization would resent this intrusion into their private lives.

The statement by one of the fired workers that "self-preservation" kept them from revealing their plans to the company is indicative of lack of trust in General Electronics by the employees and that they do not feel they can be honest and aboveboard with the management. This is bound to thwart the upward communication so vital to effective management. It also tends to deprive the workers of concern for the company and a feeling of being a part of it, which are two essentials for good morale and productivity. The issues in this situation therefore involve much more than the dismissal of employees. They strongly suggest that the practices of management and the way they look at their workers is not in the best interests of any business. In other words, this incident is not simply a question of who was right or wrong and whether or not management was justified in its action.

Even from the short-term viewpoint and from the aspect of the decision itself, one can seriously question what the company hoped to gain by the dismissal of the five employees. They were viewed as key workers who looked upon themselves as contributing significantly to the Brasstown plant, and it would seem that the longer they remained on the payroll the better off the company would be. Also, these workers appear to have ambition, drive, and imagination, attributes that they would undoubtedly —even though perhaps unconsciously—continue to contribute to their jobs as long as they remained with General Electronics. The company admits that nothing illegal was done by the employees and that they did not take any business away from it. Their firm, Advanced Board Circuitries, Inc., even hoped to do business with General Electronic's Brasstown plant. It appears that the only reason for their action was "these five people did not ask us or do this in the open," particularly in view of Stone's admission that many General Electronic workers had part-time jobs on the side. No doubt the employees of the company will be adversely affected in their attitude toward the company and their work and will strive even harder to keep their outside activities secret from General Electronics. The incident ends with a hint that legal action against General Electronics may be forthcoming, and one would well imagine that the company already regrets its decision. Strange indeed how an established free enterprise looks upon employees who want to give birth to another free enterprise.

MAX B. JONES
Professor of Management
Old Dominion University

First, let us consider some general observations concerning the practice of moonlighting and company policies to curb the practice. Employers often are unaware of the extent to which their employees engage in moonlighting and make little or no effort to control the practice unless or until a problem develops. Even when a problem does develop, most firms probably would prefer to handle moonlighting on an individual case approach rather than become committed to an inflexible policy on the matter.

A concerted effort to track down and make an example of moonlighting practices can have some serious unsought consequences. A sudden and unexpected crackdown on moonlighting may create a general attitude of suspicion and mistrust among employees. It may also generate a feeling among employees that management is attempting to overextend its influence into employees' private lives and their freedom to use their leisure time as they best see fit. For these reasons many firms do not care to publicize their policy on moonlighting formally—if they have a policy at all. Where firms do have a policy of prohibiting moonlighting, the tendency is to restrict such policy to those situations where moonlighting (1) adversely affects work performance or (2) develops a situation involving a conflict of interest.

In this case the management of General Electronics had discharged five employees who started their own business. Discharge is a severe penalty. The management of the firm leaves itself open to a serious charge of being arbitrary and capricious when it takes such actions—unless its policy against moonlighting is clearly stated and has been communicated clearly to the employees involved. Can management establish that its policy on moonlighting was clearly stated and communicated? It not, it could expect some difficulty, particularly if the five employees were represented by an organized employee association.

Apparently the five employees do not seek to challenge the discharge, if Garfield's statements of "no animosity" and "no ax to grind" can be taken literally. It is Stone who sees the matter as "an unpleasant situation." Furthermore, there is no indication that these employees have, to date, damaged the firm or not performed as expected. For these reasons management would do well to ask itself the following questions and possibly reconsider their position on moonlighting, depending on the answers:

1. Can General Electronics afford to lose five employees with the ability and initiative to set up Advanced Board Circuitries, Inc.?
2. Garfield stated that it was the "challenge" as much as anything that led the five to set up their own business. Why could General Electronics not provide sufficient challenge to absorb their employees' energies?
3. Why did the five employees not find sufficient incentive to develop their ideas within the structure of General Electronics?

Discussion items

1. Do you agree or disagree with Garfield's statement that "every company has the prerogative to manage as it sees fit"?
2. Do employees generally have the right to engage in moonlighting? What constraints should reasonably be placed on this right, if it exists?
3. How would you respond to the three questions that Professor Jones indicates management should ask itself?

Suggested reading list

BOOKS

Carroll, Stephen J., and **Tosi, Henry L.** *Organizational Behavior.* Chicago: St. Clair Press, 1977. Chap. 11.

Davis, Keith. *Human Behavior at Work.* 5th ed. New York: McGraw-Hill Book Co., 1977. Chaps. 2, 19.

Duncan, W. Jack. *Organizational Behavior.* Boston: Houghton Mifflin Co., 1978. Chap. 9.

Flippo, Edwin B., and **Munsinger, Gary M.** *Management.* 4th ed. Boston: Allyn and Bacon, Inc., 1978. Chap. 4.

Hicks, Herbert G., and **Gullett, C. Ray.** *The Management of Organizations.* 3d ed. New York: McGraw-Hill Book Co., 1976. Chaps. 13–15.

Jucius, Michael J. *Personnel Management.* 9th ed. Homewood, Ill.: Richard D. Irwin, Inc., 1979. Chap. 27.

Kast, Fremont E., and **Rosenzweig, James E.** *Organizations and Management: A Systems Approach.* 3d ed. New York: McGraw-Hill Book Co., 1979. Chap. 6.

Koontz, Harold, and **O'Donnell, Cyril.** *Management: A Systems and Contingency Analysis of Managerial Functions.* 6th ed. New York: McGraw-Hill Book Co., 1976. Part 2.

Longnecker, Justin G. *Principles of Management and Organizational Behavior.* 4th ed. Columbus, Ohio: Charles E. Merrill Publishing Co., 1977. Chap. 5.

Miner, John B. *The Management Process.* 2d ed. New York: Macmillan Publishing Co., Inc., 1978. Chaps. 11–13, 30.

Terry, George R. *Principles of Management.* 7th ed. Homewood, Ill.: Richard D. Irwin, Inc., 1977. Chaps. 3–5.

JOURNALS

Botterman, Ralph Z., and **Schwitter, Joseph P.** "Engineer-Manager Conflicts." *Advanced Management Journal* vol. 31, no. 4 (October 1966):66–69.

Cummings, Larry L., and **El Salmi, Aly M.** "The Impact of Role Diversity, Job Level, and Organizational Size on Managerial Satisfaction." *Administrative Science Quarterly* vol. 15, no. 1 (March 1970):1–10.

Dunnettee, Marvin D.; Arvey, Richard D.; and **Banas, Paul A.** "Why Do They Leave?" *Personnel* vol. 50, no. 3 (May/June 1973):25–38.

Flowers, Vincent S., and **Hughes, Charles L.** "Why Employees Stay." *Harvard Business Review* vol. 51, no. 4 (July/August 1973):49–60.

Gilman, Glenn. "The Managerial Profile." *Business Horizons* vol. 8, no. 2 (Summer 1965):31–44.

Goodman, Steven E. "Quality of Life: The Role of Business." *Business Horizons* vol. 21, no. 3 (June 1978):36, 37.

Greiner, Larry. "Evolution and Revolution as Organizations Grow." *Harvard Business Review* vol. 50, no. 4 (July/August 1972):37–46.

Kierulff, Herbert E. "Finding and Keeping Corporate Entrepreneurs." *Business Horizons* vol. 22, no. 1 (February 1979):6–15.

Levinson, Harry. "Who Is to Blame for Maladaptive Managers?" *Harvard Business Review* vol. 43, no. 6 (November/December 1965):143–58.

Liles, Patrick R. "Who Are the Entrepreneurs?" *MSU Business Topics* vol. 22, no. 1 (Winter 1974):5–14.

McCelland, Daniel C. "Money as a Motivator: Some Research Insights." *Management Review* vol. 57, no. 2 (February 1968):23–28.

Pruden, Henry O. "The Upward Mobile, Indifferent, and Ambivalent Typology of Managers." *Academy of Management Journal* vol. 16, no. 3 (September 1973):454–64.

Rosenthal, Edmond M. "Greener Pastures: Why Employees Change Jobs." *Personnel* vol. 46, no. 1 (January/February 1969):22–30.

Shetty, Y. K. "Is There a Best Way to Organize a Business Enterprise?" *Advanced Management Journal* vol. 38, no. 2 (April 1973):47–52.

Woodward, Herbert N. "Management Strategies for Small Companies." *Harvard Business Review* vol. 54, no. 1 (January/February 1976):113–21.

18

FIERY PROVOCATION

Affirmative action, external pressure groups, social changes, organizational constraints

Incident

PLEASANTVILLE, A SOUTHEASTERN CITY of 100,000 residents, earned the coveted designation of "All-American City" last year as a progressive municipality. Among other notable accomplishments, the city has established human rights councils and has supported affirmative action and equal employment opportunity programs. In fact, the first female firefighter ever to complete training in the city recently has been assigned for duty at Fire Station No. 5. Rookie firefighter Nancy Williams was welcomed for duty as a fully qualified combat firefighter by Fire Chief Dunmore.

The firefighters' work schedule of 24 hours on duty followed by 48 hours off duty required them to eat and sleep at the fire station. Station living facilities, designed for males only, included an open bay with closely spaced single beds, one toilet, a large unpartitioned shower room, and a common kitchen for cooking and eating. The only private bedroom was assigned to and occupied by the shift lieutenant. To accommodate Ms. Williams's presence, a shower schedule was arranged to afford her solitary showering privileges, and most of the men voluntarily began wearing bathrobes over their underwear, in which it was their custom to sleep.

This system worked well and seemed satisfactory until wives of the firefighters began to complain bitterly that they didn't want another woman living with their husbands under the conditions at Fire Station No. 5. It's only a matter of time until some romance blossoms, they argued. Besides that, the wives insisted, under intimate living conditions, the presence of Ms. Williams infringed upon their husbands' right of privacy. These complaints and others became front page news in the local press. Neither the husbands nor Ms. Williams commented publicly on the issue. In rapid succession the wives banded together and hired a prominent lawyer, who implied that legal action was being considered; the city manager (see organization chart, Figure 1) stated publicly that the fire chief ran the fire department and was solely responsible for resolving the issue; and the city commissioners declared the problem to be beyond their jurisdiction under the city manager form of government.

FIGURE 1
ORGANIZATION OF FIRE DEPARTMENT

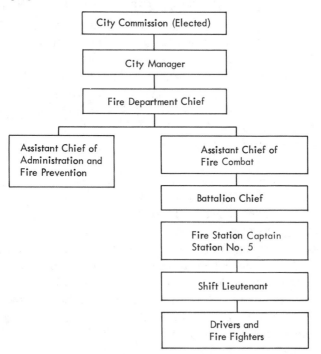

Realizing that he had been tossed the ball but not knowing what to do with it, the chief pondered his options, which included but were not limited to: reassigning Ms. Williams to the fire department's Administration and Fire Prevention unit where she would have day-shift duty only; moving the shift lieutenant out of

his private bedroom and assigning it to the female rookie firefighter; meeting personally with the wives and assuring them their
complaints were unfounded; suspending Ms. Williams from duty,
with pay, until the furor blew over; seeking a solution through the
local firefighter's union; doing nothing; or doing whatever best
would protect his position as fire chief.

As several wives of firemen began picketing Fire Station No. 5,
Chief Dunmore felt increased pressure for immediate decision
and action.

Critiques

W. JACK DUNCAN
*Professor of Management and
Associate Dean
University of Alabama in
Birmingham*

Chief Dunmore has a *hot* potato. The commission has correctly left an administrative problem to the appropriate administrative personnel. The city manager will not likely be so lucky in
"delegating" the problem.

It is tempting to approach problems of this nature from a
legalistic or moralistic perspective. Such approaches at this point
in time are of little consequence since obviously the employment
of Ms. Williams is legal and her dismissal because she is female
would be illegal. Most people would probably agree that her
employment as a firefighter is "right." Certainly, Pleasantville,
with its human rights councils, affirmative action programs, and
progressive reputation is behaving consistently with its desired
image. Therefore, these comments will attempt to look at the
management problem(s) facing Chief Dunmore and the city
manager as the municipality's chief administrative officer.

The options generated by the chief can be quickly eliminated.
Reassignment of Ms. Williams would not only be unsatisfactory to
a "qualified combat firefighter" but the avoidance of a problem
that must ultimately be confronted. Moving the lieutenant would
be counter to the entire sexual equality concept and place the city

in danger of criticism on the basis of reverse discrimination. Besides, rank has certain privileges that are indeed legitimate. Suspending Ms. Williams with pay until the trouble blows over is wishful thinking and the union is not likely to be foolish enough to get involved in a problem like this.

Probably the most challenging aspect of this problem is that the complainants are outside the organization—the wives of firemen. This complicates the issue but does not make it impossible to solve. Therefore, what should be done?

First, the fire chief and the city manager, as the administrative chief of the municipality, must determine if Pleasantville is really serious about its progressiveness. This could be done through a discussion with the commission as the elected representatives of the voters. Assuming the city is serious about human rights and affirmative action, the administrators must act not defensively but with conviction.

A favorite trick of pressure groups, especially relative to sensitive issues, is to threaten the use of a lawyer. In an effort to gain the advantage, the city manager should request a meeting with the wives and their lawyer if they choose. A good counter move would be to insist that the city attorney be present to neutralize the presence of the other lawyer.

An attempt should be made to present the city's and the fire department's position rationally. Care should be taken to explain the commitment to equality of rights and the necessity of equal hiring especially in traditionally male-dominated areas such as law and fire protection. No doubt a city such as Pleasantville has male and female partners in patrol cars that are physically proximate to one another throughout the night shift. Police departments generally employ more women in "line" positions than fire departments.

The basic problems concerning the wives is understandable. Most husbands would probably feel the same if the circumstances were reversed. The point is, however, that if equality of employment opportunities is to be a reality, inconvenient and potentially compromising situations are sure to arise. Fire departments are particularly subject to criticism because of 24-hour shifts and the fact that there are many career opportunities for women in the area. For example, a large percentage of emergency medical and paramedical personnel are female and must be available at all hours of the day and night. Therefore, sooner or later male and female assignments on all shifts in many, perhaps most jobs, is necessary for genuine equality. There simply is no other way.

It would be helpful if administrators such as the fire chief and city manager would "push" for the design of new facilities with this in mind. There is no reason why fire stations and other facilities cannot be designed with "separate but equal" facilities that ensure everyone's privacy. Hopefully, the wives will understand this rational approach. There is no way anyone can guarantee that an affair will not take place. Nor, can it be guaranteed in any other work or leisure time setting. This is one place where the city must stand its ground or concede that firefighting is really a man's world after all.

As a concluding note, it should be noted that the city's problem may be just beginning. In early 1979 a case receiving national attention related to a female firefighter in Iowa who sought to nurse her infant at the fire station during her "personal time." The wives of other firefighters once again complained and one woman firefighter in Kentucky said such behavior was "in very poor taste." Nonetheless, at the time of this writing the courts had taken the first step to enjoin the fire department from taking any further disciplinary action.

This incident is important because it highlights the reality, or the nuts and bolts, of social change. Understanding and compromising will be essential if these changes occur. The ramifications are difficult for some, but the goal seems just.

ROSEMARY PLEDGER

*Dean of the School of
Professional Studies   and
University of Houston at
Clear Lake City*

LINDA McGEE CALVERT

*Assistant Professor of
Management
University of Houston at
Clear Lake City*

The basic issue this incident forces us to consider is commitment to equality in hiring policies and the acceptance of women in nontraditional job roles. Pertinent questions to be asked are:

(1) Who sets organizational policies? (2) Who should be supporting whom in this situation? and the larger issue of, (3) What is the fire department's position on human rights? Once the overall question of commitment to equality is resolved, what to do right now becomes more straightforward.

Is this organization committed to full integration of qualified people, to equal treatment of qualified employees whatever their sex? If the answer is yes, and in today's enlightened social climate that would seem a rational answer, then the other problems become somewhat simpler. Once the decision is made, the rest is execution.

Obviously, Ms. Williams should not be suspended with pay. No, Ms. Williams, a fully qualified combat firefighter, should not be reassigned to the fire department's Administration and Fire Prevention Unit. In fact with the commitment decision made, the options no longer revolve strictly around what to do with Ms. Williams.

A broader, problem-solving approach is needed. An approach is needed that considers the impact of any decision on the organization's internal climate, as well as its immediate and future legal position. The rationale for this approach can be found in a number of relevant organizational or management theories such as systems theory and decision theory. However, the basic point is to avoid treating symptoms and start identifying the fundamental issues so that viable, long-term solutions can be found.

In the case of the fire department, a number of alternatives are available and can be implemented rather quickly, for example; (a) providing separate sleeping quarters for all the firefighters, men and women, (b) actively recruiting more women firefighters, and (c) arranging informal meetings between the various levels of employees and their immediate supervisors to discuss this problem as well as others.

Would any of these alternatives be too costly? Are they impractical? Do they compound the problems? Not if commitment to equality is to be the goal. Present societal norms dictate separate bathrooms and sleeping quarters for the two sexes. However, since the present quarters were built when women were not considered equal members of the work force, we have a dilemma.

Can we use cost as an excuse to perpetuate an outdated system? If our basic goal is equality, what is our next step?

Currently, no one in Fire Station No. 5 has any privacy. Partitioned sleeping areas and other arrangement for privacy may have been a very real need for the firefighters before Ms. Williams arrived on the scene. Private sleeping quarters for all firefighters then is one step toward improving conditions for both sexes.

Another strategy the chief could pursue is to hire more qualified women as soon as possible. Such a move would diffuse some of the attention and pressure being focused on Ms. Williams. Of course, this kind of reasoning causes the politically astute manager to simply shake his, or her, head. So, pragmatically speaking, what can be done during the next few working days? For one thing, Ms. Williams may have to stay in the shift lieutenant's bedroom (without the shift lieutenant, of course). However, the fire chief must make it clear that this is a temporary solution, both for his own credibility and to protect the lieutenant's earned status. Also tied to the issue of Ms. Williams and other women who will be hired is the anger of the wives.

A strategy that is always an option is not to do anything. This strategy may be used regarding the wives. Chief Dunmore is not likely to accomplish anything by assuring the wives that their fears are unfounded. In fact, meeting with the wives would probably compound the issues and would set a poor precedent for solving future problems. This case is a management-employee problem and should be resolved internally.

Finally, the last alternative discussed here is the more complex issue of communication. Informal meetings between various levels of the hierarchy would facilitate discussion of the immediate problem as well as other issues. Almost every organization needs to improve communication flow, both upwards and downwards. For managers, staying in touch with all levels of the organization is a form of preventive maintenance which means fewer surprises in terms of employee problems, concerns, and complaints. Furthermore, better decisions can be made with better data.

To conclude, in a committed organization the city manager and commissioners would be providing positive support for the fire chief's position. However, in this instance, Fire Chief Dunmore himself must make his decisions.

Discussion items

1. Identify advantages and disadvantages of each of the optional courses of action that are available to Chief Dunmore.
2. What course of action would you recommend be taken by Chief Dunmore?
3. Justify or challenge the action by the city commission and the city administrator in telling the chief that only he had authority to deal with the issue.

Suggested reading list

BOOKS

Burack, Elmer H. *Organization Analysis: Theory and Applications.* Hinsdale, Ill.: The Dryden Press, 1975. Chaps. 13–15.

Carroll, Stephen J., and **Tosi, Henry L.** *Organizational Behavior.* Chicago: St. Clair Press, 1977. Chap. 16.

Davis, Keith. *Human Behavior at Work.* 5th ed. New York: McGraw-Hill Book Co., 1977. Chaps. 2, 10, 16, 24.

Duncan, W. Jack. *Organizational Behavior.* Boston: Houghton Mifflin Co., 1978. Chaps. 7–9.

Flippo, Edwin B., and **Munsinger, Gary M.** *Management.* 4th ed. Boston: Allyn and Bacon, Inc., 1978. Chap. 10.

Jucius, Michael J. *Personnel Management.* 9th ed. Homewood, Ill.: Richard D. Irwin, Inc., 1979. Chap. 2.

Kast, Fremont E., and **Rosenzweig, James E.** *Organizations and Management: A Systems Approach.* 3d ed. New York: McGraw-Hill Book Co., 1979. Chap. 22.

Koontz, Harold, and **O'Donnell, Cyril.** *Management: A Systems and Contingency Analysis of Managerial Functions.* 6th ed. New York: McGraw-Hill Book Co., 1976. Chap. 4.

Longnecker, Justin G. *Principles of Management and Organizational Behavior.* 4th ed. Columbus, Ohio: Charles E. Merrill Publishing Co., 1977. Chaps. 16–18.

Megginson, Leon C. *Personnel and Human Resources Administration.* 3d ed. Homewood, Ill.: Richard D. Irwin, Inc., 1977. Chaps. 4, 7.

Terry, George R. *Principles of Management.* 7th ed. Homewood, Ill.: Richard D. Irwin, Inc., 1977. Chap. 15.

JOURNALS

Anthony, William, and **Bowen, Marshall.** "Affirmative Action: Problems and Promises." *Personnel Journal* vol. 56, no. 12 (December 1977):616–21.

Brooker, W. Michael A. "Eliminating Intergroup Conflicts through Interdepartmental Problem Solving." *Advanced Management Journal* vol. 40, no. 2 (Spring 1975):16–25.

Bunke, Harvey C. "Women Working (The Editor's Chair)." *Business Horizons* vol. 21, no. 4 (August 1978):4–8.

Dodson, Charles, and **Haskew, Barbara.** "Why Public Workers Stay." *Public Personnel Management* vol. 4, no. 2 (March/April 1976):132–38.

Emery, Douglas R., and **Tuggle, Francis D.** "On the Evaluation of Decisions." *MSU Business Topics* vol. 24, no. 2 (Spring 1976):42–48.

Gibbons, Charles C. "Marks of a Mature Manager." *Business Horizons* vol. 19, no. 5 (October 1975):54–56.

Gilbreath, Jerri D. "Sex Discrimination and Title VII of the Civil Rights Act." *Personnel Journal* vol. 56, no. 1 (January 1977):23–26.

Levinson, Robert E. "How to Conquer the Panic of Change." *Management Review* vol. 66, no. 7 (July 1977):20–24.

Likert, Rensis. "Management Styles and the Human Component." *Management Review* vol. 66, no. 10 (October 1977):23–28.

Morano, Richard A. "Managing Conflict For Problem Solving." *Personnel Journal* vol. 55, no. 8 (August 1976):393, 394.

Roach, John M. "Managing Psychological Man." *Management Review* vol. 66, no. 6 (June 1977):27, 28.

Weiss, Alan Jay. "How to Influence People Outside Your Control" *Supervisory Management* vol. 22, no. 12 (December 1977):2–9.

Yerys, Arlene. "Why Women Need Assertiveness Training." *Supervisory Management* vol. 22, no. 10 (October 1977):2–7.

19
HEROIC BANKER

Policies: formulation, flexibility, violations, communication and interpretation

Incident

AT NOON ONE DAY JACK HARVEY, a teller in a local suburban bank, was suddenly confronted by a man, pistol in hand, who demanded all the currency in the teller's cage. Harvey complied and put all his money in a paper bag. The bandit left unobtrusively through the front door, jumped in a car, and drove away. Harvey immediately sounded the alarm, ran to his own car, and pursued the bandit. Driving at high speed, he overtook the bandit, forced him to a stop, and chased him on foot until overtaking him. There ensued a struggle in which Harvey was shot in the leg, but he successfully detained the bandit until the local police arrived.

The local press gave Harvey wide coverage for his heroism. He also received recognition from various individuals and groups for his bravery. The bank officials, however, had mixed emotions about the incident. The bank had a long-standing policy that a teller, when confronted with an attempt at robbery, was to comply completely with demands, so as not to endanger employees and customers. Each teller had been further instructed to give alarm only when it was safe to do so and then to await action by police and insurance agents. Any bank employee who failed to follow this procedure would be immediately discharged.

The bank president felt that Harvey, by violating a written and well-understood policy, should be discharged. The personnel director argued that his bravery, devotion to duty, and loyalty to the bank should mitigate his infraction of policy. The director of public relations reminded the president that the public might view Harvey's discharge with misgivings since he, after all, had saved their deposits. The training director said that a dangerous precedent would be established if any exception to policy were permitted.

Critiques

WILLIAM M. FOX

*Professor of Industrial
Relations and Management
University of Florida*

Policies are not ends in themselves, but rather means to the end of facilitating the achievement of organizational objectives. Two bank objectives that are relevant to this case are avoidance of danger to employees and customers in the event of attempted robbery, and safeguarding of the deposits of the customers. Did Jack Harvey violate stated policy in any significant way, as he understood it?

He *did* comply completely with the robber's demands, thus *not* endangering employees and customers. It appears, also that he *did not* sound the alarm until it was safe to do so. Evidently, then, his only violation had to do with that part of the policy statement which required that he "await action by police and insurance agents."

It could well be that this constituted an unnecessary risk to his person and would be discouraged by the bank in view of modern theft insurance coverage. It is quite possible that the bank would face uncovered liability and very poor publicity were one of its tellers killed in such an action. Certainly, the values of such heroism to the bank and the community which prevailed in the pre-theft-insurance days of the frontier are no longer real except in a symbolic way.

To the extent that such underlying *reasons* for the last part of the policy statement had *not* been communicated to employees, it seems plausible to assume that Harvey in his own mind as well as the minds of others, was sincerely pursuing the goals of the bank while scrupulously observing the "important" part of the policy.

It would be better if the policy statement had read that "any bank employee who fails to follow this procedure will be *subject* to immediate discharge." This would publicly acknowledge the need for "breathing room" for such situations as the present one. Actually, assuming Harvey's ignorance of the reasons for the last part of the policy, he showed intelligent initiative on the bank's behalf—an admirable quality for the management to reward and nurture.

The purpose of disciplinary action is to influence the future behavior of organizational personnel along desired lines. If the assumptions above are valid (we need more information as to the manner in which the policy had been explained and Harvey's understanding of it), then commendation of Harvey's intelligent initiative "within the framework of understanding" he had at the time would be in order, as well as, a clear explanation to Harvey as well as others of why this type of action in the future would not be necessary and might prove quite disadvantageous to the bank. This approach would stand a much better chance of achieving future compliance with the policy while, at the same time, conserving and strengthening present harmonious relations.

If officials had determined that Harvey had endangered himself *despite* clear understanding of the reasons for the policy against such action, then different issues would be before us. Was Harvey an immature, publicity-seeking grandstander, or was this behavior inconsistent with usual past behavior? Is Harvey ill? If so, understanding and professional attention are needed, not disciplinary action. Whatever the case, apparently no one reserved judgement and invited Harvey to discuss the matter!

With regard to the training director's position, it seems to me that the *undesirable precedent* would be for management to make the decision without due regard to anything but the fact that a "literal" breach of policy has occurred. Any organization that commands and expects nothing more than robot-like compliance with its policies, regardless of the circumstances, is doomed to mediocrity or failure!

LOUIS J. SHUSTER

Professor of Management
California State College at
Bakersfield

The bank's policy regarding employee action during a robbery attempt fails to consider the implications of different kinds of traumatic experience. Human reactions to this type of situation cannot be prescribed by company policy. At this point in the situation, it appears that the bank officials have an obligation to commend Jack Harvey for his actions and accomplishment.

Perhaps a policy can be established that would adequately inform employees of the legalities regarding bank robberies and the implications of the hazards involved. Employees need to be urged to avoid jeopardizing themselves and others. They need to be informed of the manual processes of law enforcement in these situations. They need to be made aware of the emotional involvement of an individual committing robbery action. Perhaps the bank's employees need to be given a further understanding of the appropriate bank procedures regarding robbery attempts.

In any event Mr. Harvey's injuries are covered by Workmen's Compensation Insurance, and the time is inappropriate to look upon his action as a precedent. The determination of policies covering events of this type need to consider the reactions of an individual and his personal inclinations.

Discussion items

1.   What action do you think the bank president should take with regard to Jack Harvey's behavior? Why?

2.   If Jack Harvey is not reprimanded for violating the bank policy will it have any effect on how other employees regard policies? Explain your views.

3.   In what way should policies be communicated to employees so there can be no possibility of misunderstanding?

Suggested reading list

BOOKS

Carroll, Stephen J., and **Tosi, Henry L.** *Organizational Behavior.* Chicago: St. Clair Press, 1977. Chap. 9.

Davis, Keith. *Human Behavior at Work.* 5th ed. New York: McGraw-Hill Book Co., 1977. Chaps. 21–23.

Flippo, Edwin B., and **Munsinger, Gary M.** *Management.* 4th ed. Boston: Allyn and Bacon, Inc., 1978. Chap. 17.

Jucius, Michael J. *Personnel Management.* 9th ed. Homewood, Ill.: Richard D. Irwin, Inc., 1979. Chaps. 4, 27.

Koontz, Harold, and **O'Donnell, Cyril.** *Management: A Systems and Contingency Analysis of Managerial Functions.* 6th ed. New York: McGraw-Hill Book Co., 1976. Chaps. 10, 26.

Longnecker, Justin G. *Principles of Management and Organizational Behavior.* 4th ed. Columbus, Ohio: Charles E. Merrill Publishing Co., 1977. Chap. 23.

Megginson, Leon C. *Personnel and Human Resources Administration.* 3d ed. Homewood, Ill.: Richard D. Irwin, Inc., 1977. Chap. 23.

Miner, John B. *The Management Process.* 2d ed. New York: Macmillan Publishing Co., Inc., 1978. Chaps. 11–13.

Reitz, H. Joseph. *Behavior in Organizations.* Homewood, Ill.: Richard D. Irwin, Inc., 1977. Chap. 21.

Terry, George R. *Principles of Management.* 7th ed. Homewood, Ill.: Richard D. Irwin, Inc., 1977. Chaps. 9, 11, 20.

JOURNALS

Barton, Richard R. "Reality and Policy Decisions." *Academy of Management Journal* vol. 9, no. 2 (June 1966):117–22.

Bushnell, David S., and **Wood, William R.** "Getting Across to Your Employees." *Management Review* vol. 54, no. 8 (August 1965):53–56.

Business Week ed. "Where Skinner's Theories Work." vol. 2257 (December 1972):64–66.

Healey, James H. "Why Not a Paul Principle?" *Business Horizons* vol. 16, no. 6 (December 1973):51–54.

Henry, Kenneth. "Perspective on Public Relations." *Harvard Business Review* vol. 45, no. 4 (July/August 1967):14–26, 30–34, 162–65.

Hoover, John Edgar. "Banks Can Be Protected." *Banking* vol. 51, no. 12 (June 1959):42–43, 116–19.

Huberman, John E. "Discipline Without Punishment Lives." *Harvard Business Review* vol. 53, no. 4 (July/August 1975):6–8.

McMurry, Robert N. "Clear Communications for Chief Executives." *Harvard Business Review* vol. 43, no. 2 (March/April 1965):131–47.

Miller, Mungo. "Understanding Human Behavior and Employee Motivation." *Advanced Management Journal* vol. 33, no. 2 (April 1968):47–52.

Murray, Richard K. "Behavioral Management Objectives." *Personnel Journal* vol. 52, no. 4 (April 1973):304–6.

Myers, M. Scott. "Every Employee a Manager." *California Management Review,* vol. 10, no. 3 (Spring 1968):9–20.

Penfield, Robert V. "Identifying Effective Supervisors." *Personnel Journal* vol. 50, no. 3 (March 1971):209.

Personnel Management ed. "Fair and Effective Discipline." vol. 9, no. 2 (February 1977):5.

Schleh, Edward C. "Managing For Success: Capitalizing on Each Individual." *Advanced Management Journal* vol. 40, no. 3 (Summer 1975):13–21.

20

INDIGENOUS LEADER

Leadership types: handling grievances, listening skills, two-way communication

Incident

AT 4:45 P.M. ON FRIDAY, Mike Henry, an employee in the Machine Accounting Department, walked to the office of Mr. Herschel Jones, department head, and asked to see him privately. Henry told Mr. Jones that he had been elected by the other employees of the Machine Accounting Department, some 75 persons, to speak on their behalf about company practices which they wished modified or eliminated. One practice concerned the merit rating system, which the employees thought was unfair, poorly used, and utilized as a reason for not paying higher salaries. A second practice not well accepted by the employees was the arbitrary way in which management determined vacation time for employees. Henry said that one employee told him that last year she was given two days' notice before she received her first week of vacation in October and five days' notice before she was told that she could take off another week in April.

Mr. Jones listened attentively and told Henry that since it was so late in the day, he would consider these requests again the first part of next week. During the next week, Henry noticed that Mr. Jones was out of town, and no action was taken concerning his remarks. However, his fellow employees tended to treat him much like a hero for representing them in front of Mr. Jones.

On picking up his check on Friday afternoon, Henry was shocked to find his discharge notice and two weeks of additional pay in his envelope.

Critiques

LAWRENCE L. SCHKADE
Professor of Systems Analysis
and Urban Affairs
University of Texas at Arlington

The principal source of difficulty in this incident lies in the insensitivity and a lack of good faith on the part of management as evidenced by Mr. Jones's actions. As a consequence, an informal organization emerged from within the employee group to communicate their displeasure with existing policies and practices.

Employees desire a sense of security by knowing what to expect from management. Even consistent enforcement of stringent policies is generally more acceptable than the arbitrary application of more lenient policies. Further, there has been no apparent attempt to inform employees as to the reasons for policy decisions or involve them in these decisions.

Perhaps the clearest evidence management can give of its desire to deal fairly with employees lies in the development of a sound wage structure. In this case, merit rating may have been instituted in good faith, but the manner in which it was used, coupled with other circumstances, led employees to suspect management's motives. Negative employee reaction to over-all policy can have a marked effect on merit ratings. Poor morale can result in low productivity, high turnover, and increased costs.

The procedure for selecting vacation periods in this case reflects poor planning on the part of management and precluded any substantial degree of planning for the employee concerned —further evidence that management didn't feel that employee desires are important.

Management can help to create a favorable relationship by utilizing employee participation in decisions that affect them. Mr. Jones, if he reflects the general attitude of management, apparently looked upon the employee views as being rebellious and insubordinate. The summary dismissal of Mr. Henry, the employees' champion, is clearly a rejection of employee "impertinence." and also served to frighten the group into continued submission. There is no evidence that management looked upon employee views as being beneficial.

It is clear that management, particularly Mr. Jones, needs to adopt a new philosophy toward employee relations. It must be recognized that employees have personal desires and rights. Mike Henry should be reinstated and his leadership abilities used in creating a positive relationship with the employees. A grievance procedure should be established to settle complaints and keep management apprised of employee feelings. Existing policies should be reviewed, utilizing where possible employee views and suggestions. Employees should be informed in a timely manner about all decisions that affect them. Finally, management should make every attempt to deal fairly with employees to maintain positive motivation, once achieved.

RALPH N. TRAXLER, JR.

Professor and Dean, School of
Management and Business Sciences
Oklahoma City University

Every organization has the right to set any reasonable policy for evaluating its personnel. Establishing vacation policies is also the prerogative of management. But the company that Mike Henry worked for had undoubtedly failed to do two things concerning these two matters that are basic in building a good relationship with employees. First, the policies on evaluation and vacation had not been made completely clear to the employees. Second, the employees did not seem to have anyone to go to when they had questions or complaints about these two subjects. Anyone in the group represented by Mike Henry should have felt free to talk with Jones before the stage was reached where an employee representative had to be "elected."

At the very least, Jones should have been able to explain the reasons for these policies to Mike Henry. Certainly there was no logical reason for Jones to refuse to discuss these issues. Evidently Jones was not sure why the policies existed or what the attitude of higher management would be toward either changing the policies or explaining them in more detail to the employees. Since Jones probably knew he would be away all the next week, he should have made some kind of decision or explained to Mike Henry why he would have to delay action.

Mike Henry was turned into a hero by the fact that he had the courage to talk to Jones. The fact that he became a "hero" indicates a very poor relationship between employees and employer that was probably long-standing. This might also mean that other issues would develop into major problems as the employee group sought to gain its "rights" by sending representation to the boss. If there was no union in this organization, management was certainly building a wonderful foundation for an aggressive union organizer to start active agitation.

Under these conditions the discharge of Mike Henry was completely unjustified. At the very least Jones should have faced Mike Henry with some reason for his discharge. Jones seemed to believe that the easiest solution to this complaint was to dispose of the source of the problem by discharging Mike Henry. Now Mike Henry was more than a hero; he was a martyr. The problem still existed, and the employees would without doubt take much more aggressive action to gain their rights in the future.

Discussion items

1. If Mike Henry is reinstated, as suggested by Professor Schkade, how can his leadership abilities be used in a positive manner?
2. Do you think, as Professor Traxler suggests, that Mike Henry is now a martyr? If so, what is the significance of this?
3. What basic human relations principles have been violated in this incident?

Suggested reading list

BOOKS

Burack, Elmer H. *Organizational Analysis: Theory and Applications.* Hinsdale, Ill.: The Dryden Press, 1975. Chap. 9.

Carroll, Stephen J., and **Tosi, Henry L.** *Organizational Behavior.* Chicago: St. Clair Press, 1977. Chap. 8.

Davis, Keith. *Human Behavior at Work.* 5th ed. New York: McGraw-Hill Book Co., 1977. Chaps. 7, 8, 21–23.

Dressler, Gary. *Personnel Management: Modern · Concepts and Techniques.* Reston, Va.: Reston Publishing Co., 1978. Chap. 13.

Jucius, Michael J. *Personnel Management.* 9th ed. Homewood, Ill.: Richard D. Irwin, Inc., 1979. Chap. 26.

Kast, Fremont E., and **Rosenzweig, James E.** *Organizations and Management: A Systems Approach.* 3d ed. New York: McGraw-Hill Book Co., 1979. Chaps. 10–13.

Longnecker, Justin G. *Principles of Management and Organizational Behavior.* 4th ed. Columbus, Ohio: Charles E. Merrill Publishing Co., 1977. Chaps. 20–23.

Luthans, Fred. *Introduction to Management.* New York: McGraw-Hill Book Co., 1976. Chaps. 2, 8.

Megginson, Leon C. *Personnel and Human Resources Administration.* 3d ed. Homewood, Ill.: Richard D. Irwin, Inc., 1977. Chaps. 1, 2, 15.

Miner, John B. *The Management Process.* 2d ed. New York: Macmillan Publishing Co., Inc., 1978. Chaps. 1–5.

Terry, George R. *Principles of Management.* 7th ed. Homewood, Ill.: Richard D. Irwin, Inc., 1977. Chaps. 19, 20.

JOURNALS

Allen, Louis A. "M For Management: Theory Y Updated." *Personnel Journal* vol. 52, no. 12 (December 1973):1061–67.

Business Week ed. "A Productive Way to Vent Employee Gripes." No. 2556 (October 16, 1979):168–70, 171.

Carlisle, Howard M. "The Bond Between You and Your Subordinates." *Supervisory Management* vol. 16, no. 4 (April 1971):12–16.

Dale, L. A. "The Foreman as Manager." *Personnel* vol. 48, no. 5 (July/ August 1971):61–64.

Ewing, David W. "What Business Thinks About Employee Rights." *Harvard Business Review* vol. 55, no. 5 (September/October 1977):81–94.

Falcione, Raymond L. "The Relationship of Supervisor Credibility to Subordinate Satisfaction." *Personnel Journal* vol. 52, no. 9 (September 1973):800–3.

Greene, Charles N., and **Organ, Dennis W.** "An Evaluation of Causal Models Linking the Perceived Role with Job Satisfaction." *Administrative Science Quarterly* vol. 18, no. 1 (March 1973):95–103.

Grindle, C. R. "What's Wrong with Performance Appraisals." *Management Review* vol. 56, no. 6 (June 1967):45–49.

House, Robert J.; Filley, Alan C.; and **Kerr, Steven.** "Relation of Leader Consideration and Initiating Structure to Subordinate Satisfaction." *Administrative Science Quarterly* vol. 16, no. 1 (March 1971):19–29.

Kreitner, Robert. "People are Systems, Too: Filling the Feedback Vacuum." *Business Horizons* vol. 20, no. 6 (November 1977):54–61.

McConkie, Mark L. "A Clarification of the Goal Setting and Appraisal Process in MBO." *Academy of Management Review* vol. 4, no. 1 (January 1979):29–40.

Oshry, Barry I. "Clearing the Air in Human Relations." *Business Horizons* vol. 9, no. 1 (Spring 1966):35–46.

Smith, John P. "Personal Behavior in the Performance Appraisal Interview." *Advanced Management Journal* vol. 33, no. 1 (January 1968):57–62.

Welch, Barry. "Keeping the Discipliners in Line." *Personnel Management* vol. 10, no. 8 (August 1978):21–24.

Werther, William B., Jr., and **Weihrich, Heinz.** "Refining MBO Through Negotiations." *MSU Business Topics* vol. 23, no. 3 (Summer 1975):53–59.

21

INVASION OF PRIVACY

Psychological tests: validation, ethical considerations, issuing orders

Incident

THE FOLLOWING NOTICE was posted on the bulletin board for the 20 employees of the Atkins Finance Agency:

This company recently retained the services of Consultants, Inc., and they have recommended that we include in our selection program the polygraph test. Since this test is to be included as part of our employment program, we are requiring all presently employed persons to take the test also. You will be told the time and date to appear for the test. Your usual cooperation in this matter will be appreciated.

Three days later appeared the following statement, signed by 15 employees:

We, the undersigned, do at this time serve notice to the president of Atkins Finance Company that we consider the requirement that we take the polygraph test an invasion of our privacy, and therefore refuse to comply with the requirement.

The president immediately met with representatives of Consultants, Inc., to decide on a course of action.

Critiques

ROBERT M. GUION
Professor of Psychology
Bowling Green State University

Both the author of the notice and his consultant betray their ignorance of sound personnel research as well as their lack of

140

concern for the feelings of people. The tone of the notice is almost military in its terseness; people who have been employed in reasonably responsible positions are not likely to take any such notice in good grace. The fact that a polygraph test is better known popularly as a "lie detector" and the fact that it was not so identified in the notice combine to add further to the emotionality with which such an announcement would be greeted. One can, of course, only speculate; speculation, however, suggests a three-day period filled with much gossip, much fear, much emotion, and very little work! My sympathies are entirely with the employees!

Psychological testing has been effective primarily where the tests measure aptitude or specific ability. Personality tests are seldom useful except for sales and some managerial jobs. The polygraph detects, instead of lies, an emotionality in response; it is, therefore, properly classified in broad terms with personality measures. The prospects for it to be valid in this situation are dim.

In addition, personality testing offers another serious problem for the competent personnel research person: the lack of correspondence between "concurrent" and "predictive" validity. In a selection program a person is hired because of an at least implicit prediction that he or she will do well on the job. A selection test is, therefore, valid to the extent that scores on the test are correlated with some measure of on-the-job behavior. "Predictive" validity is determined by testing applicants and then waiting until they've held the job long enough to be evaluated on it. "Concurrent" validity is computed by using people whose performance on the job is already known. This is an example of attempted concurrent validity and clearly shows one of the dangers. Employees will not have the same motivation as will applicants—a fact that can seriously distort personality test scores. When this happens, there is no way to use the concurrent validities as estimates of the *predictive* value of the test.

In short, the practice illustrated here can be condemned on purely technical grounds; it is poor testing technique. The ethical aspects of the case also deserve some attention, but they are probably more obvious since they have been well publicized in television network news features. I would suggest as a generalization that personality probes may be ethically justified only in situations in which it can be clearly demonstrated that the information obtained helps the employer make more accurate predictions about an applicant's future work-related behavior. From this generalization, it follows that technically incompetent testing is necessarily unethical testing.

W. T. TUCKER
Professor of Marketing
Administration
University of Texas

In an incident of this kind two questions must be asked: (1) Was the management decision wise? (2) Was the decision carried out well? It is my impression that the answer to both of these questions is negative.

The polygraph test is an extremely unpleasant one that depends in large measure on subjecting the person being tested to threats, browbeating, and pointed questions about his morals. In the course of the test many subjects confess to illicit love affairs, autoeroticism, childhood thefts, and other matters on which they feel various degrees of guilt. Much of the value of the test lies in putting the fear of the polygraph in the subject.

A test of this sort is thought to be morally indefensible by many persons. Others point out that it screens those who are likely to steal from their employers and is, consequently, appropriate in hiring stockroom helpers and others subject to the temptations of petty theft. It may be appropriate when theft becomes chronic in an operation. In general, however, existing employees should not be subject to such a degrading experience nor should anyone above the lowest employee levels ever be subjected to it. Atkins Finance should not subject existing employees to the process unless losses are heavy. Even if the company is experiencing losses, a system of internal control that works is necessary to any financial institution, and polygraph testing is no substitute for adequate internal controls.

Should it become necessary to use a technique as extreme as the polygraph, employee relations are bound to suffer. Their deterioration could be kept to a minimum if management explained the circumstances (normally chronic theft of some magnitude) that required the testing, made testing voluntary, and guaranteed complete privacy of all results that did not refer to the problem at hand. The last two considerations require some discussion. Where theft has been rampant a good number of employees will volunteer to undergo polygraph testing in order to "clear" themselves. Others normally will volunteer, where management has set the stage carefully, because they feel that a failure to volunteer will be interpreted as a sign of guilt.

A guarantee of privacy can be of help, especially if it is agreed that the testing organization will give company management no information beyond that which clearly relates to specific losses or irregularities within the company. An assurance of this sort is always a bit weak; it is nearly valueless where employees do not have considerable confidence in management promises.

In summary, a resort to the polygraph is normally a symptom of management failure, except where it is used in the hiring of low-paid employees subject to temptation. Employee morale will always suffer on its introduction, even when management does a skillful job of persuading employees that the tests are necessary and that personal privacy will be protected insofar as possible.

Discussion items

1. As president of Atkins Finance Agency, what course of action should you take? Justify your position.

2. In what ways could management of the Atkins Finance Agency have gained acceptance for their decision to require employees to take the polygraph test?

3. Professor Tucker, in his critique, states that the polygraph test is thought to be morally indefensible by many persons. Do you agree or disagree? Why?

Suggested reading list

BOOKS

Carroll, Stephen J., and **Tosi, Henry L.** *Organizational Behavior.* Chicago: St. Clair Press, 1977. Chap. 10.

Davis, Keith. *Human Behavior at Work.* 5th ed. New York: McGraw-Hill Book Co., 1977. Chap. 15.

Flippo, Edwin B., and **Munsinger, Gary M.** *Management.* 4th ed. Boston: Allyn and Bacon, Inc., 1978. Chap. 9.

Jucius, Michael J. *Personnel Management.* 9th ed. Homewood, Ill.: Richard D. Irwin, Inc., 1979. Chap. 10.

Koontz, Harold, and **O'Donnell, Cyril.** *Management: A Systems and Contingency Analysis of Managerial Functions.* 6th ed. New York: McGraw-Hill Book Co., 1976. Chap. 4.

Longnecker, Justin G. *Principles of Management and Organizational Behavior.* 4th ed. Columbus, Ohio: Charles E. Merrill Publishing Co., 1977. Chap. 5.

McCormick, Ernest J., and **Tiffin, Joseph.** *Industrial Psychology.* 6th ed. Englewood Cliffs, N.J.: Prentice Hall, Inc., 1974. Chaps. 5–7.

Megginson, Leon C. *Personnel and Human Resources Administration.* 3d ed. Homewood, Ill.: Richard D. Irwin, Inc., 1977. Chaps. 7–11.

Miner, John B. *The Management Process.* 2d ed. New York: Macmillan Publishing Co., Inc., 1978. Chap. 28.

Terry, George R. *Principles of Management.* 7th ed. Homewood, Ill.: Richard D. Irwin, Inc., 1977. Chaps. 3, 17, 20.

JOURNALS

Aram, John D.; Morgan, Cyril; and **Esbeck, Edward S.** "Relation of Collaborative Interpersonnel Relationships to Individual Satisfaction and Organization Performance." *Administrative Science Quarterly* vol. 16, no. 3 (September 1971):289–96.

Bradford, Leland P., and **Harvey, Jerry B.** "Dealing with Dysfunctional Organization Myths." *Training and Development Journal* vol. 24, no. 9 (September 1970):2–6.

Business Management ed. "How to Plug Holes in Company Security." Vol. 22, no. 4 (July 1962):40–42, 66.

Carlile, William M., Jr. "City Uses Polygraph to Screen Applicants." *Public Management* vol. 41, no. 10 (October 1959):237–38.

Cary, Frank T. "IBM's Guidelines to Employee Privacy." *Harvard Business Review* vol. 54, no. 5 (September/October 1976):82–90.

Cherrington, David. "The Values of Younger Workers." *Business Horizons* vol. 20, no. 6 (November 1977):18–30.

Child, John. "Strategies of Control and Organizational Behavior." *Administrative Science Quarterly* vol. 18, no. 1 (March 1973):1–16.

Factory ed. "Lie Detector Weeds Out Misfits." Vol. 119, no. 1 (January 1961):240.

Greiner, Larry E. "Evolution and Revolution as Organizations Grow." *Harvard Business Review* vol. 50, no. 4 (July/August 1972):37–46.

Hersey, Paul, and **Blanchard, Kenneth H.** "Changes: Their Influence on Organizational Structure and Management Behavior." *Training and Development Journal* vol. 24, no. 10 (October 1970):2, 3.

Kirchner, Wayne K. "A Basic Fallacy in Personnel Testing." *Personnel* vol. 42, no. 1 (January/February 1965):50–52.

Schein, Virginia E. "Privacy and Personnel: Time for Action." *Personnel Journal* vol. 55, no. 12 (December 1976):604–7.

Schwartz, Barry. "The Sociology of Privacy." *American Journal of Sociology* vol. 73, no. 6 (May 1968):741–53.

Sternbach, Richard; Gustafson, Lawrence; and **Colier, Ronald L.** "Don't Trust the Lie Detector." *Harvard Business Review* vol. 40, no. 6 (November/December 1962):127–34.

Washnis, George J. "Polygraphs Aid in Choosing Policemen and Firemen." *Public Management* vol. 43, no. 6 (June 1961):134.

Yoder, Dale. "Management Policy and Manager Dissidence." *Personnel Administration* vol. 31, no. 2 (March/April 1968):8–18.

22

JOE LAMB

Developing a personal value structure: Does the end justify the means? Pressure groups, cliques

Incident

AT THE REGULAR MEETING of the National Office Managers Association, Ms. Joan Smith, office manager of a local mortgage company, asked the speaker, the manager of a local psychological consulting firm, for advice on a problem. The problem concerned a decision she had to make immediately relative to an employee in her department, Joe Lamb, who had been with the company for eight years as clerk-typist, bookkeeper, and more recently as chief file clerk. Lamb was described as a mild-tempered, introverted bachelor of 43, who usually preferred to keep to himself. His employment record was described as good.

On a recent evening after work, Lamb took his evening meal alone at a local restaurant and went to a movie. Returning to his one-room apartment four blocks away, he took a short cut through a park, and it was here that the local policeman on duty was attracted by the shouts of a girl who said that she had been attacked. Lamb was described as the assailant, arrested, and subsequently brought to trial on a rape charge. The jury brought forth a verdict of not guilty due to insufficient evidence.

Inasmuch as Lamb was declared not guilty by a court of law, Ms. Smith could see no justifiable reason for terminating his employment. Within a short time, however, Ms. Smith noticed that much antagonism and hostility were directed toward Lamb by other employees in the office. Many of the workers, male and female, refused to associate with Lamb, or they failed to coordinate their work activities with the file department, and office procedure was disrupted. The matter finally resulted in a demand from some of the employees that Lamb be discharged. They stated it was their feeling that Lamb was guilty of the crime, and some were quite fearful of him.

Ms. Smith decided to talk with Lamb in an attempt to persuade him to resign voluntarily. Lamb refused to resign and implied that if he was discharged, he would bring criminal action against the company for damaging his reputation and jeopardizing his opportunity for employment elsewhere.

The consultant, after some thought, recommended that Lamb be discharged on the basis of suspicion of guilt. Ms. Smith also considered the option of transferring Lamb to a different department, even though retraining him would then probably be required.

Critiques

C. B. GAMBRELL, JR.
Vice President for Academic Affairs
University of Central Florida

The consultant's decision was one of taking the path of least resistance. In this case such a decision offers the advantages of placating the disturbance among the other office workers and avoiding the risk of damaging customer good will. However, there are serious disadvantages to such a solution in that there were no technical grounds for discharge, and management runs the risk of setting a precedent by supporting a breach of policy, as well as of incurring a severe court investigation. It must be remembered that federal as well as many state and local regulations require that a due process procedure be followed in the discharge of persons and especially those employees who have successfully passed any required probationary period. In addition, constitutionally impermissible grounds may not be used for terminating an employee. Thus, Lamb might very well sue for job retention and damages and, if successful in his suit, which is certainly a strong possibility, the reputation of management would be greatly marred, a result carrying with it the threat of a severe loss of trade in the future, not to mention statements by competitors and others familiar with the case.

Keeping Lamb would, of course, impair office efficiency while upholding the torch of management integrity. It is felt that Lamb's future success and chances for promotion within his department may have been irreparably damaged.

It is, therefore, recommended that Lamb be transferred to another location if this is possible, and that the incident never be officially revealed to anyone other than the personnel director and Lamb's new superior. It is believed that Lamb may gain acceptance among new associates, that the other workers in his department would be partially satisfied, and that management's integrity would be maintained by such a solution. The risks that Lamb may not approve of a transfer or that he might have to be demoted and/or retrained, are unavoidable if this procedure is adopted. There is also the possibility that some customer good will may be lost, but this would be small indeed compared to that which would result from Lamb's suit following his dismissal.

Regardless of whether management is successful in moving Lamb to another location, it is the *responsibility* of Ms. Smith, as the office manager, to counsel, persuade, and ultimately to convince other office personnel that overt discrimination on the basis of unsubstantiated and hearsay evidence cannot and will not be tolerated. Under the circumstances, the risk of losing one or two good employees is more acceptable than a lawsuit and the ensuing bad publicity.

A. T. HOLLINGSWORTH

Professor of Management
University of South Carolina

Hindsight is always 20–20 so there is no sense in looking back at what Smith should have done. The question is what does Smith do now? The alternatives are: firing, transferring, seeking a voluntary resignation, ignoring, or keeping Lamb on the job.

Recently an attorney gave a group of business executives the following advice: "You may fire an individual for no reason, you may fire an individual for the wrong reason, or you may fire an individual for the right reason, but you cannot fire an individual for an illegal reason." This is the initial question confronting Smith; can Joe Lamb be fired legally. Yes, he can. The only way that the firm could get into legal difficulty is if when asked for references, they gave the reason for the firing as Lamb's arrest for rape. He could then sue the firm for slandering his reputation.

However, simply because it is legal is not a good reason for the firing. It would set a dangerous precedent and could cause future EEOC problems if a similar occurrence happened and concerned an individual in a protected class instead of Lamb. Voluntary resignation is obviously out of the question given Lamb's reaction to this suggestion. A transfer does offer a possible out, but it is not the best answer from a managerial point of view.

The solution to the problem must be initiated by Smith. It is clear the problem cannot simply be ignored. All employees should be made aware, by Smith personally, either in an open meeting or through personal conversations, that the only reason for which individuals will be discharged is job-related performance. Lamb's accusation and subsequent acquittal is not job related and therefore as long as his work is "good," he will remain on the job. Smith should point out that this policy will be applied equitably to all individuals. People will not be required to like Lamb, only to perform needed job activities with him.

It is quite possible that ostracism would ultimately cause Lamb's resignation, but the manager's position would be quite clear: that the organization is interested in performance. This should demonstrate to the employees that Smith intends to keep this matter on an objective basis, not an emotive basis, and should minimize these types of problems in the future.

Discussion items

1. If you were Ms. Smith would you accept the consultant's recommendation to discharge Joe Lamb on the basis of suspicion of guilt? Defend your position.

2. Professor Gambrell states that keeping Joe Lamb will uphold the torch of management integrity. Do you agree? Why or why not?

3. How should the company have planned for Joe Lamb's return to work?

Suggested reading list

BOOKS

Carroll, Stephen J., and **Tosi, Henry L.** *Organizational Behavior.* Chicago: St. Clair Press, 1977. Chap. 3.

Davis, Keith. *Human Behavior at Work.* 5th ed. New York: McGraw-Hill Book Co., 1977. Chaps. 1, 23, 24.

Donnelly, James H.; Gibson, James L.; and **Ivancevich, John M.** *Fundamentals of Management.* 3d ed. Dallas, Texas: Business Publications, Inc., 1978. Chap. 9.

Flippo, Edwin B., and **Munsinger, Gary M.** *Management.* 4th ed. Boston: Allyn and Bacon, Inc., 1978. Chaps. 3, 22.

Jucius, Michael J. *Personnel Management.* 9th ed. Homewood, Ill.: Richard D. Irwin, Inc., 1979. Chaps. 11, 23.

Kast, Fremont E., and **Rosenzweig, James E.** *Organizations and Management: A Systems Approach.* 3d ed. New York: McGraw-Hill Book Co., 1979. Chap. 6.

Koontz, Harold, and **O'Donnell, Cyril.** *Management: A Systems and Contingency Analysis of Managerial Functions.* 6th ed. New York: McGraw-Hill Book Co., 1976. Chap. 4.

Longnecker, Justin G. *Principles of Management and Organizational Behavior.* 4th ed. Columbus, Ohio: Charles E. Merrill Publishing Co., 1977. Chap. 20.

Megginson, Leon C. *Personnel and Human Resources Administration.* 3d ed. Homewood, Ill.: Richard D. Irwin, Inc., 1977. Chaps. 4, 15, 23.

Miner, John B. *The Management Process.* 2d ed. New York: Macmillan Publishing Co., Inc., 1978. Chaps. 6–8.

Terry, George R. *Principles of Management.* 7th ed. Homewood, Ill.: Richard D. Irwin, Inc., 1977. Chaps. 3, 4, 6, 14.

JOURNALS

Bower, Marvin. "A New Look at the Company Philosophy." *Management Review* vol. 55, no. 5 (May 1966):4–14.

Davis, Keith. "The Care and Cultivation of the Corporate Grapevine." *Management Review* vol. 62, no. 10 (October 1973):53–55.

Doutt, John T. "Management Must Manage the Informal Groups Too." *Advanced Management* vol. 24, no. 5 (May 1959):26–28.

Finkelstein, James A., and **Ziegenfus, James T., Jr.** "Diagnosing Employee's Personal Problems." *Personnel Journal* vol. 57, no. 11 (November 1978):653–55, ff.

Harvey, J. B. "Neurotic Organization Symptoms, Causes and Treatment." *Personnel Journal* vol. 50, no. 6 (June 1971):694–99.

Heisler, W. J. "Patterns of OD in Practice." *Business Horizons* vol. 18, no. 1 (February 1975):77–84.

Hill, Jack A. "The Decision-Making Process of the Employee Discharge." *Advanced Management Journal* vol. 30, no. 4 (October 1965):68–77.

Hill, Raymond E. "Managing Interpersonal Conflict in Project Teams." *Sloans Management Review* vol. 18, no. 1 (Winter 1977):45–60.

Hollingsworth, A. Thomas. "Improving Managerial Decisions that Affect Human Resources." *Personnel Journal* vol. 52, no. 6 (June 1973):446–50.

Johnson, Gary R. "Supervision: A Two Way Street to Somewhere." *Personnel Journal* vol. 50, no. 9 (September 1971):683–86, 723.

Kuehl, Charles R. "Leader Effectiveness in Commitment Type Groups." *Journal of Business* vol. 50, no. 2 (April 1977):223–29.

Learned, Edmund P.; Dooley, Arch R.; and **Katz, Robert L.** "Personal Values and Business Decisions." *Harvard Business Review* vol. 37, no. 2 (March/April 1959):111–20.

Loban, Lawrence N. "Mental Health and Company Progress." *Management Review* vol. 55, no. 12 (December 1966):29–33.

McAdams, Tony. "Dismissal: A Decline in Employer Autonomy?" *Business Horizons* vol. 21, no. 1 (February 1978):67–72.

Maier, N. R. F. "How to Get Rid of an Unwanted Employee." *Personnel Administration* vol. 28, no. 6 (November/December 1965):25–27.

Petit, Thomas A. "Making Socially Responsible Decisions." *Academy of Management Journal* vol. 9, no. 4 (December 1966):308–17.

Singer, Henry A. "Human Values and Leadership." *Business Horizons* vol. 18, no. 4 (August 1975):85–88.

23

LITSON COMPANY

Planning: forecasting labor needs, company image, public relations

Incident

THE LITSON COTTON YARN MANUFACTURING COMPANY, located in Murray, New Jersey, decided, as a result of increasing labor costs, to relocate their plant in Fairlee, a southern community of 4,200. Plant construction was started, and a personnel office was opened in the State Employment Office, located in Fairlee.

Because of poor personnel practices in the other three textile mills located within a 50-mile radius of Fairlee, the Litson Company found it was receiving applications from some of the most highly skilled and best-trained textile operators in the state. After receiving applications from approximately 500 applicants, employment was offered to 260 male and female applicants. It was decided that these employees would be placed immediately on the payroll with instructions to await final installation of machinery expected within the following six weeks.

The managers of the three other textile companies, faced with resignations from their most efficient and best-trained employees, approached the managers of Litson with the complaint that their labor force was being "raided." They registered a strong protest to cease such practices and demanded an immediate cancellation of the employment of the 260 employees hired by Litson.

The managers of Litson discussed the ethical and moral considerations involved in offering employment to the 260 employees. It was clear that Litson faced a rather tight labor market in Fairlee, and the Litson management thought that if the 260 employees were discharged, the company faced cancellation of their plans and large construction losses. It was felt, in addition, that

Litson management was obligated to the 260 employees who had resigned their previous employment in favor of Litson employment.

The dilemma facing the managers of Litson was compounded when the manager of one community plant reminded Litson that his plant was part of a nationwide chain supplied with cotton yarn from Litson. It was inferred that attempts to continue operations in Fairlee by Litson could result in cancellation of orders and a possible loss to Litson of an approximate 18-percent market. It was further suggested to Litson managers that action taken on the part of the nationwide textile chain could possibly result in cancellation of orders from other textile companies friendly to them.

Critiques

THOMAS Q. GILSON

Professor and Associate Dean
of Industrial Relations
University of Hawaii

The managers of the Litson Company face the question of whether they are prepared to retreat in the face of the demand for the cancellation of the employment of the 260 employees. This demand is supported by the implied threat by the manager of one of the other companies of a boycott which might seriously hurt the business of Litson. Furthermore, the three companies who made the demand would certainly do anything in their power to undermine the Litson Company's position in the community.

On the other hand, several considerations suggest "holding the line." First, the employees were hired in the open market. They evidently chose to apply at Litson because of the unfavorable comparison with the personnel practices of their present employers. Litson may have failed to make an adequate survey of community practices, but they certainly did nothing unethical.

Second, Litson had created an obligation to the employees.

Unless they were prepared to pull out completely, this obligation should be fulfilled. If the employment of the 260 was canceled, Litson could expect to attract only marginal workers and to suffer from a seriously damaged image locally.

Third, to pull out completely appears to entail serious losses. On the other hand, if they stay, there is the threatened boycott. Litson should not be stampeded by the suggestion of one other manager. The idea that companies friendly to his company might cancel orders is certainly farfetched in today's purchasing where price, quality, and service are the primary determinants. Even the loss of his own company's orders may be questioned. Thus, a certain and substantial loss must be balanced against an uncertain one, a loss that should not be completely discounted, but which appears considerably exaggerated.

In weighing the considerations, those on the side of turning down the demand are preponderant on both business and moral bases.

This decision is made despite the poor policies evident in the fact that the problem arose. A more gradual approach, an adequate survey of personnel policies of other employers, and work with other employers are all suggested by the events in the case.

Assuming that the Litson Company decided to stay in Fairlee and continue the employment of the 260 employees, there remain some major policy questions that are pointed up in the case.

There was no evidence that the company had surveyed the personnel policies and practices of other companies in the area before they located. Favoritism, arbitrary actions, and poor organization may have accounted for some of the applications. But it would appear that wages, fringe benefits, and similar policies must account for much of the attractiveness of the Litson Company. The company should consider whether it is not a more effective policy to fit its personnel policies reasonably close to those of existing companies, both for community relationships and long-range competitiveness.

Secondly, the policy of hiring a large number of employees on a stand-by basis appears questionable. Aside from the cost, the problem of getting a large group started at once is almost insurmountable. Further, the impact on other employers, as in this case, is much greater. A more gradual start-up would appear preferable from cost, technical, and strategic standpoints.

A third question raised by the case is the relation of the company to existing institutions·in the community. The company evidently did not find out the reactions of the other companies until after employment had begun. Furthermore, even though Litson used the State Employment Office for hiring, it apparently did not check out the possible implications of Litson policies or the employment of large numbers from other firms. The State Employment Office could undoubtedly have provided help on both questions if asked.

Next, the Litson Company should consider carefully what actions they should take now or in the future in the face of threats such as the one made in this case. Even if new policies were effectively applied, such a question might arise again. Therefore, the company should consider its position vis-à-vis such a threat.

Finally, the company should consider how it may offset any damage which has been done locally. Some revision of policies and efforts to develop cooperative relations may be in order.

JACK W. MARTIN
Professor Emeritus of Management
University of Denver

The management of the Litson Company is faced with the problem of whether or not to incur the ill will of two local textile mills by hiring former employees of these mills. Litson is staffing a new plant, to open soon in Fairlee, where the other mills are located. The employees are evidently unhappy with the personnel practices of the mills and are eager to work for Litson. Definite promises of future employment have evidently been made to 260 employees by Litson management. Reprisals by the two mills are threatened in the form of dropping Litson as a source of yarn supply if Litson goes ahead with hiring the employees.

Litson should proceed with their decision to hire the employees and risk the wrath of the other firms if these conditions can be

satisfied: Can Litson offer the employees a more favorable working situation within their present cost-price structure? Can Litson
offer these employees long-run employment and security equivalent to or better than that to be had with the other firms? Have the
negotiations proceeded to a point where there is no turning back
in that bad relations have been generated between the other mills
and their employees and changing the course of action would
serve no purpose? It appears that the answer to these questions is
in the affirmative; therefore, Litson should stick with its decision.

The settlement of the issue, once positive action is taken, is one
that will rest with public opinion. While the other companies
could carry out their threats and Litson may suffer some loss of
sales as a result, if the reason the employees left the other concerns was ever brought to light in the public press the other mills
would suffer far more in comparison. Litson has a powerful
weapon in a well-planned public relations campaign explaining
just what benefits have been given the employees, and so forth.
While it is hoped that this tactic would never come into play,
Litson could use it to advantage.

Also, since 260 employees and their families are involved, this
would affect over one fourth of the population of Fairlee. The
repercussion in the community would far overshadow the
threatened loss of sales. Certainly the other mills must be aware
of this.

Litson management is to be sharply criticized for getting into
this situation, since it shows faulty planning on their part. They
should have gone into the labor market more thoroughly, including a discussion of the labor situation in the community with the
top executives of the mills before they started building. However,
having gone as far as they have they had better stick to their high
standards and follow through on their initial decision.

Discussion items

1. What course of action should be taken by management of the Litson Company? Support your position.

2. While the Litson Company may be guilty of faulty planning, as
suggested by Professor Martin, do you think it has engaged in any
unethical or immoral employment practices? Defend your answer.

3. Professor Gilson, in his critique, states that the Litson Company should consider whether it is not a more effective policy to fit its personnel policies reasonably close to those of existing companies. Do you agree or disagree? Why?

Suggested reading list

BOOKS

Burack, Elmer H., and **Smith, Robert D.** *Personnel Management.* New York: West Publishing Co., 1977. Chap. 5.

Carroll, Stephen J., and **Tosi, Henry L.** *Organizational Behavior.* Chicago: St. Clair Press, 1977. Chaps. 6, 7, 11.

Donnelly, James H.; Gibson, James L.; and **Ivancevich, John M.** *Fundamentals of Management.* 3d ed. Dallas, Tex.: Business Publications, Inc., 1978. Chaps. 3, 4.

Flippo, Edwin B., and **Munsinger, Gary M.** *Management.* 4th ed. Boston: Allyn and Bacon, Inc., 1978. Chaps. 4–6.

Kast, Fremont E., and **Rosenzweig, James E.** *Organizations and Management: A Systems Approach.* 3d ed. New York: McGraw-Hill Book Co., 1979. Chaps. 8, 9, 17.

Koontz, Harold, and **O'Donnell, Cyril.** *Management: A Systems and Contingency Analysis of Managerial Functions.* 6th ed. New York: McGraw-Hill Book Co., 1976. Part 2.

Longnecker, Justin G. *Principles of Management and Organizational Behavior.* 4th ed. Columbus, Ohio: Charles E. Merrill Publishing Co., 1977. Chaps. 5–9.

Luthans, Fred. *Introduction to Management.* New York: McGraw-Hill Book Co., 1976. Chap. 4.

Megginson, Leon C. *Personnel and Human Resources Administration.* 3d ed. Homewood, Ill.: Richard D. Irwin, Inc., 1977. Chap. 6.

Terry, George R. *Principles of Management.* 7th ed. Homewood, Ill.: Richard D. Irwin, Inc., 1977. Part 3.

JOURNALS

Andersen, Theodore A. "Coordinating Strategic and Operational Planning." *Business Horizons* vol. 8, no. 2 (Summer 1965):49–54.

Cassell, Frank H. "Manpower Planning: State of the Art at the Micro Level." *MSU Business Topics* vol. 21, no. 4 (Autumn 1973):13–21.

Ebert, Ronald J., and **Adam, Everette E., Jr.** "The Human Factor in Facilities Location Planning." *Business Horizons* vol. 20, no. 6 (November 1977):35–42.

Ewing, David W. "A New Basis for Company Planning." *International Management* vol. 25, no. 7 (July 1970):34–39.

Hampton, David R. "The Planning-Motivation Dilemma." *Business Horizons* vol. 16, no. 3 (June 1973):79–87.

Hartman, Richard I. "Managerial Manpower Planning: A Key to Survival." *Personnel Journal* vol. 44, no. 2 (February 1965):86–91.

Holbert, Neil B. "The Life of Staff." *Business Horizons* vol. 21, no. 3 (June 1978):79–82.

Mintzberg, Henry. "Strategy Making in Three Modes." *California Management Review* vol. 16, no. 2 (Winter 1973):44–53.

Rank, John D., and **Lundgren, Earl F.** "Easing the Pangs of Plant Closing." *Personnel* vol. 42, no. 3 (May/June 1965):67–73.

Reid, Douglas, M. "Human Resource Planning: A Tool For People Planning." *Personnel* vol. 54, no. 2 (March/April 1977):15–25.

Rue, Leslie W. "The How and Who of Long-Range Planning." *Business Horizons* vol. 16, no. 6 (December 1973):23–30.

Schaffer, Robert H. "Putting Action into Planning." *Harvard Business Review* vol. 45, no. 6 (November/December 1967):158–66.

Schmenner, Roger W. "Look Beyond the Obvious in Plant Location." *Harvard Business Review* vol. 57, no. 1 (January-February 1979):126–32.

Shank, J. K.; Niblock, E. G.; and **Sandalls, W. T., Jr.** "Balance 'Creativity' and 'Practicality' in Formal Planning." *Harvard Business Review* vol. 51, no. 1 (January/February 1973):87–95.

Student, Kurt R. "Cost vs. Human Values in Plant Location." *Business Horizons* vol. 19, no. 2 (April 1976):5–14.

24

LOCKS VERSUS LIVES

*Decision making, responsibility, control,
ethical considerations*

Incident

THE ADMINISTRATOR of the State Mental Hospital learned
that keys to security wards for dangerous criminals had been lost
or stolen when he received an early morning telephone call the
first of May from the night administrator of the hospital. Since
duplicate keys were available in the hospital safe, the administrator, Mr. Jackson, knew that loss of the keys would not interfere
with the routine functioning of the hospital. But he decided to call
a general staff meeting the next morning to consider the problem.

At the meeting, Mr. Jackson explained the problem of the missing keys and asked for suggestions on what to do. The assistant administrator suggested that the matter be kept confidential
among the staff since public knowledge could lead to damaging
publicity and possibly to an investigation by higher officials in the
Department of Health and Rehabilitative Services.

The head of security for the hospital reported that only two
keys were missing and that, although he could not yet determine
if the keys had been stolen or lost, he thought they probably had
been stolen. He emphasized that the missing keys were "master
keys" that could open the doors to all the security wards where
the most dangerous criminals were housed. In his opinion immediate replacement of the locks on those doors was required.

The director of accounting estimated the cost of replacing the
locks at over $5,000. She reminded the meeting that the operat-
ing costs of the hospital already exceeded its operating budget by
about 10 percent due to unexpected inflation and other unfore-
seen expenses and that an emergency request for a supplemental
budget appropriation to cover the deficit had been sent to the

Department of Health and Rehabilitative Services the previous week. In sum, she concluded, no funds were available in the budget for replacing the locks and an additional request for $5,000 might jeopardize the request for supplementary operating funds that had already been submitted. Besides, since it was early May, the hospital would begin operating under the budget for the next fiscal year in approximately 60 days. The locks could then be replaced and the costs charged against the new budget. Another staff member reasoned aloud that if the keys had been lost, any person finding them would not be likely to know of their purpose and that if the keys had been stolen they probably would never be used in any unauthorized way.

Mr. Jackson thanked the staff members for their contributions, ended the meeting, and faced the decision. He reflected upon the fact that behind the doors to the security wards were convicted first-degree murderers and sexual psychopaths, among others. He also remembered his impeccable 13-year record as an efficient and effective hospital administrator.

As Mr. Jackson continued his deliberations, the thought occurred to him that perhaps the most important action would be to find and place the blame upon the person who was responsible for the disappearance of the two keys. Moreover, security procedures might need reviewing. Mr. Jackson could not clearly see how best to proceed.

Critiques

ANDRÉ L. DELBECQ
Professor of Administration
University of Wisconsin

If Mr. Jackson had had a managerially trained guardian angel on duty prior to his staff meeting, it might have whispered three aphorisms often found in management literature in Mr. Jackson's ear:

1. "Remain problem-centered and explore integrative combinations of alternative solutions."

2. "Focus on system weaknesses, don't scapegoat individuals."
3. "Confront difficulties, don't smooth or resort to authority."

Alas, the managerial angel must have been visiting a journal editor instead. Let's look at each of these three concerns.

PROBLEM CENTEREDNESS

Problem exploration at best was symptomatic. For example, the staff meeting did not explore how the keys might have been lost or stolen, whether there were differing degrees of security needs as between patients or wards, or the exact nature of the public-relations concerns. In like fashion, round-robin, off-the-cuff opinion giving does not constitute exploration of alternative solutions. The few solutions proposed were deeply embedded in subgroup biases. Security stressed security, Accounting stressed budgets, and Administration stressed public relations. In each instance, there was a single alternative suggested. There are, doubtless, a variety of security options (for example, change some, not all, locks and increase ward observation), budget options (such as, cash flow and resource variations), and external relations options (such as, contacting few key people).

FOCUSING ON SYSTEM WEAKNESSES

The present tension, once a short-run solution is reached, offers the opportunity for reexamination of security systems as an organization issue. Any tendency to scapegoat individuals will decrease attention to systemic weaknesses and increase information absorption. Unless rule violation or serious negligence is involved, focusing on individuals is inappropriate.

CONFRONTING DIFFICULTIES

In the "era of Watergate," one is sensitized to the fact that smoothing over errors leads to later charges of an even more serious nature. Direct confrontation of the problem, sharing information with key authority figures, and admission of organizational failures indicate a manager's ability to confront crisis. Neither benign neglect nor negligence based on attempts to maintain illusions of omniscience are coping strategies for system errors. A cover-up only exacerbates later suspicions that private ambition has been placed above managerial responsibilities and, in this case, public trust and safety.

PUBLIC SAFETY

Finally, in an emergency involving public safety, short-run coping procedures must be instituted even while intermediate and long-run solutions are explored. Early A.M., several hours prior to the staff meeting, was the time to respond with increased temporary security measures.

THOMAS A. NATIELLO
Professor of Management and
Health Administration
University of Miami

Any organization requires identification of its objectives, goals, priorities, and strategies. A state mental hospital is no exception. Important actions in any situation must be based on these criteria. Mr. Jackson, the administrator, and his staff must understand the reasons for the organization's existence, at least within the realm of security and institutional responsibility for dangerous criminals and the attendant systems that discharge this responsibility.

The assignment of individual responsibility for the disappearance of the keys would have a lower initial priority than the maintenance of institutional security. It would be hoped that additional security systems have been brought into play to prevent the keys from being used in a destructive manner. Systems did not exist for control of security keys at all times. It is now clear that a review of security procedures is necessary.

There is, however, a deeper implication in the apparent inadequacy of the administrator and the department heads involved to act decisively and effectively. The organizational environment seems to be one of reluctant innovation and extreme personal caution with little feedback to the administrator or staff;

each individual considers only his or her point of view within the structure, clearly indicating a divergence of individual goals between each of the functional areas. The assistant administrator's suggestion of confidentiality among the staff, the director of accounting being concerned about the cost and the possible jeopardy of other requests for funds, and the administrator being concerned with his impeccable 13-year record and assignment of blame all indicate a lack of understanding of organizational priorities and departmental responsibilities toward them. The head of security, after learning of the loss and recommending the replacement of all locks, appears to take no further responsibility for future actions but rather has abdicated this responsibility, as it seems everyone else has, to the administrator who is to make the decision for the organization.

Often, organizations use approaches that allow individual goals to replace the overall goals of the organization. Organization leaders should take action not to avoid blame but to attempt to find solutions and set up effective systems that are in the best interests of the total organization. The organization must also have a means of external communication, particularly with the Department of Health and Rehabilitative Services. Easy communication, rather than an adversary relationship, should provide information to aid decisions in such circumstances. Therefore, expenditures required, in whatever form they may take, because of the loss of the keys should be considered in terms of their contribution to organizational effectiveness and the institution's satisfaction of societal requirements.

Further, the administrator should analyze the organizational systems within the hospital. Overreliance on individuals behaving properly under unusual situations rather than developing the systems necessary to meet contingencies in a more positive manner is a dangerous approach to high priority organizational requirements. There should exist within the organization some means by which the organization's readiness to act effectively can be constantly reviewed and a crisis orientation averted.

The administrator must develop an understanding of the critical variables associated with his institution. Identification of these variables will enable him to develop appropriate organizational systems for their support, thereby enabling him to control effectively the situation within the organizational framework with a sensitivity to the external environment.

But what to do now? The administrator must decide to take some action, even if the decision is to do nothing. A problem-solving decision structure could be useful, such as Kepner-Tregoe, which lends itself to risk-cost analysis.

The lost key situation can be analyzed in terms of the problems it has caused and the resultant risks to hospital personnel, to patients, to the community, and to the operation of the organization. The risk and cost of alternative feasible solutions can be compared. Immediate action can then be taken to intervene in situations that result in a threat to life, morally or ethically undesirable situations, or prevention of the successful discharge of the hospital's responsibilities in its role as an agent of the state.

A careful analysis of the incident will provide information for the formulation of conclusions involving decisions, organizational and individual responsibilities, control processes, and moral and ethical considerations.

Discussion items

1. Evaluate the recommendations that various staff members of State Mental Hospital made at their meeting.

2. Who, if anyone, should be blamed for allowing the keys to become unaccounted for? What penalities would you consider appropriate?

3. What is the most immediate responsibility of the hospital administrator? Why? What is involved in using the Kepner-Tregore technique suggested by Professor Natiello?

Suggested reading list

BOOKS

Burack, Elmer H. *Organization Analysis: Theory and Applications.* Hinsdale, Ill.: The Dryden Press, 1975. Chap. 11.

Carroll, Stephen J., and **Tosi, Henry L.** *Organizational Behavior.* Chicago: St. Clair Press, 1977. Chap. 12.

Davis, Keith. *Human Behavior at Work.* 5th ed. New York: McGraw-Hill Book Co., 1977. Chap. 9.

Donnelly, James H.; Gibson, James L.; and **Ivancevich, John M.** *Fundamentals of Management.* 3d ed. Dallas, Tex.: Business Publications, Inc., 1978. Chap. 13.

Filley, Alan C.; House, Robert J.; and **Kerr, Steven.** *Managerial Process and Organizational Behavior.* 2d ed. Glenview, Ill.: Scott, Foresman and Co., 1976. Chaps. 7, 19.

Flippo, Edwin B., and **Munsinger, Gary M.** *Management.* 4th ed. Boston: Allyn and Bacon, Inc., 1978. Chaps. 18–21.

Kast, Fremont E., and **Rosenzweig, James E.** *Organizations and Management: A Systems Approach.* 3d ed. New York: McGraw-Hill Book Co., 1979. Chaps. 14–16.

Koontz, Harold, and **O'Donnell, Cyril.** *Management: A Systems and Contingency Analysis of Managerial Functions.* 6th ed. New York: McGraw-Hill Book Co., 1976. Chap. 9.

Longnecker, Justin G. *Principles of Management and Organizational Behavior.* 4th ed. Columbus, Ohio: Charles E. Merrill Publishing Co., 1977. Chap. 8.

Miner, John B. *The Management Process.* 2d ed. New York: Macmillan Publishing Co., Inc., 1978. Chaps. 6, 7.

Terry, George R. *Principles of Management.* 7th ed. Homewood, Ill.: Richard D. Irwin, Inc., 1977. Part 1, Chaps. 6–8.

JOURNALS

Albanese, Robert. "Criteria for Evaluating Authority Patterns." *Academy of Management Journal* vol. 16, no. 1 (March 1973):102–11.

Cecil, Earl A.; Cummings, Larry L.; and **Chertkoff, Jerome M.** "Group Composition and Choice Shift: Implications for Administration." *Academy of Management Journal* vol. 16, no. 3 (September 1973):412–22.

Ericsson, Tore, and **Mirsberger, Gerald E.** "Responsibility in Management—What Does It Really Mean?" *Advanced Management Journal* vol. 38, no. 4 (October 1973):36–45.

Hair, Joseph F., Jr.; Bush, Ronald F.; and **Busch, Paul.** "Employee Theft: Two Views From Two Sides." *Business Horizons* vol. 19, no. 6 (December 1976):25–9.

Holloman, Charles R., and **Hendrick, Hal W.** "Adequacy of Group Decisions as a Function of the Decision-Making Process." *Academy of Management Journal* vol. 15, no. 2 (June 1972):175–84.

Huber, George P., and **Delbecq, André.** "Guidelines for Combining the Judgments of Individual Members in Decision Conferences." *Academy of Management Journal* vol. 15, no. 2 (June 1972):161–74.

Ivancevich, John M., and **Donnelly, James H., Jr.** "Relation of Organizational Structure to Job Satisfaction, Anxiety-Stress and Performance." *Administrative Science Quarterly* vol. 20, no. 2 (June 1975):272–79.

Ives, Brian D. "Decision Theory and the Practicing Manager." *Business Horizons* vol. 16, no. 3 (June 1973):38–40.

McConkey, Dale D. "Applying Management by Objectives to Non-Profit Organizations." *Advanced Management Journal* vol. 38, no. 1 (January 1973):10–20.

McMurry, Robert N. "Management's Achilles Heel: Over-Dependence." *Michigan Business Review* vol. 25, no. 5 (November 1973):14–23.

Maier, Norman R. F. "Prior Commitment as a Deterrent to Group Problem Solving." *Personnel Psychology* vol. 26, no. 1 (Spring 1973):117–26.

Scheips, Charles D. "Eight Ways to Improve Your Chances of Success as a Manager." *Advanced Management Journal* vol. 38, no. 1 (January 1973):42–49.

Simon, Herbert A. "On the Concept of Organizational Goal." *Administrative Science Quarterly* vol. 9, no. 2 (June 1964):1–22.

Stimson, David H. "Utility Measurement in Public Health Decision Making." *Management Science* vol. 16, no. 2 (October 1969):17–30.

25

MISINTERPRETED PROCEDURE

Effective response to provocation, communicating,
grievance procedures, personal value structure

Incident

JACK HARRIS, HEAD OF PRODUCTION of a medium-size, single-plant, nonunion firm producing top-quality ceramic tile, had just received another memorandum from Robert Dace, director of personnel, which he considered to be demeaning and filled with irrelevancies. Harris had been with the company in key management capacities for ten years. Robert Dace had joined the firm as personnel director about a year ago. Dace had learned rapidly and was confident that he thoroughly understood company policies and procedures, a number of which he had revised personally. Being somewhat skilled in writing, Dace had also drafted several proposed policy statements that he hoped would be implemented by Mr. Hampton, president of the firm.

The hot memo, which Jack still had in his hand, was the latest of a flurry of memos that he and Dace had exchanged regarding the firm's grievance procedure. Six years ago, when the firm was much smaller, Jack and Mr. Hampton together had developed the written grievance procedure as follows:

California Tile Company, Inc.
Uniform Grievance Appeal Procedure

1. Members of management are urged to maintain an open-door policy with employees and to fully discuss any questions raised pertaining to grievances regarding work rules, work conditions, compensation, or other complaints arising from the work situation.
2. Grievance appeals can be made only after the employee has discussed the matter with the Head of Production.
3. Employee complaints, explaining the situation and the steps taken

to clear it with the Head of Production, should be filed in writing with the Director of Personnel.

4. The Grievance Appeals Board will review the situation with the employee and with the Head of Production. If it seems appropriate and likely to be beneficial, a meeting with the employee and the Head of Production should be arranged.

5. A report of each complaint will be made by the Grievance Board with copies to the employee, the Head of Production, the Director of Personnel, and the President of the Company.

Jack recalled that the grievance procedure had worked well over the years and that it was well understood by the workers, foremen, and managers. But now, for some curious reason, Dace seemed unable or perhaps unwilling to follow the well-established written grievance procedures. Jack removed the sheaf of memos from the file, arranged them by date on his desk, and read them over again.

February 15, Memorandum
To: Jack Harris, Head of Production
From: Robert Dace, Director of Personnel
Mr. Barnwell Simons is appealing a decision that you made in connection with his work-assignment grievance. As we discussed, as part of the grievance procedure you are supposed to nominate a person to serve on the Grievance Appeals Board. Since I would like to have this matter resolved with some dispatch, I would very much appreciate it if you would provide me with a name by February 18.

February 16, Memorandum
To: Robert Dace
From: Jack Harris
1. In compliance with your February 15 memo concerning the grievance appeal of Mr. Barnwell Simons, I nominate Cord Meyer to the Grievance Appeals Board.
2. I assume that Mr. Simons has provided a written statement of the grounds upon which his grievance appeal is founded, since that is a required step in the appeal procedure, as I recall. I therefore would appreciate receiving a copy of his written statement.

February 21, Memorandum
To: Jack Harris
From: Robert Dace
With respect to your memo of February 16, I am requesting that Cord Meyer serve on the Grievance Appeals Board. With respect to your

second request, for a copy of Mr. Simon's written statement, this was submitted to me as what I assume to be a confidential communication, and inasmuch as the grievance appeals procedure of this company does not indicate that the Head of Production is to receive a copy of the employee's original letter of appeal, I do not feel that I can, in good conscience, provide you with a copy of this statement, irrespective of my own personal feelings about the matter.

February 23, Memorandum
To: Robert Dace
From: Jack Harris
Thank you for your memo dated February 21. Your negative response to my routine request for a copy of the written statement of the grounds upon which Mr. Simons has based his grievance appeal appears to depart markedly from past practice in similar situations with which I am familiar. Also with respect to your memo of that date, your interpretation of the Uniform Grievance Appeal Procedure of this company appears to be at variance with the interpretation of others known to me. I do respect your personal decisions and feelings about the matter; however it remains a fact that both your interpretation of the grievance appeal procedures and your response generate several questions, the answers to which will be forthcoming sometime later during the grievance review procedure, I suppose. I share your desire that this grievance appeal be resolved with some dispatch, as stated in your memo of February 15. Let me assure you again that I remain prepared to cooperate toward that end.

February 28, Memorandum
To: Jack Harris
From: Robert Dace
Before this matter gets out of hand, I hasten to assure you that my *only* reasons for not wanting to make Mr. Simons's letter to me available to you were, first, my desire to respect and affirm the basic principle that letters written to me are not in the public domain, and, second, the fact that there is nothing in the Uniform Grievance Appeals Procedure of this company that indicates that the Head of Production (or, indeed, the members of the Grievance Appeal Board) should receive a copy of the employee's letter of appeal. Mr presumption, based in part on our discussions of company policy since I have been Director of Personnel, has been that you would want me to *scrupulously adhere* to company procedures as set out in writing, rather than as they may have been carried out—or more precisely, ignored—in the past. I concede and regret the fact that I erred in this presumption. Moreover, it was never my intention to keep you uninformed as to the nature of the grievance appeal. In

point of fact, having recalled our detailed conversation of some two weeks ago when we discussed the specific situation and you *explicitly* indicated that Mr. Simons had seen you, presented his case to you, and finding it rejected might appeal your decision, I had no reason to believe that within this short span of time you would have forgotten the reasons for the grievance appeal. Here, too, I have apparently erred, since Cord Meyer also called me to task because of your assertion to him that you did not know the grounds on which Mr. Simons had based his appeal and that I was doing nothing to enlighten you. Although two errors are two more than I normally care to make, and while I think I am making a third error, I am providing you with a copy of Mr. Simons's original letter to me in the hope that this will be taken as a nonprecedent-setting act of good faith and, more importantly, in some measure rectify the first two errors. If you would like additional copies of this letter, my secretary would be happy to provide these; if I can provide any additional information, please do not hesitate to ask and I will do my best to oblige should that information be available to me. I might point out to you however, that now that others (you and Cord Meyer) have copies of the letter, I cannot be responsible for who else may obtain a copy.

Jack felt no responsibility for the escalation of the intensity of the personnel director's memos, but he did feel strongly that an appropriate response was required. What response? What action? How best to proceed? These questions filled Jack's mind and prevented him from continuing with his other work.

Critiques

RICHARD I. HARTMAN
*Professor and Chairman of
Management and Administration
Bradley University*

The Uniform Grievance Appeals Procedure of California Tile Company, Inc., is vague, inadequate, and incomplete. The interchange of memos between Jack Harris, head of production, and Robert Dace, director of personnel, indicates that the two men have different interpretations of the workings of the Uniform Grievance Appeals Procedure.

Jack Harris and Mr. Hampton, president of the firm, wrote the grievance procedure six years ago. Consequently, Jack is probably very confident that he thoroughly understands all aspects of the grievance procedure. In addition, Jack has experience in actually processing grievances through this procedure. Jack Harris's position in his dispute with Robert Dace appears to rely quite heavily upon past practice or history in handling grievances.

On the other hand, Robert Dace has been with the firm for only one year. As a result, his experience with the workings of the grievance procedure is limited. Robert Dace's position is that the company grievance procedure must be scrupulously adhered to as set out in writing rather than how the procedure has been carried out in the past.

Jack Harris should attempt to de-escalate the "memo madness" that has arisen with Robert Dace. A written response to Robert Dace's February 28 memo would undoubtedly further escalate the conflict situation that is building between the two men.

In light of the situation, Jack Harris should respond by requesting a meeting with Robert Dace for the express purpose of rewriting the Uniform Grievance Appeals Procedure and settling the grievance of Mr. Barnwell Simons. This meeting, if successful, would undoubtedly involve considerable give-and-take and a willingness by Robert Dace and Jack Harris to compromise.

A review of the grievance procedure is in order, since it was written more than six years ago. In addition, the size of the firm has increased during the six-year period. It would behoove Jack Harris and Robert Dace to consult with other individuals in the firm during the process of evaluating and rewriting the grievance procedure.

The rewritten grievance procedure should be more explicit, detailed, and complete than the existing procedure. It is important that the procedure carefully spell out the steps to be followed in processing a grievance and the appropriate role of the various individuals involved.

Once Robert Dace and Jack Harris have agreed upon a new written grievance procedure they should seek the approval of Mr. Hampton, president of the firm. After the president approves the rewritten grievance procedure it would be necessary to communicate the procedure effectively to all employees of the firm.

WILLIAM J. WASMUTH

*Professor of Human Resources
and Personnel Administration
Cornell University*

While varied interpretations of a grievance appeals procedure is the basis for much of this case, there is a more fundamental issue that needs to be examined, namely the basis of the line-staff conflict. Prior to considering what might be an appropriate response by Jack Harris it is necessary to try to determine whether he is currently in an organizational and personal position of strength or weakness.

On the one hand Jack's position to counter Robert Dace effectively would be relatively *weak* if the case material, supported by reasonable assumptions, were interpreted as follows:

1. Dace has the backing of Mr. Hampton to act as a "watchdog" over personnel practices to insure that employees are treated fairly and to help resist unionization.
2. Company procedures, including grievance handling, *have in fact been ignored* in the past, as stated by Dace in the February 28 memo.
3. Prior experience indicates that grievances to Jack have been treated lightly or possibly squelched (implied by the comments of Mr. Simons and Cord Meyer in the February 28 memo).

Given the above circumstances Jack would be well advised to pay a personal visit to Dace's office, talk face to face, and initially try to stop the memo warfare. Next he should try to get Dace to tell him what he expects Jack's role and actions should be in order to fulfill step 2 of the grievance procedure effectively even if this means "eating a bit of crow." If Dace's suggestions are procedurally or morally unacceptable, Jack should then take a stand and be willing to bring the matter to a head with Mr. Hampton if necessary.

If, on the other hand, the following set of conditions were operative, Jack's strategy in dealing with Dace could be quite different, namely from a position of *strength*.

1. Jack has high status with Mr. Hampton, supported by ten years in key management positions.
2. Dace is playing the dangerous game of blocking an established and workable grievance procedure in order to set up a procedure of his own to gain personal power (this assumes Jack is correct in stating the old procedure has worked well for six years).
3. Dace's effective role as Director of Personnel is dependent in large measure on the cooperation and support of line management. This would seem likely unless Mr. Hampton wants controls to tighten up on loose informal practices that evolved when the company was much smaller.

In this situation, as with the one cited earlier, the memo war should cease. Jack can take firm initiative and ask Dace to come to *his* office for a serious face-to-face discussion of their *personal* differences. While memos may have eventually settled procedural difficulties involving the grievance procedure, they are inappropriate for reconciling the fundamental causes of interpersonal conflict involving organizational status, line-staff authority, and leadership style.

Discussion items

1. What action would you recommend that Jack Harris take? Why? What action would you recommend be taken by Robert Dace? Why?
2. Would you classify this conflict as being organizational, that is, a line and staff conflict, or as a personal conflict? Why?
3. Should the guide for resolving the conflict over the grievance procedure be "traditional past practice" or "current requirements and interpretations"? Why?

Suggested reading list

BOOKS

Carroll, Stephen J., and **Tosi, Henry L.** *Organizational Behavior.* Chicago: St. Clair Press, 1977. Chap. 9.

Davis, Keith. *Human Behavior at Work.* 5th ed. New York: McGraw-Hill Book Co., 1977. Chaps. 21–22.

Filley, Alan C.; House, Robert J.; and **Kerr, Steven.** *Managerial Process and Organizational Behavior.* 2d ed. Glenview, Ill.: Scott, Foresman and Co., 1976. Chaps. 8, 9.

Flippo, Edwin B., and **Munsinger, Gary M.** *Management.* 4th ed. Boston: Allyn and Bacon, Inc., 1978. Chap. 17.

Hicks, Herbert G., and **Gullett, C. Ray.** *The Management of Organizations.* 3d ed. New York: McGraw-Hill Book Co., 1976. Chaps. 25, 26.

Jucius, Michael J. *Personnel Management.* 9th ed. Homewood, Ill.: Richard D. Irwin, Inc., 1979. Chap. 15.

Kast, Fremont E., and **Rosenzweig, James E.** *Organizations and Management: A Systems Approach.* 3d ed. New York: McGraw-Hill Book Co., 1979. Chaps. 10–13.

Koontz, Harold and **O'Donnell, Cyril.** *Management: A Systems and Contingency Analysis of Managerial Functions.* 6th ed. New York: McGraw-Hill Book Co., 1976. Chap. 26.

Longnecker, Justin G. *Principles of Management and Organizational Behavior.* 4th ed. Columbus, Ohio: Charles E. Merrill Publishing Co., 1977. Chaps. 16, 23.

Miner, John B. *The Management Process.* 2d ed. New York: Macmillan Publishing Co., Inc., 1978. Chap. 8.

Terry, George R. *Principles of Management.* 7th ed. Homewood, Ill.: Richard D. Irwin, Inc., 1977. Chap. 20.

JOURNALS

Adizes, Ichak. "Mismanagement Styles." *California Management Review* vol. 19, no. 2 (Winter 1976):5–20.

Anthony, William P. "Living with Managerial Incompetence." *Business Horizons* vol. 21, no. 3 (June 1978):57–64.

Bacharach, Samuel B., and **Aiken, Michael.** "Communication in Administrative Bureaucracies." *Academy of Management Journal* vol. 20, no. 3 (September 1977):365–77.

Bassett, Glenn A. "What Is Communication and How Can I Do It Better." *Management Review* vol. 64, no 2 (February 1974):25–32.

Blai, Boris, Jr. "Some Basics of Sound Human Relations." *Personnel Journal* vol. 52, no. 8 (August 1973):710–14.

Chase, Andrew B., Jr. "How to Make Downward Communication Work." *Personnel Journal* vol. 49, no. 6 (June 1970):478–83.

Davis, Keith. Communication within Management." *Personnel* vol. 31, no. 3 (November 1954):212–18.

Fern, Dan H., and **Yankelovich, Daniel.** "Responding to the Employee Voice." *Harvard Business Review* vol. 50, no. 3 (May/June 1972):83–91.

Golightly, Henry O. "The What, What Not, and How." *Business Horizons* vol. 16, no. 6 (January 1974):47–50.

Girkscheit, Gary M., and **Crissy, William J. E.** "Improving Interpersonal Communications Skills." *MSU Business Topics* vol. 21, no. 4 (Autumn 1973):63–68.

Harvey, Jerry B., and **Boettger, C. Russell.** "Improving Communications Within a Managerial Workgroup." *Journal of Applied Behavioral Science* vol. 7, no. 2 (November 1971):164–79.

Poole, Marshall Scott. "An Information-Task Approach to Organizational Communication." *Academy of Management Review* vol. 3, no. 3 (July 1978):493–504.

Watson, Goodwin, and **Glaser, Edward M.** "What We Have Learned about Planning for Change." *Management Review* vol. 54, no. 11 (November 1965):34–46.

Whitehead, Carlton J. "Communication—A Key to Managerial Effectiveness." *Business Topics* vol. 15, no. 2 (Spring 1967):54–58.

Woodruff, W. R. "Are You in Communication With Your Subordinates?" *Supervisory Management* vol. 16, no. 7 (July 1971):20–23.

26

MORAL QUESTION

Inservice training of hospital employees, ethical and moral considerations in setting hospital charges

Incident

THE 12-MEMBER BOARD OF TRUSTEES of Salem County Hospital met to consider a proposal made by the hospital's administrator to discontinue the hospital's specialty and technical training programs for clinical personnel such as laboratory technicians, licensed practical nurses, and radiological technicians.

The hospital's administrator emphasized that the present trend is away from hospitals providing training programs for such personnel. Instead, the trend is toward locating these programs in community colleges. A significant increase in the cost of providing such training during the past decade has been responsible for the trend. In order to provide such training activities, general hospital funds derived from patient charges or from funds appropriated for patient care must be diverted to support the effort. At Salem County Hospital it means each patient must be charged an additional $2.10 for each day that patient is in the hospital.

The chief of the medical staff, who vehemently opposes the move, pointed out some of the benefits to be derived from continuation. Most important, in his view, was the retention of trainees. With the serious shortage of paramedical personnel, both nationally and locally, he considers this an inappropriate time to stop training. In addition, trainees render a service to the hospital during the period they are being trained. Lastly, he feels a health care facility such as Salem, a 200-bed voluntary general hospital, has an educational responsibility to the community.

The administrator made a final plea that in view of steadily increasing hospital costs and corresponding patient charges, continuation of the training could not be justified. In his opinion it reduced to a moral consideration; it simply isn't equitable to require a hospitalized sick person to bear the burden of training paramedical personnel. The board must decide what action to take.

Critiques

ROBERT BOISSONEAU
Professor and Dean of Human Resources
Eastern Michigan University

The board finds itself with several important unanswered questions, such as:

1. What effect will the discontinuation of technical training programs have on the supply of these technicians?
2. Has the administrator approached a college to assume responsibility for these programs?
3. Has the administrator discussed this issue with others in the hospital, for example, the chief of the medical staff?
4. Is cost the only important consideration?
5. Are there other funding sources for the training programs?
6. Is it reasonable to reduce this complex issue to simply a moral question?

Based on what is known about this incident, the administrator has not given the board a comprehensive report. It does need one.

The key element is to determine whether elimination of the training programs will reduce the supply of trained technicians. The modern hospital must have trained technicians to fulfill its purpose.

It is important to know whether other institutions in that geographic area train these particular technicians. If the answer is affirmative and Salem County Hospital is able to employ adequate numbers, there may be no problem.

If there are not other training programs that could be expected to supply technicians, the administrator has the obligation to approach an appropriate college with a request that the college assume responsibility for the training program. It is likely that a community with a 200-bed general hospital would have such a college.

In communicating with others, such as the chief of the medical staff, the administrator would want to point out the trend of locating training programs in educational institutions. While the hospital may want to offer use of its facilities for the clinical portion of the training program, it can no longer provide blanket educational opportunities as it once did because of changing expectations regarding cost control. The development of an affiliation agreement with a college for the use of its clinical facilities could be an important recruitment device as well as possibly being income producing for the hospital.

The importance of the cost factor cannot be denied. Hospital administrators seem to be under fire from every direction to control costs. The $2.10 charge per patient day amounts to over $100,000 a year based on a 70 percent occupancy rate.

If a relationship with an appropriate college is not developed, the administrator would want to explore other funding sources. Since the chief of the medical staff is so interested, he may want to lead an effort directed at having the organized medical staff assume full or part of the financial responsibility for the training program by assessing each physician's professional fee account. After all, the trainees serve physicians as well as the hospital.

However, to base the entire decision on the moral issue of unfair charges is too simplistic in this situation. The patient care and training components must also be considered.

Finally, by the very nature of moral questions, some other people have a different view. There is no question that thousands of health providers are charging sick people for the training of health personnel. Possibly more important is that millions are accepting those charges with hardly a question.

JAMES O. HEPNER

Professor and Director of
Health Administration and
Planning
Washington University

The 12-member board of trustees of Salem County Hospital should approve the proposal made by the hospital's administrator to terminate the clinical training program for laboratory technicians, licensed practical nurses, and radiological technicians.

It is traditional for hospitalized patients to pay additional fees to support training programs in medical-school-affiliated teaching hospitals. The cost per patient day in teaching hospitals is substantially higher because of educational programs, primarily for medical students, interns, and residents. It is inappropriate for a 200-bed community hospital to carry the primary accountability for training programs. Not only is the hospital too small to support such training totally, but it is also evident from the incident that there is a nearby community college that may be willing to assume this responsibility. The rationale for supporting the administrator's proposal goes beyond that of a moral question wherein inpatients must pay $2.10 additional per day to support these three training programs. There is serious question regarding the quality of such hospital-based training programs because of the inability of hospitals to attract full-time certified faculty who will devote their entire efforts to education as opposed to patient service. The community college most certainly would have a broader base and has greater potential for attracting qualified faculty.

In terms of quality, the didactic aspects of the training could be carried out at the community college. However, it is extremely important that the students be offered clinical exposure, which might well be completed under supervision at the community hospital. By so doing, the cost to the hospital would be less, the quality of education would be higher, and the hospital would still have the opportunity of retaining the best graduates in the laboratories, the x-ray department, and the nursing divisions.

There have been serious questions raised by various third-party payors of hospital care regarding their responsibility for supporting training programs at the expense of the insured hospitalized patient. Therefore, various hospital insurance plans have eliminated training expense from their reimbursement formulas. This means that such training expense must be made up by "full pay" patients, that is, those who do not have insurance or who pay the full billed charges over and above the insurance coverage.

By working out appropriate responsibility for didactic and clinical education between the community college and the hospital, one of the points in opposition to closing the training programs made by the chief of the medical staff would be resolved. Furthermore, the physician's concern regarding the educational responsibility of the hospital to the community would also be met. However, the doctor is in error making an argument favoring the service that the trainees could render to the hospital. Accreditation bodies such as the American Medical Association and the National League of Nursing who are concerned with the quality of allied health and nursing education, vehemently oppose using students as "cheap labor" for the benefit of the hospital or the attending medical staff. In fact, they make a very strong distinction between education and service starting with the dominant profession, undergraduate and graduate medical education, where medical students, interns, and residents complete their clinical training in the teaching hospital setting.

In conclusion, with the board of trustees approving the administrator's proposal, it would be very important that the administrator have a detailed action plan for transferring the didactic responsibility for education to the community college and working out arrangements for clinical training within the hospital. In transferring the primary responsibility for education to the community college, the hospital staff, medical staff, program alumni, and most importantly students in training must be informed and their cooperation sought in supporting the change before the plan is implemented.

Discussion items

1. Do you agree or disagree with the administrator that it is not equita-

ble to require a hospitalized sick person to bear the burden of training clinical personnel? Why?

2. Write a critique that reflects the relevant issues your examination of the incident reveals. Be sure to decide what should be done about continuing specialty and technical training at Salem County Hospital.

3. Are nonprofit organizations faced with the same primary goals and objectives as a profit-oriented organization? How would the establishment of goals and objectives be affected?

Suggested readings

BOOKS

Carroll, Stephen J., and **Tosi, Henry L.** *Organizational Behavior.* Chicago: St. Clair Press, 1977. Chap. 17.

Hepner, James O., and **Hepner, Donna M.** *The Health Strategy Game.* St. Louis: The C. V. Mosby Co., 1973. Chap. 6.

Herkimer, Allen G. *Understanding Hospital Financial Management.* Germantown, Md.: Aspen Systems Corp., 1978. Chaps. 3, 8.

Jucius, Michael J. *Personnel Management.* 9th ed. Homewood, Ill.: Richard D. Irwin, Inc., 1979. Chap. 13.

Koontz, Harold, and **O'Donnell, Cyril.** *Management: A Systems and Contingency Analysis of Managerial Functions.* 6th ed. New York: McGraw-Hill Book Co., 1976. Chap. 4.

McCormick, Ernest J., and **Tiffin, Joseph.** *Industrial Psychology.* 6th ed. Englewood Cliffs, N.J.: Prentice Hall, Inc., 1974. Chaps. 9, 10.

Megginson, Leon C. *Personnel and Human Resources Administration.* 3d ed. Homewood, Ill.: Richard D. Irwin, Inc., 1977. Chap. 12.

Schultz, Rockwell, and **Johnson, Alton C.** *Management of Hospitals.* New York: McGraw-Hill Book Co., 1976. Chaps. 6, 12, 16.

Terry, George R. *Principles of Management.* 7th ed. Homewood, Ill.: Richard D. Irwin, Inc., 1977. Chaps. 3, 11.

Wilson, Florence A., and **Neuhauser, Duncan.** *Health Services in the United States.* Cambridge, Mass.: Ballinger Publishing Co., 1976. Chap. 2.

JOURNALS

Agee, William M. "The Moral and Ethical Climate in Today's Business World." *MSU Business Topics* vol. 26, no. 1 (Winter 1978):16–19.

Aldag, Ramon J., and **Jackson, Donald W., Jr.** "A Managerial Framework For Social Decision Making." *MSU Business Topics* vol. 23, no. 2 (Spring 1975):33–40.

Brooker, W. Michael A. "Eliminating Intergroup Conflict Through Interdepartmental Problem Solving." *Advanced Management Journal* vol. 40, no. 2 (Spring 1975):17–25.

Cabot, Louis W. "On an Effective Board." *Harvard Business Review* vol. 54, no. 5 (September/October 1976):40–42, 46.

Davis, Keith. "Five Propositions For Social Responsibility." *Business Horizons* vol. 18, no. 3 (June 1975):19–24.

Estes, Robert M. "The Case For Counsel to Outside Directors." *Harvard Business Review* vol. 54, no. 4 (July/August 1976):125–32.

Holms, Sandra L. "Executive Perceptions of Corporate Social Responsibility." *Business Horizons* vol. 9, no. 3 (June 1976):34–40.

Macnaughton, Donald S. "Managing Social Responsiveness." *Business Horizons* vol. 19, no. 6 (December 1976):19–24.

Morano, Richard A. "How to Manage Change to Reduce Stress." *Management Review* vol. 66, no. 11 (November 1977):21–25.

Morris, Thomas L. "Effective Employee Development in Hospitals." *Training and Development Journal* vol. 28, no. 4 (August 1974):26–30.

Parket, I. Robert, and **Eilbirt, Henry.** "Social Responsibility: The Underlying Factors." *Business Horizons* vol. 18, no. 4 (August 1975):5–10.

Personnel Journal ed. "Sources and Resolution of Conflict in Management." vol. 56, no. 5 (May 1977):225–6, 253.

Rassam, Clive. "How to Solve Interdepartmental Conflict." *International Management* vol. 31, no. 10 (October 1976):47–50.

Sethi, S. Prakash. "A Conceptual Framework for Environmental Analysis of Social Issues and Evaluation of Business Response Patterns." *Academy of Management Review* vol. 4, no. 1 (January 1979):63–86.

Student, Kurt R. "Changing Values and Management Stress." *Personnel* vol. 54, no. 1 (January/February 1977):48–55.

27
MOTOWN SLOWDOWN

Gaining acceptance of change, use of authority, grievances, motivation

Incident

FREDERICK WOOLSEY HAD BEEN MADE SUPERVISOR of one production line at Motown Metal Fabrication, Inc. In this position he was responsible for operating the entire production line efficiently and effectively. He supervised 6 foremen and 48 assembly-line workers. He said his job was to keep the assembly line going at the scheduled 71 units per hour.

When Woolsey took over the job of supervisor two months ago, the production line was losing 90 minutes of production a day. Line stoppages, maintenance problems, absenteeism, and workers stopping the line for repair were some of the causes of production loss. The 90-minute-per-day loss was approximately 20 percent of the daily operating schedule.

Woolsey reduced absenteeism and took other steps to prevent the loss of scheduled production time. He frankly admitted that he had discharged several persons. Moreover, he kept the main line going even when some "feeder" lines stopped. "The workers don't like it," said Woolsey. "They resent working the required 7 hours and 45 minutes a day instead of only 6 hours and 30 minutes."

The disgruntlement of the production line workers seemed to be centered in Robert Long and Vick Green. They claimed that Woolsey was guilty of using "speed-up" tactics and filed a formal grievance two weeks ago, with Woolsey as the target. Woolsey is also the target of their increasingly vitriolic verbal protests. Green and Long are black and Woolsey is white, but workers in the plant feel there are no racial implications in the situation.

The complaints against Woolsey are varied and include the

following: Both Green and Long said that Woolsey removed benches on which the workers sat to take breaks during gaps in the line. Green said that Woolsey laid off workers for being two minutes late. He also said that Woolsey had foremen running around picking up papers. Green added that Woolsey had threatened to fire him after the model changeover in two weeks. Long said that Woolsey had threatened him with an iron bar about eight inches long. Both Long and Green are openly defiant and imply that they are ready to take matters into their own hands.

The plant manager is convinced that the situation is explosive, but he is uncertain how to proceed.

Critiques

LYMAN W. PORTER
Dean of the Graduate School of Administration
University of California in Irvine

There seem to be at least three salient points to be examined with respect to this incident:

1. The supervisor, Woolsey, has failed to obtain the commitment of his subordinates to the goal of 71 units per hour. (Whether this is a realistic goal is a separate question.) There is no indication that they had any voice in formulating goals or even in helping to determine how goals are to be reached. The situation appears to be a strictly "top down" type of operation, with the subordinates being given little credit for possibly having ideas to contribute to planning how the production line should be operated. Indeed, Woolsey almost seems more interested in making sure no one misses a minute on the line than he does in reaching the 71-unit goal. (A case of the means becoming more important than the ends, or goal.) Woolsey is operating more as a watchdog than as a facilitator.

2. The supervisor seems not to have gained the support of, or even rapport with, the informal leadership structure existing among his subordinates (that is, Green and Long, who, if not

informal leaders, are at least vocal). Green and Long, for their part, seem more upset at Woolsey than at having to produce 71 units per hour.

3. It is not at all clear how the production line workers see themselves benefiting from reaching the goal of 71 units (or any other particular goal, whether lower or higher than 71). Similarly, we do not know what they believe will happen if the line does not produce at precisely 71 units. In other words, the reward/punishment structure in this particular situation is unclear.

If improvements are to be made, both from the company and the workers' point of view, it would appear that the following would need to take place:

1. An objective analysis should be carried out to determine if the goal of 71 units is reasonable and feasible. If it is not, then Woolsey should take the issue up with his superiors. In that way, he would be demonstrating to his subordinates that he is as concerned with their welfare as with the company's and would gain their increased confidence in him. If the goal is reasonable, then the employees should be given some opportunity to help determine how it is to be reached. The superior needs to try to gain acceptance of and commitment to the goal.

2. The supervisor needs to try to obtain the cooperation and assistance of the two apparent informal leaders. To do so may not be easy, but there may be ways to turn their outspokenness into positive acts of leadership among their peers. That is, there may be opportunities for them to simultaneously help Woolsey *and* gain further respect from their fellow workers.

3. The reward structure needs to be clarified, so that the subordinates can see and feel some connection between their efforts and performance, on the one hand, and the kinds of positive outcomes they can obtain if they meet the goal on the other hand. Simply an opportunity to have some control over the variation in the work pace during the day, as long as the goal of 71 units (or whatever other goal is adopted) is reached, could be a positive incentive for goal attainment. An effective supervisor ought to be able to think of other additional possibilities for linking rewarding outcomes to adequate or outstanding performance.

Critiques

FRANK J. SCHILAGI
Professor and Dean, Babcock
Graduate School of Management
Wake Forest University

Two issues immediately present themselves as obvious challenges to the plant manager: first, the managerial style of Woolsey and second, the disgruntlement of Long and Green. The situation is delineated in the Long and Green frame of reference, and we have no information about Woolsey's perception of the situation. The single comment about his job ". . . to keep the assembly line going at the scheduled 71 units per hour . . ." seems to indicate a tendency to lead in a 9.1 managerial grid style. The interpersonal conflict between Green, Long, and Woolsey is obvious.

What, then, are the alternative actions available to the plant manager? Broadly defined, he could decide to utilize the authosity he has as a function of his position and dismiss Long, and/or Green, and/or Woolsey, or any combination thereof. Assuming, however, that a manager is responsible for more than short-run stability vis-à-vis the work force, the plant manager should elect to invest some time and effort in an attempt to understand the situation. While a number of theoretically useful answers are available, we would like to suggest an alternative that involves additional questions. Interest in this approach developed as a result of experience in learning at the Creative Education Foundation (CEF), State University of New York at Buffalo.

Without explaining the numerous specific techniques that have been developed by the CEF over the past 18 years, it would suffice to say that the philosophy is that of asking questions in a creative way. The following questions were raised within a short time period and are the start of the process that provides the manager with the appropriate information. This approach considers the development of the right questions as the first and most important step in solving the problem.

I.   Is Woolsey's style consistent with the plant manager's phi-
     losophy of working with people?
     A. If yes, consider in what way the plant manager might
         encourage and support Woolsey's style.
     B. If no, consider alternatives available to change his be-
         havior.
II. What is Woolsey's perception of the situation?
     A. Has he been exposed to other ways of managing
         people?
         1. What managerial style did Woolsey's supervisor
             have?
     B. How does he perceive the organization's reward sys-
         tem vis-à-vis effectiveness and efficiency?
     C. Why does he think he was promoted?
     D. Why did the company promote him?
III. What information is available on Robert Long and Vick
     Green?
     A. Does the Personnel Department have performance,
         grievance records?
     B. What do the foreman and other production-line
         people know about Long and Green?
IV. What information is available about the situation?
     A. What is the extent of disgruntlement? (Two out of 48?
         Twenty out of 48?).
     B. What is the turnover rate on that production line?
         1. As compared to other lines?
         2. Before and after Woolsey's promotion?
V.   What historical information is available?
     A. What type of managerial style did the former supervisor
         exhibit?
     B. Why was he replaced?
         1. In the company's view?
         2. In Woolsey's view?

The above questions should not be considered as a comprehensive list. They are intended as an example of an approach
for increasing the plant manager's perception of the situation.
Thus, the *primary* consideration at this point should be a free
form of asking questions. And, in many cases, the potential an-
swer(s) can be found in the questions.

For example, Woolsey may not know of any other way to manage people (Question II). If this is true, exposure to alternative ways of managing may be appropriate. Or, Long and Green may be reacting to a change in supervisors (Question V). Further, the plant manager may encourage a 9.1 managerial style by his behavior (Questions II and V).

Whatever the answers, they will probably not be discovered if the proper questions are not developed.

It should be noted that the ability to develop additional questions is, in fact, available to all competent managers. The difficult aspect of the process seems to be our desire to find an answer as soon as possible. To be considered an effective approach to problem solving, the manager must be willing to develop as many questions as time permits. And, from this additional information, he should be able to develop an effective solution to the problem.

Discussion items

1. How may employees be given an opportunity to react to the production goal of 71 units per hour and be given an opportunity to help determine how the goal is to be achieved?

2. What approaches would you recommend in trying to gain the cooperation of Green and Long, the two apparent informal leaders? Explain.

3. How might the reward/penalty structure be clarified so that the workers can see the connection between their efforts toward improved production and some positive outcomes for them in terms of rewards?

Suggested reading list

BOOKS

Carroll, Stephen J., and **Tosi, Henry L.** *Organizational Behavior.* Chicago: St. Clair Press, 1977. Chap. 13.

Davis, Keith. *Human Behavior at Work.* 5th ed. New York: McGraw-Hill Book Co., 1977. Chaps. 3, 4, 10, 26.

Donnelly, James H.; Gibson, James L.; and **Ivancevich, John M.** *Fundamentals of Management.* 3d ed. Dallas, Texas: Business Publications, Inc., 1978. Chap. 11.

Filley, Alan C.; House, Robert J.; and **Kerr, Steven.** *Managerial Process and Organizational Behavior.* 2d ed. Glenview, Ill.: Scott, Foresman and Co., 1976. Chap. 6.

Flippo, Edwin B., and **Munsinger, Gary M.** *Management.* 4th ed. Boston: Allyn and Bacon, Inc., 1978. Chap. 21.

Jucius, Michael J. *Personnel Management.* 9th ed. Homewood, Ill.: Richard D. Irwin, Inc., 1979. Chap. 26.

Kast, Fremont E., and **Rosenzweig, James E.** *Organizations and Management: A Systems Approach.* 3d ed. New York: McGraw-Hill Book Co., 1979. Chap. 23.

Koontz, Harold, and **O'Donnell, Cyril.** *Management: A Systems and Contingency Analysis of Managerial Functions.* 6th ed. New York: McGraw-Hill Book Co., 1976. Chaps. 14–16.

Longnecker, Justin G. *Principles of Management and Organizational Behavior.* 4th ed. Columbus, Ohio: Charles E. Merrill Publishing Co., 1977. Chap. 12.

Megginson, Leon C. *Personnel and Human Resources Administration.* 3d ed. Homewood, Ill.: Richard D. Irwin, Inc., 1977. Chaps. 16, 17.

Terry, George R. *Principles of Management.* 7th ed. Homewood, Ill.: Richard D. Irwin, Inc., 1977. Chaps. 14, 18.

JOURNALS

Clutterback, David. "General Motors Strives to Motivate Its Workers." *International Management* vol. 30, no. 1 (January 1975):13–19.

Deming, Donald D. "Reevaluating the Assembly Line." *Supervisory Management* vol. 22, no. 9 (September 1977):2–7.

Drasler, Daren. "What Makes People Work Harder." *Supervisory Management* vol. 13, no. 10 (October 1968):25–28.

Faush, David. "The Humanistic Way of Managing People." *Business Week* vol. 2238 (July 1972):48–49.

Gokuc, Mitchell. "Motivating the Worker." *Personnel Journal* vol. 52, no. 11 (November 1973):988–91.

Herrick, Neal Q., and **Quinn, Robert P.** "The Working Conditions Survey as a Source of Social Indicators." *Monthly Labor Review* vol. 94, no. 4 (April 1971):15–24.

Huberman, John. "Discipline Without Punishment." *Harvard Business Review* vol. 42, no. 4 (July/August 1965):62–68.

Korach, Kenneth A. "Blacks in the U.S. Labor Movement." *MSU Business Topics* vol. 25, no. 4 (Winter 1977):11–16.

Levitan, Sar A., and **Belous, Richard S.** "Thank God It's Thursday." *Across the Board* vol. 14, no. 3 (March 1977):28–31.

Luthans, Fred, and **Krietner, Robert.** "The Role of Punishment in Organizational Behavior Modification." *Public Personnel Management* vol. 2, no. 3 (May/June 1973):156–61.

Mayfield, Harold. "Understanding the Needs of Your Subordinates." *Supervisory Management* vol. 16, no. 1 (January 1971):10–12.

Prather, Dirk C. "Managing Human Resources." *Journal of Systems Management* vol. 22, no. 12 (December 1971):22–25.

Scott, D. "Motivation from the Transactional Analysis Viewpoint." *Personnel* vol. 51, no. 1 (January/February 1974):8–20.

Strauss, George. "Worker Dissatisfaction: A Look at the Causes." *Monthly Labor Review* vol. 97, no. 2 (February 1974):57.

White, Harold C. "How the Leader Looks to the Led." *Administrative Management* vol. 35, no. 3 (March 1974):58–60.

Wool, Harold. "What's Wrong With Work in America." *Monthly Labor Review* vol. 96, no. 3 (March 1973):38–44.

28

NO COMMENT

Personal value structure, ethical responsibilities, consultant relations

Incident

WHILE SERVING AS EDUCATIONAL CONSULTANT to the State Real Estate Board, Robin Rostow, Professor of Real Estate at Keowee State University, discovered that applicants to the board who wished to become registered state realtors were required to study a variety of topics including the legal and financial aspects of real estate transactions, contracts, calculations, and many other subjects important for persons in the field of real estate to know. Professor Rostow further found that as a result of the wide variety of topics no single satisfactory source contained the required materials.

Because of this scatter of required materials among different sources and because of the geographic scatter of applicants throughout the state, members of the State Real Estate Board faced the continuing problem of assembling the required materials into study packets and then distributing these packets to applicants. This procedure was awkward, time consuming to the board, and costly to the applicants.

Professor Rostow proposed a solution to these difficulties. He proposed to write a textbook expressly tailored to the requirements of the state board. The real estate book would cover the required topics in the sequence and with the emphasis preferred by the state board, so that it would meet their needs exactly. This one source of information could then be reproduced in quantity and conveniently distributed to applicants. Moreover, it was proposed that each applicant be required to purchase the special text. Other advantages were (1) reduced cost to the applicant, (2) increased convenience for the applicant, and (3) improved preparation of the applicant and thus a reduced failure rate on the state realtor license examination.

The real estate board accepted the professor's proposal in toto. The book was written and published, and it served its intended purpose for three years. Then came the newspaper headlines, PROF GIVES NO COMMENT TO PROBE INTO BOOK SALE, followed by the lead paragraph: "A Keowee State University professor whose state-commissioned book earned $300,000 for himself and his wife would not comment Thursday on a planned investigation into the circumstances surrounding the preparation, publication, and sale of the book."

The newspaper account was based on the state auditor's report, which, in part, contained the following facts: The real estate board had retained Rostow as a consultant and had paid him consultant fees for developing the book for them. After the book was written, however, Rostow retained the copyright and established the T-A-T Publishing Company to produce the book. During the three-year period covered by the auditor's report, Rostow received $10,000 in consultant fees from the State Real Estate Board and $105,000 in royalties from the book, while his wife received $225,000 in the form of profit as president and treasurer of the publishing company. The auditor's report asserted that the real estate board could have published the textbook on its own at a saving for the license applicants and as a source of funds for the real estate board. Moreover, publication of the book by the board would have allowed a sale price to applicants of $3.90 instead of $6.40, the actual selling price. The T-A-T Publishing Company was the sole publisher of the book, and the book was the sole product of the T-A-T Publishing Company.

The members of the joint legislative auditing committee, which was investigating the situation, were outspoken in expressing their concern. "I think they (the State Real Estate Board) gave away the public's assets," said State Representative Mary Krause, a member of the investigating committee. The committee unanimously approved a motion that a close investigation be made into the profit made by Rostow and his wife in the publishing venture. Other areas of possible investigation discussed by committee members included various legal issues, questions of professional ethics, collusion, conflicts of interest, and recovery of some part of the royalties and publishing profits.

When reached by telephone and asked about the situation and the forthcoming investigations, Rostow's only comment was, "No comment."

Critiques

DANIEL D. ROMAN
Professor of Management Science
George Washington University

Professor Rostow's finding that no single satisfactory source existed for the required study material was not very profound based on the information already available. As a consultant, he merely confirmed known facts. He was operating within ethical bounds when he suggested that a special text could be written that would incorporate all of the required information. He would still not transcend an ethical position by suggesting that he could provide such a text to the state for additional consulting compensation. Where Rostow was guilty of poor judgment and questionable ethics was in establishing a conflict of interest situation when he proposed himself as author and recommended that the State Real Estate Board *require each applicant to purchase the special text.*

Rostow's recommendation for a single information source had merit, but there were alternatives that the board could have considered:

1. Reference to applicable material with responsibility for acquiring this information left in the hands of the applicants.
2. Refer to applicable material and indicate its availability for a nominal fee.
3. Commission Professor Rostow to write a book for a consulting fee. This is a common governmental practice. The results of government-sponsored research are often made available to the public for a nominal sum.
4. If Professor Rostow decided to write a book independently

that would meet the board's requirements and be exclusive of the consulting arrangement, the board should at most include the book as a reference and not as required reading. Had the board followed this course of action, it would have avoided being criticized for establishing a monopolistic position for Rostow. Rostow would then have had to assume the responsibility for the promotion and sale of the book outside the auspices of state sponsorship. This is reasonable—to perceive a need and take an entrepreneurial position. It is compatible with free-enterprise doctrine.

5. A fifth possibility might have also been explored. If the board felt such a book was essential and should be required of all applicants, it could have acquired ownership rights to the book and offered the author a royalty arrangement if such an inducement was needed to have him undertake the project.

Some additional observations:

The issue of excessive profits would not be germane if the state board had not established a captive market for the author.

In the academic profession it is not unusual to publish for prestige. Often, academic publication affords little or no direct monetary returns. However, professional recognition, establishing expertise in a given area, and potential consulting fees may be inducements to undertake such ventures.

What constitutes excessive profits is a matter for conjecture where creative effort is involved. It is not unusual for authors of good-selling books to enjoy financial returns in six figures. The price of the book in question was not unreasonable based on current textbook pricing practices.

The real estate board erred in not considering its alternatives. Additionally, the board should have obtained a legal opinion relative to the ownership rights to the book since they had already paid Rostow a consulting fee for developing the project.

The profit issue was incidental; the real problem was procedural.

OGDEN H. HALL
Professor of Management
University of New Orleans

Was Rostow hired as an "educational consultant" to develop instructional materials and methods for those applying for licenses to the State Real Estate Board? If so, it would seem that any materials produced would be the property of the board rather than the professor. If not, ownership may be a moot question.

On the other hand, is there any reason why the professor should be precluded from personal gain just because he developed the materials? It seems that the appropriate basis for this decision is the extent to which the board's objectives can be accomplished by T-A-T Publishing Company or by other alternatives. I think we must conclude from the information presented that there was a significant improvement in the service rendered to applicants when compared with previous efforts. Whether the new approach is the best available has not been tested.

Two actions by the board are questionable to say the least. One of these actions is the requirement that applicants purchase Professor Rostow's book. Making the material conveniently available at a lower price is a distinct service. Requiring its use may suggest the possibility of a collusion. The other questionable action is the retention of Professor Rostow as a consultant *after* publication of the book. If he was, in fact, employed to provide services other than producing the materials, continuation of the relationship could be desirable. If not, there is strong implication of collusion.

The incident must also be examined from the perspective of Professor Rostow as a professional educator, applying standards that are incumbent to the profession. The professor's principal allegiance must be to his academic affiliation. Typically, any extra-mural activities should contribute to his competence as a teacher and researcher and/or provide service to the community. There is nothing reported in the incident that could not conceivably raise his productivity in each of these categories. There is, however, a serious question arising from his role as an entrepreneur.

With the required purchase of the book, T-A-T Publishing has a virtual monopoly. A pricing policy that would yield profits and royalties of the magnitude reported is exploitative, to say the least. Also, his acceptance of royalties under the monopolistic arrangement has overtones of violating professional ethical standards. And if Rostow was paid by the board to prepare the materials, his rights to the property and any personal gains could be reasonably questioned.

Finally, "no comment" should not be too readily interpreted as nolo contendere or prima facie evidence of wrongdoing. However, both the board (as custodian of state assets) and Professor Rostow (as a professional educator and consultant) have implicit obligations for full disclosure of the nature of their relationship. The appropriate forum is quite probably the legislative committee rather than the press. I suggest that they take the initiative, if their intentions are honorable.

Discussion items

1. Are the issues in this incident mainly political? Ethical? Personal? Organizational? Or other? Explain.

2. On what grounds would you justify preventing the professor (consultant) from realizing personal gain from the materials he created and developed?

3. Do you agree with Representative Mary Krause that the state real estate board gave away the public's assets? Explain your position.

Suggested reading list

BOOKS

Carroll, Stephen J., and **Tosi, Henry L.** *Organizational Behavior.* Chicago: St. Clair Press, 1977. Chap. 15.

Davis, Keith. *Human Behavior at Work.* 5th ed. New York: McGraw-Hill Book Co., 1977. Chaps. 19, 20.

Flippo, Edwin B., and **Munsinger, Gary M.** *Management.* 4th ed. Boston: Allyn and Bacon, Inc., 1978. Chap. 3.

Hicks, Herbert G., and **Gullett, C. Ray.** *The Management of Organizations.* 3d ed. New York: McGraw-Hill Book Co., 1976. Chaps. 6, 7.

Kast, Fremont E., and **Rosenzweig, James E.** *Organizations and Management: A Systems Approach.* 3d ed. New York: McGraw-Hill Book Co., 1979. Chaps. 2, 6.

Koontz, Harold, and **O'Donnell, Cyril.** *Management: A Systems and Contingency Analysis of Managerial Functions.* 6th ed. New York: McGraw-Hill Book Co., 1976. Chap. 4.

Longnecker, Justin G. *Principles of Management and Organizational Behavior.* 4th ed. Columbus, Ohio: Charles E. Merrill Publishing Co., 1977. Chaps. 3–5.

Megginson, Leon C. *Personnel and Human Resources Administration.* 3d ed. Homewood, Ill.: Richard D. Irwin, Inc., 1977. Chaps. 15, 20, 23.

Miner, John B. *The Management Process.* 2d ed. New York: Macmillan Publishing Co., Inc., 1978. Chap. 30.

Terry, George R. *Principles of Management.* 7th ed. Homewood, Ill.: Richard D. Irwin, Inc., 1977. Chap. 3.

JOURNALS

Adler, N. A. "Sounds of Executive Silence." *Harvard Business Review* vol. 49, no. 4 (July/August 1971):100–105.

Cartun, Walter P. "Fact And Fiction of Social Responsibility." *Advanced Management Journal* vol. 38, no. 1 (January 1973):34–37.

Davis, Keith. "The Case for and against Business Assumption of Social Responsibilities." *Academy of Management Journal* vol. 16, no. 2 (June 1973):312–21.

———. "Understanding the Social Responsibility Puzzle." *Business Horizons* vol. 10, no. 4 (Winter 1967):45–50.

Ehrle, Raymond A. "The Credibility and Survival of the Professional." *Advanced Management Journal* vol. 38, no. 2 (April 1973):37–41.

Fitzpatrick, George D. "Good Business and Good Ethics." *Advanced Management Journal* vol. 30, no. 4 (October 1965):23–28.

Gillis, J. G. "Legal Consequences of Unethical Conduct." *Financial Analysts Journal* vol. 29, no. 11 (November 1973):12, 13.

Jones, D. "Confessions of a Consultant." *Management Review* vol. 62, no. 6 (June 1973):42–44.

Lederer, A. M. "Selecting a Management Consultant." *Administrative Management* vol. 34, no. 8 (August 1973):61–63.

Lodge, George Cabot. "Ethics and the New Ideology." *Management Review* vol. 66, no. 7 (July 1977):10–19.

Miller, Samuel H. "The Tangle of Ethics." *Harvard Business Review* vol. 38, no. 1 (January/February 1960):59–62.

Robertson, J. "Good Will beyond the Balance Sheet." *Electronic News* vol. 16 (December 1971):9.

Steiner, George A. "New Patterns in Government Regulation of Business." *MSU Business Topics* vol. 26, no. 4 (Fall 1978):53–61.

Tierney, Ernest T. "Change—A Great Motivator." *Advanced Management Journal* vol. 38, no. 4 (October 1973):20–27.

Walker, F. W. "Productivity, Profits and Business Ethics." *Advanced Management Journal* vol. 38, no. 3 (July 1973):2–8.

29

ORGANIZATION STUDY

Organization: evaluation of departmental effectiveness, span of control, delegation

Incident

IN A RECENT CONFIDENTIAL SURVEY among 25 members of the Cordle Manufacturing Company's middle management group, each participant was asked to evaluate other operating departments. The survey was designed to determine, if possible, the respect and good will generated from one department to another.

In studying the results of the survey, Floyd Morgan, executive vice president, wondered whether the opinions and answers given could be classified as valid. Of the functional departments evaluated, all had been rated reasonably satisfactory in terms of being efficient, well organized, easy to work with, and cooperative, except for the sales department. From the 25 questionnaires returned, 18 participants said the sales department needed reorganizing. They stated that it was difficult to work with and rarely cooperated with the other departments.

Later in the week Mr. Morgan reported the results of the survey to the company president. The president listened attentively and then said to the executive vice president:

Floyd, obviously something has to be done about this. You and I know that the sales department is probably the most profitable and energetic group we have. We have poured more money and more new blood into sales than into any other area. It is high time they realize they have to fit into the organization in more ways than just dollars and cents. My suggestion to you is simple. Take the results of this survey over to Bill Lee, director of sales, and tell him to straighten it out fast. We do not operate just for the benefit of that department.

Critiques

ROBERT G. COOK
Professor of Management
University of Missouri

The president of the Cordle Manufacturing Company made a hasty decision and issued instructions prematurely where time was not the critical factor. His impulsive action may create problems rather than solve them. Two general factors underly an evaluation: survey validity and the approach for corrective action. Should the validity be high, contrary to my expectations, it is possible that time is needed to digest changes in the sales department due to new personnel and revised operations. Alternatively, there may be some inept individuals and/or faulty operations and hence a real problem.

It is more likely that the validity of the survey is low. The president may be trying to solve a nonexistent problem. This would tend to create problems, possibly very serious ones. There could be difficulties within the sales department but the low validity survey would not tell us that. Though the survey may not measure what it was intended to measure, it may have some value if it leads to research behind the opinions expressed. That managers in other departments are disturbed about the sales department should not necessarily be interpreted as something wrong in that department. Variations in customer demand filter through a sales department and necessarily affect operations and personnel in other units of organization. Too, new sales personnel with more money may be making needed changes in generating demand and servicing customers. Such changes may be disturbing established patterns of behavior and arise principally from changes in institutional factors. This type of problem is often less obvious than those arising from conflicts of personality. Unfortunately, the president concludes that the sales personnel are at fault and implies that it is due to their shortcomings. Even cursory research might lead to other conclusions.

The survey designer should have dealt with validity before the survey became operational. Mr. Morgan reported "results" to the president without expressing his serious reservations. He implied validity by failing to raise the issue. Even so, the president should have questioned validity early in the decision-making process. The approach to corrective action seems certain to breed frustration and resentment even if the survey were sound. Bill Lee's opinions have been ignored. He has responsibility with uncertain authority. The effect upon sales and personnel has not been considered. It could lead to loss of capable managers and decreased achievement of organizational objectives.

ALFRED L. THIMM
Professor of Industrial Administration
Union College in Schenectady

The most profitable and aggressive department in an organization has just lost a popularity contest. Unfortunately cooperativeness and "good fellowship" are neither necessary nor sufficient conditions for excellence. Frequently "difficult" though truly superior individuals or departments serve as a welcome though painful irritant in an organization by conducting continuous guerrilla warfare with mediocrity and red tape. After all, Taylor was very difficult to administer and Steinmetz practically invented the term *uncooperative.*

There is abundant evidence on the other hand that the "happy" "cooperative" organization, filled with smooth, homogeneous mediocrities, does not necessarily run an efficient or a profitable enterprise. In this specific case it was "the most profitable and energetic group" that was found "difficult" by the "reasonably satisfactory" departments.

As an immediate step, the results of the survey should be brought to the attention of the sales department. The young and aggressive nature of the "new blood" in the department probably prevented them from being aware of their impact upon the rest of the enterprise. A certain amount of additional maturity and tenure might go far to remove quickly the most flagrant personality clashes. It would be much more important, however, to collect as many examples of incidents of lack of cooperation to determine to what extent these occurrences were due to outmoded procedures and mediocrity in the rest of the organization. A "straightening out" of the sales department without these considerations might easily change the department into a cooperative but merely "reasonably satisfactory" group. A study of the underlying causes that produced the ill feeling between the sales department and the rest of the firm might lead to a rejuvenation of the entire organization.

Discussion items

1. Did the president use good judgment in ordering Floyd Morgan, the executive vice president, to "straighten out" the sales department? Explain your position. Assuming that you were in the position of Morgan, how would you proceed to carry out the president's orders?

2. Is it important that respect and goodwill prevail in the relationships among various departments in an organization? Explain your position on this question.

3. What is involved in reorganizing a department? What type of changes are required? What might managers expect a reorganization to accomplish?

Suggested reading list

BOOKS

Burack, Elmer H. *Organization Analysis: Theory and Applications.* Hinsdale, Ill.: The Dryden Press, 1975. Chap. 2.

Carroll, Stephen J., and **Tosi, Henry L.** *Organizational Behavior.* Chicago: St. Clair Press, 1977. Chap. 18.

Davis, Keith. *Human Behavior at Work.* 5th ed. New York: McGraw-Hill Book Co., 1977. Part 3.

Donnelly, James H.; Gibson, James L.; and **Ivancevich, John M.** *Fundamentals of Management.* 3d ed. Dallas, Texas: Business Publications, Inc., 1978. Chaps. 11, 12.

Flippo, Edwin B., and **Munsinger, Gary M.** *Management.* 4th ed. Boston: Allyn and Bacon, Inc., 1978. Chaps. 7, 8.

Jucius, Michael J. *Personnel Management.* 9th ed. Homewood, Ill.: Richard D. Irwin, Inc., 1979. Chap. 28.

Koontz, Harold, and **O'Donnell, Cyril.** *Management: A Systems and Contingency Analysis of Managerial Functions.* 6th ed. New York: McGraw-Hill Book Co., 1976. Part 3.

Longnecker, Justin G. *Principles of Management and Organizational Behavior.* 4th ed. Columbus, Ohio: Charles E. Merrill Publishing Co., 1977. Chaps. 10–14.

Miner, John B. *The Management Process.* 2d ed. New York: Macmillan Publishing Co., Inc., 1978. Chaps. 14–16.

Terry, George R. *Principles of Management.* 7th ed. Homewood, Ill.: Richard D. Irwin, Inc., 1977. Part 4, Chap. 24.

JOURNALS

Argyris, Chris. "Interpersonal Barriers to Decision Making." *Harvard Business Review* vol. 44, no. 2 (March/April 1966):84–97.

Booker, Gene S., and **Miller, Ronald W.** "A Closer Look at Peer Ratings." *Personnel* vol. 43, no. 1 (January/February 1966):42–47.

Buck, Vernon E. "Too Much Control—Too Little Quality." *Business Horizons* vol. 8, no. 3 (Fall 1965):34–44.

Cornman, Guy L., Jr. "Aspects of an Attitude Survey." *Advanced Management Journal* vol. 31, no. 4 (October 1966):62–65.

Desi, G. R. "Dealing with Organizational Conflict." *Management Review* vol. 54, no. 10 (October 1965):37–41.

Dodd, William E., and **Pesci, Michael L.** "Managing Morale Through Survey Feedback." *Business Horizons* vol. 20, no. 3 (June 1977):36–45.

Greiner, Larry E. "Patterns of Organization Change." *Harvard Business Review* vol. 45, no. 3 (May/June 1967):119–30.

Gumpert, David E. "Growing Concerns: Performance Measures for Small Business." *Harvard Business Review* vol. 57, no. 1 (January/February 1979):172–76.

House, Robert. "A Path Goal Theory of Leader Effectiveness." *Administrative Science Quarterly* vol. 16, no. 3 (September 1971):321–39.

Khandwalla, Pradip N. "Viable and Effective Organizational Designs of Firms." *Academy of Management Journal* vol. 16, no. 3 (September 1973):481–95.

Kochen, M., and **Deutsch, K. W.** "Delegation and Control in Organizations with Varying Degrees of Decentralization." *Behavioral Science* vol. 22, no. 4 (July 1977):258–64.

Mali, Paul. "A Practical Scheme that Motivates People." *Administrative Management* vol. 34, no. 3 (March 1973):64–66.

Nielsen, Warren R., and **Kimberly, John R.** "Smoothing the Way for Managerial Change." *Advanced Management Journal* vol. 41, no. 2 (Spring 1976):4–16.

Van De Vliert, Evert. "The Organization Consultant: Controller? Pilot? Coach?" *Advanced Management Journal* vol. 36, no. 3 (July 1971):19–26.

Werhrich, Heinz. "MBO in Four Management Systems." *MSU Business Topics* vol. 24, no. 4 (Fall 1967):51–57.

Zaleznik, Abraham. "The Dynamics of Subordinacy." *Harvard Business Review* vol. 43, no. 3 (May/June 1965):119–31.

30

PROMOTION OF CARLA JUDSON

Improving organizational efficiency: reducing turnover, accidents, absences

Incident

MS. CARLA JUDSON was one of six production department heads under consideration for the recently vacated post of plant manager in charge of production. All those under consideration were close friends socially as well as professionally. During the past year employee productivity had decreased, absenteeism had risen, employee turnover had increased, and the accident record had soared. Unable to control the situation and under pressure from top management, the former plant manager had resigned.

The total situation in production was alarming if not critical. The employees sensed the problem. They openly discussed the possible successor and quietly wagered how long he or she would last.

At a private luncheon with Mr. Priest, the company president, Ms. Judson learned that she had been selected to fill on an acting basis the job of plant manager in charge of production. If she could eliminate production problems during the next six months, she would be given all authority and responsibility for the post. Mr. Priest informed her, furthermore, that a meeting of all company officers and department heads was scheduled for the following morning. At that time Ms. Judson was supposed to outline a program of action to straighten out the situation in production.

Critiques

HAROLD F. PUFF
Professor of Management
Miami University at Oxford

Basically, management must recognize what contributed to the failure of the recent plant manager in order to prevent a repetition. The immediate issue is to appoint a competent successor and to help counteract low employee productivity, excessive absenteeism, and accidents.

These morale symptoms of managerial failure can usually be traced to poor planning, organizing, motivating, and controlling, with the entire chain of command accountable. Evidently, a block in communications has led to the accumulation of unsatisfied employee grievances and dissension, with ultimate refusal to cooperate with management to achieve company objectives.

The new plant manager will have to cope with three groups, which constitute three strikes against her. First, top management's appointing Judson on an "acting" basis indicates a reluctance to give complete authority and backing, yet intention to hold her accountable for success or failure of her program. If this was the attitude taken with her predecessor, it may doom Judson also to failure. Second, the former colleagues who are also her friends socially may be jealous of her appointment, considering themselves candidates for her job upon her failure. Knowing her well, they could contrive to obstruct her plans and upset her home life too. Orders and directives from a former friend holding only acting authority will elicit poor response. Third, workers who are already gambling on the date of her demise will not readily become more interested in their production schedules and safety record.

What is needed is a strong leader to set objectives and standards, review and revise policies, and then set procedures and controls for implementing them. She must use positive motivation, but have full authority and backing of top management to carry out her plans. As a department head with a first-hand grasp of plant deficiencies, Ms. Judson should be able to pinpoint trouble areas and produce ideas for coping with them, even upon short notice.

After reviewing Ms. Judson's proposals, the next step for Mr. Priest and top management is to help her formulate strategy and then delegate full authority to act positively. Mr. Priest should make available specialized staff assistance, such as production planning and control and personnel. An attitude survey could become the basis of a personnel program that would restore confidence and loyalty toward management and the company. Attention should be given to opening up the channels of communication.

If the immediate need for a plant manager were not so pressing, an outside qualified person who could bring a fresh approach, unhampered by old prejudices and ill will, might be considered. However, recruiting and selecting a competent person would take time, and an outsider would need more time and a free hand to analyze existing problems and to build respect and followership.

ALBERT N. SCHRIEBER

Professor of Business Policy
and Operations Management
University of Washington

With the luncheon coming to a close, Ms. Judson has to make a fast decision to accept or reject the job of acting plant manager. She probably has some ideas regarding the difficulties in the plant, although it is not likely that she fully understands the situation, nor is it likely that she has a simple panacea.

What risks will she encounter by refusing to accept the new position? Is it likely that she will not again receive an opportunity for promotion? If she refuses, will top management consider her a block in the organization structure preventing the advancement of her subordinates? Is Mr. Priest assigning her the acting plant manager's job as an order, so that Ms. Judson has no choice and refusal will really be a resignation?

There are apparently some very serious plant problems to deal with that might well turn into a major crisis within the next six months. If she accepts the job but is not capable of meeting the problems, she may find it impossible to return to her former position, and may be terminated as was the previous plant manager. Does she have the ambition to take on this challenge? Does she have the broader knowledge and skills required? Undoubtedly, many of these factors are in her favor or else the top management would not have selected her. She should recognize that every crisis involving difficult and unpleasant problems also represents an opportunity.

If Ms. Judson decides to accept, she has several choices. She can assume the job on a temporary basis and limit herself to expedient action, thus leaving fundamental changes to her successor. Another approach would be to try for a complete solution so that the new position would become a permanent assignment for her. Still another alternative would be to protect herself by establishing limited expectations for results during the next six months. This latter direction would involve a kind of "bargaining" with Mr. Priest that would depend largely on Mr. Priest's personality and the way he relates himself to Ms. Judson and other executives.

Ms. Judson should be aware that this job involves a radical change for her. One of the more serious difficulties will be the change in relationship with many of her close friends. Some may be jealous that she, rather than they, were promoted. Some may become her adversaries if she is required to take actions they disapprove or find unpleasant.

Ms. Judson faces the immediate task of how to conduct herself the following morning at the meeting of all company officers and department heads. One approach would be to come in with a complete program of action. But does she actually know enough about the situation to prepare a complete solution within the 24 hours or less that she has available? If a simple solution could have solved the problem, it is likely that the previous manager would have found it. A more effective approach might be to describe her method of studying the problem and to suggest when she would have a solution to recommend.

Before she undertakes the study, it would be necessary that

her authority and responsibilities be clearly understood by all. One way to establish this would be by a positive statement by Mr. Priest. This might or might not create an environment conducive to cooperation. A better way would be to evolve the statement after an open and frank discussion in which all the executives have an opportunity to express their ideas. When this has been done, Ms. Judson would be ready to outline her method of study as follows:

1. Determine the significant facts regarding the current situation. What are the specific factors that have caused the unfavorable changes of the past year? Can these be measured in specific quantitative terms? How much did exterior environmental factors, such as a hostile union, or unfavorable economic conditions contribute to the difficulties? She should discuss the problem with the previous manager if possible and with the other department heads. She might even want to discuss the matter with union leaders or selected employees.
2. Establish the "real" problems. There may be many apparent problems that are not necessarily the "real" problems. Thus, employee morale may prove to be poor. But what has brought about the poor morale? Usually the difficult task of determining the real problems clearly leads to the correct action to be taken.
3. Consider the possible alternate courses of action. This would also involve anticipating the effects of each course of action.
4. Evaluate the significance and probability of each effect for each alternative, and establish the criterion for a successful solution. Each alternative will probably have some favorable factors and some negative factors.
5. Make the decision by choosing the alternative that appears to have the greatest promise for success and plan the detailed steps for implementation.
6. Test or check the decision with the company officers and/or department heads. This would involve a "selling job" on the part of Ms. Judson to convince others of the wisdom of her decision. After her ideas are accepted, she will then be ready to take action.

These comments merely suggest the first steps for Ms. Judson. The next steps to take will depend on the outcome of her presentation the following day to the company officers.

Discussion items

1. Do you think Carla Judson should accept the promotion? Defend your answer.

2. Outline the dangers of accepting a job on an acting basis without full authority to do what is necessary to get the job done.

3. Evaluate Professor Schrieber's six-step approach that he thinks Carla Judson should adopt if she accepts the position. Outline your own program of action that Judson might present to the company officers and department heads the following morning.

Suggested reading list

BOOKS

Carroll, Stephen J., and **Tosi, Henry L.** *Organizational Behavior.* Chicago: St. Clair Press, 1977. Chap. 18.

Davis, Keith. *Human Behavior at Work.* 5th ed. New York: McGraw-Hill Book Co., 1977. Chap. 6.

Flippo, Edwin B., and **Munsinger, Gary M.** *Management.* 4th ed. Boston: Allyn and Bacon, Inc., 1978. Chap. 9.

Jucius, Michael J. *Personnel Management.* 9th ed. Homewood, Ill.: Richard D. Irwin, Inc., 1979. Chap. 12.

Kast, Fremont E., and **Rosenzweig, James E.** *Organizations and Management: A Systems Approach.* 3d ed. New York: McGraw-Hill Book Co., 1979. Chap. 18.

Koontz, Harold, and **O'Donnell, Cyril.** *Management: A Systems and Contingency Analysis of Managerial Functions.* 6th ed. New York: McGraw-Hill Book Co., 1976. Chaps. 18, 19, 30.

Longnecker, Justin G. *Principles of Management and Organizational Behavior.* 4th ed. Columbus, Ohio: Charles E. Merrill Publishing Co., 1977. Chap. 10.

McCormick, Ernest J., and **Tiffin, Joseph.** *Industrial Psychology.* 6th ed. Englewood Cliffs, N.J.: Prentice Hall, Inc., 1974. Chap. 19.

Megginson, Leon C. *Personnel and Human Resources Administration.* 3d ed. Homewood, Ill.: Richard D. Irwin, Inc., 1977. Chap. 14.

Terry, George R. *Principles of Management.* 7th ed. Homewood, Ill.: Richard D. Irwin, Inc., 1977. Chaps. 1, 2, 15, 16.

JOURNALS

Alfred, Theodore M. "Checkers or Choice in Manpower Management." *Harvard Business Review* vol. 45, no. 1 (January/February 1967):157–69.

Baer, Walter E. "For the Supervisor—Do's and Don'ts in Handling Grievances." *Personnel* vol. 43, no. 6 (November/December 1966):27–32.

Bennis, Warren G. "Organizational Revitalization." *California Management Review* vol. 14, no. 1 (Fall 1966):51–60.

Brooker, W. M. A. "The Content and Process of Adaptive Change." *Advanced Management Journal* vol. 30, no. 2 (April 1965):21–24.

Couch, Peter D. "Learning to be a Middle Manager." *Business Horizons* vol. 22, no. 1 (February 1979):33–41.

Decotiis, Thomas, and **Petit, André.** "The Performance Appraisal Process: A Model and Some Testable Propositions." *Academy of Management Review* vol. 3, no. 3 (July 1978):635–46.

Garrison, Kathleen, and **Mochinsky, Paul M.** "Evaluating the Concept of Absentee-Proneness with Two Measures of Absence." *Personnel Psychology* vol. 30, no. 3 (Autumn 1977):389–93.

Gonen, Turan, and **Bekiroglu, Haluk."** "Motivation—The State of the Art." *Personnel Journal* vol. 56, no. 11 (November 1977):561–62.

Hartman, Richard I., and **Gibson, John J.** "The President Problem of Employee Absenteeism." *Personnel* vol. 50, no. 6 (July 1971):535–40.

Heisler, W. J. "Promotion: What Does It Take to Get Ahead?" *Business Horizons* vol. 21, no. 2 (April 1978):57–63.

Henry, James D. "Are You Good at Career Counseling?" *Supervisory Management* vol. 19, no. 3 (March 1974):22–27.

Koch, James L. "Managerial Succession in a Factory and Changes in Supervisory Leadership Patterns." *Human Relations* vol. 31, no. 1 (January 1978):49–57.

McMahon, Timothy, and **Ivancevich, John M.** "A Study of Control in a Manufacturing Organization: Managers and Non-Managers." *Administrative Science Quarterly* vol. 21, no. 1 (March 1976):66–83.

Miller, Theron F. "How to Slow the Turnover Flow." *Personnel Journal* vol. 47, no. 5 (May 1968):321–22.

Sirota, David, and **Wolfson, Alan D.** "Pragmatic Approach to People Problems." *Harvard Business Review* vol. 51, no. 1 (January/February 1973):120–28.

Snelling, Robert O., Sr. "Tackling the Turnover Problem." *Supervisory Management* vol. 16, no. 1 (January 1971):37–39.

Wherry, Robert J., Sr., and **South, John C.** "A Worker Motivation Scale." *Personnel Psychology* vol. 30, no. 4 (Winter 1977):613–36.

31

REVERSE DISCRIMINATION

Avoiding charges of discrimination in employment and promotion practices, affirmative action requirements, employee perceptions of unfair practices

Incident

AT A MEETING OF ALL MANAGEMENT PERSONNEL, the legal advisor to the Rampart Insurance Company spoke on the subject of employee discrimination with special emphasis on subjects relating to female and minority group employees. Essentially the message was that there should be no discriminatory decisions by managers relating to the selection and hiring process, promotion policies, seniority, recognition, vacations, work loads, and so forth.

The managers of the company accepted the advice seriously, and under a climate established and implemented by the president, administered the philosophy vigorously. In some cases, women who had good performance records, equal seniority with men, and other minimal qualifications were promoted to supervisory positions, even though they might be married, have several children, and could not work overtime when needed. In other cases, employees who were classed as members of minority groups were purposely rated high on employee evaluation reports so a basis could be established for justifying a forthcoming promotion.

After about a year had passed, other nonmanagement employees gave signs that they were upset, dissatisfied, and angry about the newly introduced managerial philosophy. When no attention was given to their statements that they were now being discriminated against, and when no action came forth when they requested a hearing with the president, the informal leaders of the group posted a notice on all bulletin boards which read as follows:

All employees who are dissatisfied with present management practices and who desire to meet and discuss the organization of an independent union or discuss the possibility of affiliating with a national union, please sign below.

Critiques

SHEILA DAVIS INDERLIED

Assistant Professor of Human Resources Management
California State University at Long Beach

Is there one best way to deal with problems of discrimination in a company? What factors led to the ultimate dissatisfaction at Rampart Insurance Company? Three primary issues emerge in this incident. They are:

1. The manner in which Rampart's management handled inferences concerning discrimination.
2. The charges of "reverse discrimination" by nonmanagement employees.
3. How Rampart can establish an effective affirmative action program.

Consider the factors leading up to the bulletin board notice and the implications of each factor. The first issue is that of discrimination. In the meeting with management personnel it was the legal advisor to the company who initiated discussion of employee discrimination. It seems that the message to management was a warning with no clear objectives, other than to possibly intimidate. In fact, there is no definition of discrimination provided, no figures on numbers of women or minorities are provided to management, and no direction is given regarding corrective action. It is not even clear who will direct a program if one is established.

In the spirit of equal opportunity the managers then attempted to operationalize the "philosophy." Because of a lack of clarity and direction by upper management, middle management had to implement this philosophy individually without specific instructions or guidelines. In promoting women with similar qualifications to men the manager was operating properly. If previous discrimination exists regarding women in a department, or in the company as a whole, promoting women even with minimal equal qualifications, is acceptable under the law. However, since being married, having children, or having less flexibility regarding overtime are not job-related, they cannot be factors used in consideration for promotion.

In the consideration of minority employees for promotion, it is not in the spirit of affirmative action to artificially inflate job ratings for purposes of promotion. In fact, performance appraisal ratings by supervisors should never be used solely as the basis for promotion, since they are often biased.

The second issue, reverse discrimination, is illustrated by the anger and apparent frustration of lower-level employees. After requesting several meetings with management and the president of Rampart, their understandable hostility led to notices suggesting union organizing.

As yet, it is unclear what the courts will decide regarding what constitutes reverse discrimination. However, there is no evidence to suggest that Rampart is practicing such discriminatory policies. In the case of promoting women, they are as minimally qualified as men who might be promoted. The courts have in the past decided that when a seniority system is bona fide, it can be used as the basis for selection and promotion. Artificially rating minorities high does not constitute reverse discrimination practices—just an unwise selection and promotion procedure.

In fact, the entire problem might have been alleviated if consideration of employees' concerns throughout the company had taken place. Little communication regarding the new policy was evident and, in fact, nonmanagement employees were refused access to information by management. This of course resulted in charges of reverse discrimination.

What can be done to reestablish a climate of support and encouragement for employees and to continue to deal with discrimination? This involves the third issue, which is the implementation of an effective affirmative action plan for Rampart. This may help to alleviate some of the problems that have recently occurred. The plan should take into consideration the following:

1. Since government policies that protect companies, minority employees, and women are rapidly changing, Rampart's staff must be knowledgeable in those areas that affect employment and production.
2. Rampart should hire an affirmative action coordinator whose job specifically deals with issues of discrimination. A "legal advisor" may not be enough.
3. Rampart should examine its policies regarding selection, appraisal, promotion, and retention. We do not know, for example, whether in fact there really is a paucity of women or minorities in departments of the company. Statistics and accurate records should be collected and maintained in order to substantiate claims.
4. A clear company policy on affirmative action goals, policies, and standards should be made available to all employees, management and nonmanagement.
5. If possible, an affirmative action policy committee, consisting of management and other employees should be established at Rampart. This would encourage participation by employees not previously included.
6. Providing training to women and minorities would encourage Rampart's employees to apply for upper-level positions. Sometimes women, for example, do not have the skills necessary for managerial responsibility (for example, Larwood, Wood and Inderlied, 1978). Training would also avoid the pitfalls of inflated performance appraisals.

In summary, it seems that employees at Rampart are angry because they perceive management as excluding them from decision making and possibly passing over them for promotion. By correcting poorly conceived policies and badly managed communication of philosophy, management will go a long way toward relieving some of the tensions that have resulted. However, affirmative action represents an enormous and uncomfortable change for many employees. The law provides guidelines to assist companies in meeting goals but does not always suggest ways of dealing with problems that result. Rampart could turn a bad situation into an effective solution with the proper awareness, sensitivity, and guidance for all of its employees.

JOSEPH F. McGRAW

Instructor of Business Administration
Troy State University in Montgomery

Discrimination in any form, including reverse discrimination, is wrong. The president of Rampart has clearly practiced discrimination. Perhaps some would even conclude that he is stupid and deserves the union he seems likely to get. I would hesitate to reach such a conclusion hastily based on so little evidence. Not too many stupid people get to occupy the president's office. Further, I've seen too many otherwise brilliant presidents make what would appear on the surface to be questionable decisions in actions related to the 1964 Civil Rights Act. Why do they do it? All they need to do is obey the law. Isn't it just that simple? No! There is nothing simple about it. It is one thing to discuss these matters in the safety of the classroom. Applications in real life, however, often become entwined in a jungle of inconsistencies and contradictions.

Let's look first to the law. Just how clear is it? When he was United States Attorney General, Edward H. Levi expressed an opinion on the subject. He was quoted in the 29 March 1976 edition of *United States & World Report* as saying "that if a person examined statutes banning discrimination, executive orders issued pursuant to them, and court rulings interpreting them, he would have a view of a madhouse. The resemblance between the statutes and court decisions would be purely coincidental—and usually there isn't any resemblance." Well, if the law itself is fuzzy, perhaps the federal agency charged with enforcement of the act has shed some light on our subject. Not so, according to many who have dealt with EEOC. In fact, this has been a highly criticized agency. The December 1976 edition of *Fortune* contains a lengthy article on EEOC, which claims it is among the most poorly run agencies in Washington. The article states, "The view that EEOC is badly run is not really controversial these days. Its critics have included the General Accounting Office, the investigative arm of Congress, which recently found the agency to be minimal in its effectiveness. Its own internal audits have raised questions about the destruction and falsification of files, employees doing jobs for which they had never been properly trained, and friction between district and regional offices. More remarkable is the fact that the agency's employment standards and practices have led to well-documented charges that there is discrimination in the EEOC itself. The agency has shown itself to be susceptible to the very sort of prejudice for which it takes employers to court."

It is not just the law and the EEOC that managers must contend with when fishing in these troubled waters. Many other groups and individuals bring pressure on managers that result in hasty and questionable decisions. A recent incident that occurred in a major southeastern city provides an example. A large high school selected its cheerleaders on the basis of best qualified as measured against a long-standing set of standards. As it turned out, all girls selected one year were white. This resulted in protests by black students. Immediately, a black state legislator threw himself into the incident. He demanded that cheerleaders be selected on the basis of race so that the team would be comprised of blacks and whites in the same ratio as the student body. The school was roughly 35 percent black. Newspapers gave his proposal wide publicity. Then he was advised that a majority of the football team was black. Should blacks be removed from it to make way for less competent white players? It was at this point the legislator learned that these matters are not always simple. By now the situation was getting nasty. To avoid potential violence, the principal made a decision. All girls who tried out would be declared cheerleaders without regard to qualifications. The school had a large squad that year.

Did the president of Rampart just wake up one morning and decide to implement so radical a departure from past practice? Or was he under pressure? What were his alternatives? Was he about to lose important contracts for lack of an affirmative-action program? Had he been visited by EEOC? Had a quota system been imposed? Was he so naive as to not know that his new program would demoralize his work force? We don't know the answer to these questions. We do, however, know that the woods are full of organizations that have placed incompetent people in leadership positions in the name of what is called, all too casually, "equal employment opportunity." When employees perceive that they have been discriminated against, the effects are deadly. Enthusiasm, loyalty, and performance are compromised and organizational effectiveness and efficiency suffer. I support fully the 1964 act and regard it as a milestone in American history. The implementation of the act, however, has been deplorable and has resulted in conditions just as "sick" as the ills the act was intended to cure. Perhaps, just perhaps, the highly publicized suit initiated by Sears at the time of this writing will result in a reexamination of what is happening. If not, it will be a great pity, for the insanity has gone on too long.

Discussion items

1. Review current legislation pertaining to discriminatory practices with which managers must conform. Justify or criticize the Rampart managerial policies relating to the selection, hiring, evaluation, and promotion of nonmanagerial employees.

2. Does the implementation of vigorous "Affirmative Action" and "Equal Employment Opportunity" programs inherently require that some employees receive unfair and unequal treatment in matters relating to selection, hiring, performance evaluation, and promotion? If so, defend. If not, explain.

3. Suggest the appropriate action that should be taken by management now that Rampart employees are considering the possibility of unionizing.

Suggested reading list

BOOKS

Burack, Elmer H. *Organization Analysis: Theory and Applications.* Hinsdale, Ill.: The Dryden Press, 1975. Chap. 15.

Carroll, Stephen J., and **Tosi, Henry L.** *Organizational Behavior.* Chicago: St. Clair Press, 1977. Chap. 18.

Davis, Keith. *Human Behavior at Work.* 5th ed. New York: McGraw-Hill Book Co., 1977. Chap. 18.

Dressler, Gary. *Personnel Management: Modern Concepts and Techniques.* Reston, Va.: Reston Publishing Co., 1978. Chap. 15.

Jongeward, D., and **Scott, D.** *Affirmative Action for Women.* New York: Addison-Wesley Publishing Co., Inc., 1975.

Jucius, Michael J. *Personnel Management.* 9th ed. Homewood, Ill.: Richard D. Irwin, Inc., 1979. Chaps. 1–5, 23.

Kast, Fremont E., and **Rosenzweig, James E.** *Organizations and Management: A Systems Approach.* 3d ed. New York: McGraw-Hill Book Co., 1979. Chap. 24.

Koontz, Harold, and **O'Donnell, Cyril.** *Management: A Systems and Contingency Analysis of Managerial Functions.* 6th ed. New York: McGraw-Hill Book Co., 1976. Chap. 19.

Longnecker, Justin G. *Principles of Management and Organizational Behavior.* 4th ed. Columbus, Ohio: Charles E. Merrill Publishing Co., 1977. Chaps. 3, 18, 26.

Megginson, Leon C. *Personnel and Human Resources Administration.* 3d ed. Homewood, Ill.: Richard D. Irwin, Inc., 1977. Chaps. 2–7.

Terry, George R. *Principles of Management.* 7th ed. Homewood, Ill.: Richard D. Irwin, Inc., 1977. Chap. 21.

JOURNALS

Bartol, Kathryn M. "The Sex Structure of Organizations: A Search for Possible Causes." *Academy of Management Review* vol. 3, no. 4 (October 1978):805–15.

Brookmire, David A., and **Burton, Amy A.** "A Format for Packaging Your Affirmative Action Program." *Personnel Journal* vol. 57, no. 6 (June 1978):294–304.

Burke, Ronald J., and **Weir, Tamara.** "Readying the Sexes for Women in Management." *Business Horizons* vol. 20, no. 3 (June 1977):30.

Commerce Clearing House Labor Law Reports ed. "Equal Employment Opportunity Agreement between AT&T Company and EEOC and U.S. Department of Labor." Issue no. 373 (1973):614–19.

Flast, Robert H. "Taking the Guesswork out of Affirmative Action Planning." *Personnel Journal* vol. 56, no. 2 (February 1977):68–71.

Gatewood, Robert D., and **Schoenfeldt, Lyle F.** "Content Validity and EEOC: A Useful Alternative For Selection." *Personnel Journal* vol. 56, no. 8 (August 1977):402–4, ff.

Gilbreath, Jerri D. "Sex Discrimination and Title VII of the Civil Rights Act." *Personnel Journal* vol. 56, no. 1 (January 1977):23–26.

Goodman, Carl F. "Equal Employment Opportunity: Preferential Quotas and Unrepresented Third Parties." *Public Personnel Management* vol. 6, no. 6 (November/December 1977):371–85.

Hildebrand, George H. "Evaluating the Impact of Affirmative Action: A Look at the Federal Contract Compliance Program." *Industrial and Labor Relations Review* vol. 29, no. 4 (July 1976):486–507.

Kilgour, John G. "Responding to the Union Campaign." *Personnel Journal* vol. 57, no. 5 (May 1978):238–42, 269.

Larwood, L.; Wood M.; and Inderlied, S. D. "Training Women for Management: New Problems and Issues." *Academy of Management Review* vol. 3, no. 3 (July 1978):584–93.

Newman, Jerry M. "Discrimination in Recruitment: An Empirical Analysis." *Industrial and Labor Relations Review* vol. 32, no. 1 (October 1978):15–23.

Pati, Gopal C. "Countdown on Hiring the Handicapped." *Personnel Journal* vol. 57, no. 3 (March 1978):144–53.

Robertson, David E. "New Directions in EEO Guidelines." *Personnel Journal* vol. 57, no. 7 (July 1978):360–63.

Scala, Bea. "Affirmative Action and the Bakke Case—Speculation on What it Could Mean to Management." *Administrative Management* vol. 38, no. 12 (December 1977):26–28.

Sherman, Mitchell. "Equal Employment Opportunity: Legal Issues and Societal Consequences." *Public Personnel Management* vol. 7, no. 2 (March/April 1978):127–33.

Stafford, James E., and Gelb, Betsy D. "Who's More Critical of Business: Men or Women?" *Business Horizons* vol. 21, no. 1 (Februrary 1978):5–10.

32

RIVERSIDE ACADEMY

Avoiding conflict of interest situations, governing board relationships, legal issues

Incident

MR. ROBERT WINKLE, the newly appointed headmaster of Riverside Academy, has been busy preparing for his first regular meeting of the school's board of directors. In a previous conference with the board's chairman, items that needed to be placed on the agenda for the meeting were determined. One of the items concerned the school's insurance coverage. In reviewing the school's present insurance policies, Winkle was surprised at the total cost of the coverage, which clearly appeared to be much above the average. In addition, he noted that all of the policies had been issued by one firm that is owned by none other than the chairman of his board. Further investigation revealed that the firm had held the school's coverage for the past nine years.

Mr. Winkle had recently reviewed in detail the constitution/by-laws of the board of directors and became familiar with a section that states, "No director, while serving as a member of the board of directors of Riverside Academy, shall derive personal financial gain or reward from serving on the board because of membership." Winkle must decide on a proper course of action to take with regard to what he perceives to be clearly a case of managerial conflict of interest.

Critiques

ROBERT E. ENGEL
Associate Professor and Chairman
Postsecondary and Continuing Education
University of Iowa

There are two critical aspects of this incident as far as the headmaster is concerned. The more important aspect may not be the most obvious one. The obvious problem is the apparent conflict of interest. It could be dealt with in a somewhat abstract way without regard for whom the subjects are. One would want to ascertain (probably from the school's legal counsel) whether or not the constitution/by-laws of the organization have indeed been broken. If there is an offense, it and the offender should be corrected.

Perhaps the less obvious but more crucial problem for both the headmaster and the school is how to handle this situation. In protecting the best interests of the organization, Mr. Winkle will not want to do it greater harm; nor would he wish to embarrass a director of the school unnecessarily or damage his reputation. Consequently, the headmaster has a communication and human relations challenge. Questions of power, authority, and role are foremost, along with the issue of institutional stability. This is the most critical aspect of this incident as far as the welfare of the organization is concerned.

The headmaster may be somewhat handicapped by his newness to the situation. He probably does not know the chairman well and probably is not sure how he would react to a query about this issue. On the other hand, there may be an advantage in being new on the scene. Apparent innocence based on lack of acquaintance with a situation is often excused. (For example: The little child who pointed out that the emperor was wearing no clothes.)

The dynamics of the situation and the personalities of the people involved will largely determine *how* the headmaster will broach the subject. But there is no question that he *must* raise the issue with the chairman. (Unless, of course, he should find that he is mistaken.) Whether or not the by-laws are being infringed, prudent attention to the issue will legitimize the headmaster's authority as the chief executive of the school. And it will demonstrate his thoroughness as an administrator. In any case, to ignore the issue would amount to administrative malfeasance.

While the headmaster is considering how he will approach the chairman, and while he is (perhaps) gaining expert counsel on the interpretation of the constitution/by-laws, he ought to seek some simple facts himself. For example, we are told that the school has purchased its insurance from this firm for nine years. We also note that the by-laws state that no director *while serving* shall derive financial gain or reward. It may be that the chairman was elected to the board *after* the school purchased the insurance coverage and, simply, no one has thought about it. Perhaps the chairman is not familiar with all of the by-laws. Oversight or lack of information are frequently the reason for problems of this nature, in which case the problem may be easily resolved. Typically, a reasonable person will be grateful for being informed and for being saved embarrassment.

Or it may be that in spite of Mr. Winkle's observation that the insurance costs seem too high, the coverage from this firm is the best deal available. It may be that a different by-law states that such services must be purchased after a bidding process and that this firm's bid was the lowest for the kind of coverage desired. Since school trustees or directors of private schools (as one assumes this is), are typically expected to make financial as well as service contributions to the school, the chairman may wish to return his profit from the sale of insurance to the school. Or perhaps he (or his company) is already doing this, but the headmaster does not know it.

These comments and examples suggest that (1) the incident is critical both as an apparent legal conflict of interest and as a communication challenge relative to the exercise of role, power, and authority in the organization; (2) the situation may not be what it seems to be and, therefore, the headmaster must not jump to conclusions; (3) one should not take precipitous action which might be unnecessary and which could generate a greater crisis for the organization and for the people involved than the apparent problem itself. Nevertheless, it is clear that the headmaster cannot ignore the issue.

JONATHON S. RAKICH

Professor of Management and
Director of Graduate Programs in Business
University of Akron

Before Mr. Winkle, the newly appointed headmaster of Riverside Academy, decides on a course of action with regard to his "perceived" conflict of interest on the part of the chairman of the board of directors of Riverside Academy, certain assumptions must be made. First, given the fact that there is a board of directors, it is assumed that Riverside Academy is a nonprofit corporation incorporated by a state and that it has tax-exempt status. Second, it may be assumed that the chairman has been a board member for at least the past nine years, the period of time during which the Academy's insurance coverage was written by the chairman's insurance agency. Third, it is assumed that Mr. Winkle has checked comparable rates for similar insurance coverage with other carriers in order to draw the conclusion that the total cost of the coverage ". . . clearly appeared to be much above the average." Based on these assumptions, Mr. Winkle should collect additional information before deciding on the course of action he should follow. That is, he should not blindly assume "conflict of interest" and act before he acquires additional information as described in the following paragraphs. There may indeed have been valid reasons for the past board actions. If so, unfounded accusations by the newly hired headmaster would place him in an untenable and embarrassing situation.

On the surface it appears that there is indeed a conflict of interest between the chairman and the academy's purchasing of its insurance policies. From a legal point of view, state statutes specify that any board member has a legal responsibility to disclose full information to the full board when dealings by the corporation (that is, the academy), be it profit or nonprofit, will possibly result in financial gain for any board member. This is reflected in the constitution/by-laws of the academy. In this particular incident, the chairman owned the insurance agency that wrote the insurance policies for the academy. Therefore, he has a legal duty to disclose that fact to all members of the board and to disassociate himself from any voting on the letting of the contract. Should this disclosure, "fair dealing," and voting disassociation not have been made by the chairman during the past nine years, there would be legal recourse for recovery. For example, the academy could sue the chairman and quite possibly, constituants (parents, employees) could initiate legal recovery. In addition, the tax-exempt status of the academy could be in jeopardy. Mr. Winkle should do all of his homework prior to taking any particular action. This would include a review of the minutes for all of the meetings during which the insurance contracts were awarded to determine whether the chairman had disclosed his interest and disassociated himself from the voting.

If there is evidence that the chairman disassociated himself, disclosed his interests in the insurance agency, that other agencies submitted bids, and there was good faith in the awarding of the contracts, the situation should probably stop at that point. However, it might be appropriate for Mr. Winkle to suggest that an arm's length be kept in the future awarding of contracts. Given that the academy's public image is important, the board of directors should conduct its business in such a manner that no outside observer (public) could perceive conflict of interest. If the minutes do not indicate that disclosure and disassociation had occurred, then Mr. Winkle should consult with an attorney and seek information to determine if other improprieties occurred in the past.

Presuming an impropriety occurred, the first thing that Mr. Winkle should do is approach the chairman and discuss the matter with him. He should present all of the information he has acquired: specifically, the laws of the state, copies of the minutes of the board meetings during which the contracts were awarded, and the attorney's opinion of the possible legal ramifications. If the chairman does nothing, or attempts to suppress the information, it would be Mr. Winkle's responsibility to present all of the information (along with recommendations) to the full board. Should the full board take no action to rectify the situation, (terminate the contracts, initiate a "fair dealing" process, and/or elect a new chairman), Mr. Winkle would have no recourse other than to offer his resignation to the full board. If Mr. Winkle did not present this information to the full board after conversing with the chairman, with or without his consent, meaning he chose to ignore the situation, he could be culpable and would not fulfill his responsibilities as headmaster of the academy. Furthermore, he would be practicing situational ethics—the violation of one principle in order to accomplish other objectives. Unfortunately, when an individual particpates in situational ethics, he is contaminating himself in terms of future effectiveness.

Discussion items

1. Do you feel that there is a "managerial conflict of interest" present in this incident? Explain your views.

2. Evaluate Professor Rakich's statement that Mr. Winkle would be practicing "situational ethics" if he chose to ignore the present situation he finds himself in.

3. What course of action do you think Mr. Winkle should take with regard to the perceived conflict of interest. Why?

Suggested reading list

BOOKS

Burack, Elmer H. *Organizational Analysis: Theory and Applications.* Hinsdale, Ill.: The Dryden Press, 1975. Chap. 2.

Carroll, Stephen J., and **Tosi, Henry L.** *Organizational Behavior.* Chicago: St. Clair Press, 1977. Chaps. 13–15.

Donnelly, James H.; Gibson, James L.; and **Ivancevich, John M.** *Fundamentals of Management.* 3d ed. Dallas, Tex.: Business Publications, Inc., 1978. Chaps. 3, 5.

Flippo, Edwin B., and **Munsinger, Gary M.** *Management.* 4th ed. Boston: Allyn and Bacon, Inc., 1978. Chaps. 23, 24.

Jucius, Michael J. *Personnel Management.* 9th ed. Homewood, Ill.: Richard D. Irwin, Inc., 1979. Chap. 24.

Kast, Fremont E., and **Rosenzweig, James E.** *Organizations and Management: A Systems Approach.* 3d ed. New York: McGraw-Hill Book Co., 1979. Chap. 21.

Koontz, Harold, and **O'Donnell, Cyril.** *Management: A Systems and Contingency Analysis of Managerial Functions.* 6th ed. New York: McGraw-Hill Book Co., 1976. Part 1.

Longnecker, Justin G. *Principles of Management and Organizational Behavior.* 4th ed. Columbus, Ohio: Charles E. Merrill Publishing Co., 1977. Chap. 15.

Miner, John B. *The Management Process.* 2d ed. New York: Macmillan Publishing Co., Inc., 1978. Chap. 14.

Rakich, Jonathon S.; Longest, Beaufort B., and **O'Donovan, Thomas R.** *Managing Health Care Organizations.* Philadelphia, Pa.: W. B. Saunders Co., 1977. Chap. 13.

Terry, George R. *Principles of Management.* 7th ed. Homewood, Ill.: Richard D. Irwin, Inc., 1977. Part 4.

JOURNALS

Boling, T. Edwin. "The Management Ethics 'Crises': An Organizational Perspective." *Academy of Management Review* vol. 3, no. 2 (April 1978):360–65.

Bowman, James S. "Managerial Ethics in Business and Government." *Business Horizons* vol. 19, no. 5 (October 1976):48–54.

Brenner, Steven N., and **Molander, Earl A.** "Is the Ethics of Business Changing?" *Harvard Business Review* vol. 55, no. 1 (January/February 1977):57–71.

Brown, Courtney C. "Restructuring the Board: A Director's Perspective." *Management Review* vol. 66, no. 9 (September 1976):4–13.

Chandler, Marvin. "It's Time to Clean Up the Boardroom." *Harvard Business Review* vol 53, no. 5 (September/October 1975):73–82.

Donnel, John D. "Sixteen Commandments For Corporate Directors." *Business Horizons* vol. 19, no. 1 (February 1976):45–58.

Hanson, Walter R. "Focus on Fraud." *Financial Executive* vol. 43, no. 3 (March 1975):14–19.

McCloy, John J. "On Corporate Payoffs." *Harvard Business Review* vol. 54, no. 4 (July/August 1976):14–28, ff.

Mack, Harold. "Transition Management in a Changing Environment." *Personnel Journal* vol. 57, no. 9 (September 1978):492–95, 516–17.

Mueller, Robert Kirk. "From the Boardroom: The Hidden Agenda." *Harvard Business Review* vol. 55, no. 5 (September/October 1977):40–48, 52.

Schmidt, Warren H. "Conflict: A Powerful Process For (Good or Bad) Change." *Management Review,* vol. 63, no. 12 (December 1974):5–10.

Schollhammer, Hans. "Ethics in an International Business Context." *MSU Business Topics* vol. 25, no. 2 (Spring 1977):54–61.

Ways, Max. "Business Faces Growing Pressures to Behave Better." *Fortune* vol. 89, no. 5 (May 1974):193–95.

33

ROCKWOOD NATIONAL BANK

Control: cost reduction, public reaction to controls,
customer relations, control of confidential information

Incident

IN AN EFFORT TO CONTROL COSTS of servicing customer
accounts, the vice president of Rockwood National Bank charged
Ray Shingle, manager of systems, to make a study and subsequent recommendations to reduce the operating expense of
the department.

Thirty days later, Mr. Shingle's recommendations were put
into operation. Six months later, costs of operating the department were reviewed against costs for the preceding six month
period. It was found that costs had decreased by $6,715. This
decrease was due primarily to savings in salaries charged against
the customer service department. During the preceding six
month period, 9,037 customers had been provided service.
Under the new system, 4,812 customers had been provided service.

When the vice president of the Rockwood National Bank reported the savings in the customer service department to the
president of the bank, the president expressed surprise that the
vice president thought a savings had taken place. "In the first
place," the president said, "you moved the customer service department from the main floor to the sixth floor so that fewer customers would take the trouble to check their balances and review
their statements; furthermore, you require each customer to
show positive identification before they can obtain any information about their accounts; on top of this, you have instructed the
personnel in the customer service department absolutely to
refuse to give out any banking information to anyone requesting
it over the telephone. It's my opinion," continued the president,

"that you should revert to the old system and give our customers the kind of service they deserve."

Critiques

ROBERT T. SPROUSE
Vice Chairman, Financial
Accounting Standards Board
Stamford, Connecticut

As the president has recognized, the effect of the procedures recommended by Mr. Shingle "to control costs of servicing customer accounts" appears to be reflected primarily in a reduction of customer services and only incidentally in a reduction in the cost of providing those services. Indeed, the average cost per customer accommodated may well have been increased.

A lack of effective communication among the managers of the Rockwood National Bank is evident. It is clear that the president did not intend that customer services were to be curtailed or discouraged in order to reduce costs. The vice president's instructions to Mr. Shingle, however, were quite broad. Accordingly, it is understandable that Mr. Shingle initiated changes that had the effect of reducing the services provided rather than reducing the costs of continuing to provide the same services. These are two separate matters, each of which appears to have deserved attention.

First, the practice of supplying information to customers by telephone and without positive identification needed examination. The banker-depositor relationship is a confidential one; appropriate safeguards are desirable. Past procedures were apparently lax. A letter from the president to individual depositors explaining that new procedures were being employed in order to more fully protect the confidential nature of their financial affairs might well have insured retention of customer good will, or even increased it.

Second, an appropriate policy should have been established with respect to the kind of services to be provided, under what conditions, and the extent to which it is desirable to encourage customers to avail themselves of such services. Once the bank's policy is clearly established, responsibility for implementation at the lowest cost consistent with that policy could be assigned to an appropriate individual, presumably Mr. Shingle.

Cost *reduction* can almost always be effected by eliminating some activity. Such an approach, however, can easily be "penny wise and pound foolish." Cost *control,* on the other hand, implies the implementation of policies and decisions at the lowest costs consistent therewith. Indeed, such costs are almost always a relevant factor in the determination of policy and in the decision-making process.

The president, vice president, and manager of systems (Mr. Shingle) should get together and, after considering the costs involved, agree upon an appropriate policy for operating the customer service department. In implementing that policy, customers should be informed in such a way as to minimize unfavorable reaction.

HAROLD W. STEVENSON
Professor of Finance
Arizona State University

On several counts the management of Rockwood National Bank exhibits faulty handling of a change in customer service. Starting with the bank's foggy picture of who really determines customer service policy, the plans and implementation of a significant change appear to have been botched. The attempt to justify the change on the basis of fewer customers served also appears ill-advised. Although the president should be the one foremost in the bank concerned with customer relations, he seems to be mindful of this service change only after the fact.

Since people seem to be particularly sensitive to infringements on what they consider their rights in money matters, it behooves a bank to be very cautious in instituting a service change. Irritated customers are very likely to react by withdrawing their balances.

The president, therefore, should ever be striving for bank employees to foster customer relations. A bank, after all, operates to provide services to customers. It builds its reputation slowly over the years, but it could have this confidence undermined rather quickly through sudden and poorly announced changes in service.

It is commendable for a bank to innovate in operations such as in providing drive-in services, bank-by-mail procedures, and lobby tellers. It is also commendable to seek to reduce operating expenses where feasible and to levy special charges on services for customers, where justified. In providing certain services a bank is not as efficient as would be theoretically possible, but there are dangers in reasoning along efficiency lines. From an expense standpoint it would probably be best for a bank to receive all deposits by mail and to have no pretentious banking structures. Customers differ and their needs differ, however, and some customers desire to bank in person. Banks, therefore, have banking facilities to accommodate the major needs.

Rockwell management errs in attempting to cut down on counter and telephone traffic regarding account balances merely by making this service less convenient. Perhaps the customers should first be circularized on how to keep their own running balances and also on the need for a bank to be cautious in giving account information by telephone. By directing customer attention to services already rendered that cover these needs, Rockwell may be able to effect the desired ends with less customer ill will. If certain customers require special account statement reports, consideration can be given to special fees. The true measure of satisfactory changes is not how few customers are served, but rather whether customers are content and deposit balances are favorably affected.

Discussion items

1. Professor Sprouse, in his critique, states that a lack of effective communication among the managers of the Rockwood National Bank is evident. Describe methods by which this deficiency could have been corrected.

2. Professor Stevenson indicates in his critique that the true measure of satisfactory change at Rockwood National Bank is whether customers are content. Outline a method whereby customer satisfaction can be ascertained.

3. The control process consists of several definite steps that are fundamental to all managerial controlling. In what respect did the events occurring in this incident violate good managerial controlling?

Suggested reading list

BOOKS

Burack, Elmer H. *Organization Analysis: Theory and Applications.* Hinsdale, Ill.: The Dryden Press, 1975. Chap. 5.

Carroll, Stephen J., and **Tosi, Henry L.** *Organizational Behavior.* Chicago: St. Clair Press, 1977. Chap. 16.

Davis, Keith. *Human Behavior at Work.* 5th ed. New York: McGraw-Hill Book Co., 1977. Chap. 27.

Donnelly, James H.; Gibson, James L.; and **Ivancevich, John M.** *Fundamentals of Management.* 3d ed. Dallas, Tex.: Business Publications, Inc., 1978. Chaps. 6, 12.

Duncan, W. Jack. *Organizational Behavior.* Boston: Houghton Mifflin Co., 1978. Chap. 13.

Flippo, Edwin B., and **Munsinger, Gary M.** *Management.* 4th ed. Boston: Allyn and Bacon, Inc., 1978. Chaps. 18–20.

Kast, Fremont E., and **Rosenzweig, James E.** *Organizations and Management: A Systems Approach.* 3d ed. New York: McGraw-Hill Book Co., 1979. Chap. 18.

Koontz, Harold, and **O'Donnell, Cyril.** *Management: A Systems and Contingency Analysis of Managerial Functions.* 6th ed. New York: McGraw-Hill Book Co., 1976. Part 6.

Longnecker, Justin G. *Principles of Management and Organizational Behavior.* 4th ed. Columbus, Ohio: Charles E. Merrill Publishing Co., 1977. Chaps. 24, 25.

Terry, George R. *Principles of Management.* 7th ed. Homewood, Ill.: Richard D. Irwin, Inc., 1977. Part 6.

JOURNALS

Anthony, Robert N. "The Trouble with Profit Maximization." *Harvard Business Review* vol. 38, no. 6 (November/December 1960):126–34.

Crane, Roger R. "Organizing for Productivity Improvements." *Advanced Management Journal* vol. 38, no. 2 (April 1973):28–31.

Dun's Review and Modern Industry ed. "The Dangerous Job of Cutting Costs." Vol. 80, no. 5 (November 1962):42–43, 142–43.

Furniss, James P., and **Nadler, Paul S.** "Should Banks Reprice Corporate Services?" *Harvard Business Review* vol. 44, no. 3 (May/June 1966):95–105.

Grote, Richard C. "Do You Have Trouble Delegating?" *Supervisory Management* vol. 16, no. 2 (February 1971):8–10.

Heron, John R. "Thoughts on Criticism." *Supervisory Management* vol. 22, no. 4 (April 1977):29–34.

Hershey, Robert. "Competitive Intelligence for the Smaller Company." *Management Review* vol. 66, no. 1 (January 1977):18–22.

Hocking, Ralph T., and **Hocking, Joan M.** "The Evolution of Decision Systems." *MSU Business Topics* vol. 24 no. 3 (Summer 1976):55–59.

Levenson, Harold E. "A Basic Approach to Cutting Costs." *Supervisory Management* vol. 22, no. 4 (April 1977):16–20.

Miller, H. B. "Is Business Meeting Its Obligations to the Public?" *Public Relations Journal* vol. 18, no. 5 (May 1962):14–18.

Odiorne, George S. "MBO: A Backward Glance." *Business Horizons* vol. 21, no. 5 (October 1978):14–24.

Quinn, Robert E. "Toward a Theory of Changing: A Means-End Model of the Organizational Improvement Process." *Human Relations* vol. 31, no. 5 (May 1978):395–415.

Sadler, Philip. "Designing an Organizational Structure: A Behavioral Approach." *Management International Review* vol. 11, no. 6 (April/May 1971):19–33.

Schleh, Edward C. "Handing Off to Subordinates: Delegating For Gain." *Management Review* vol. 67, no. 5 (May 1978):43–47.

Short, Larry E. "Planned Organizational Change." *MSU Business Topics* vol. 21, no. 4 (Autumn 1973):53–61.

Uhl, Kenneth P. "Better Management of Market Information." *Business Horizons* vol. 9, no. 1 (Spring 1966):75–82.

Wilson, Thomas B. "Making Negative Feedback Work." *Personnel Journal* vol. 57, no. 12 (December 1978):680, 681.

34

SUBVERSIVE EMPLOYEE

The indispensable employee: recruitment, subversion, security measures

Incident

THE SCIENTIFIC–RESEARCH CORPORATION engaged in the development of complex electronic equipment for various major producers and prime contractors who were primary suppliers to the federal government. The jobs were very individual and required the expert knowledge and experience of a group of research-oriented persons employed by Scientific-Research Corporation.

Scientific-Research Corporation was headed by Mr. Marvin Stonehill, who had organized the company six years previously. During the past fiscal year Scientific-Research's gross sales had totaled $11 million, a net profit of $910,000. Mr. Stonehill felt that the company was now in a position to bid directly on government orders since his firm had most of the ingredients necessary for qualifying as a direct producer.

In going through the steps necessary to establish the firm as a qualified bidder on certain governmental defense contracts, Mr. Stonehill had to submit the names of all employees so that a thorough security check could be made on each. Mr. Stonehill submitted the names routinely and thought very little about this requirement until he received a registered letter from the regional office of the federal government. This letter indicated that all except two employees had been given security clearance. To Mr. Stonehill's surprise, one was the chief research engineer. The other was an operative employee who was foreign-born. The letter stated that until the status of these two people had been clarified, the Scientific-Research Corporation would not be considered as a primary bidder on government defense orders.

Mr. Stonehill reviewed the situation and the possibilities. The operative employee could be given an outright release without causing any problems. However, the chief research engineer was almost indispensable. His experience, skill, creativity, and leadership had been the backbone of the research activities. The chief research engineer's salary of $53,000 a year was merely a token symbol of his value to the company. On the other hand, Mr. Stonehill estimated that the company, as a qualified bidder on government defense orders, could conservatively expect to double its sales during the coming year.

Critiques

ELWOOD S. BUFFA
Professor of Business Adminstration
University of California at Los Angeles

The major issue in the "Subversive Employee" incident relates to the magnitude of importance of government contracting to this company—"Mr. Stonehill estimated that the company, as a qualified bidder on government defense orders, could conservatively expect to double its sales during the coming year." Though apparently the loss of the chief research engineer would be a blow to the organization because of his experience, skill, creativity, and leadership, he is not indispensable. Clearly, Mr. Stonehill must find a replacement even though this may be a difficult problem.

The occurrence of this incident should bring Mr. Stonehill to a reappraisal of his entire organization from the viewpoint of the "indispensable employee." If an organization is filled with indispensable employees, then apparently a very poor job of organization has been done. The result should be a review of all positions to see if other indispensable employees exist and to develop a program of executive development which provides the needed depth.

There is a human side to this incident which should not be overlooked. The chief research engineer has apparently made great contributions to the organization. He should not be coldly cut from the company; rather, Mr. Stonehill should first discuss the case with the appropriate government officials to see if any other alternatives exist. It may be that organizational changes can be made which would put the chief research engineer in a position relative to the defense contracts which would satisfy the security needs. If this cannot be done, every attempt should be made to help place the man in a position in another organization. If separation is the only answer, the separation benefits should be quite liberal.

ROBERT D. HAY
Professor of Management
University of Arkansas

The basic decision confronting Mr. Stonehill is whether the firm should sacrifice the jobs of two employees, not known for sure to be security risks, for the possibility of the firm's being accepted as a bidder on governmental research contracts.

There are three or four factors having a bearing on Mr. Stonehill's decision. In the first place, he is not definitely sure that both employees are security risks. He needs more information before he can state that they are. He is not ready to make his basic decision until he gets additional information clarifying the status of the two employees. Some type of phone call, letter, or inquiry needs to be made.

Second, assuming that the two are security risks, Mr. Stonehill has to establish a policy on whether the company will employ security risks, government bidding or not. Is the national interest of higher importance in Mr. Stonehill's scale of values than the interest of two (probably one—the research engineer) employees? If the firm deals in secret types of research projects, then it seems to me that employment of security risks is bad policy.

Third, assuming that Mr. Stonehill wants to keep the research engineer and release the operative employee, a question of equity to all employees arises. Is it fair to release an operative employee and not to release a research engineer when both of them are security risks? I don't think so. I could not justify in my mind releasing one and not the other.

Fourth, is one person indispensable to any business? In a very small business, I would say yes. In a large one, such as Scientific-Research Corporation, I would say no. The chief engineer can be replaced and so can the operative employee.

The analogy could be made that Mr. Stonehill, as a submarine commander searching at the bottom of the sea for governmental research contracts in enemy-infested waters, has two of his crew stranded on top. Should he surface?

Alternatives available to Mr. Stonehill are to release the two and bid on the government contract, not release the two and continue as is, or seek more information on the status of the two before making his decision. I would recommend that Mr. Stonehill seek more information. If he finds that the two cannot be cleared, then he should release both of them, explaining reasons therefor, and help them obtain jobs. In addition, I would recommend that he include in his hiring policy that all employees must be cleared before permanent employment is offered to any prospective employee, operative or managerial.

Discussion items

1. Considering the available information, would it be a sound business decision if Mr. Stonehill, head of the company, decided to forego his plan of qualifying to bid directly on government contracts in order to retain the key research engineer in the organization? Why?

2. Do you agree or disagree with Professor Hay's view that it would be unfair to release an operative employee and not to release a research engineer when both are security risks? Defend your position.

3. Do you feel that this firm has been lax in its recruitment procedures and security measures? If so, what procedures do you recommend? If not, elaborate on your views.

Suggested reading list

BOOKS ꜱ

Carroll, Stephen J., and **Tosi, Henry L.** *Organizational Behavior.* Chicago: St. Clair Press, 1977. Chaps. 1, 2.

Davis, Keith. *Human Behavior at Work.* 5th ed. New York: McGraw-Hill Book Co., 1977. Chaps. 15, 19, 20.

Flippo, Edwin B., and **Munsinger, Gary M.** *Management.* 4th ed. Boston: Allyn and Bacon, Inc., 1978. Chaps. 11, 12.

Hicks, Herbert G., and **Gullett, C. Ray.** *The Management of Organizations.* 3d ed. New York: McGraw-Hill Book Co., 1976. Chaps. 4, 30.

Jucius, Michael J. *Personnel Management.* 9th ed. Homewood, Ill.: Richard D. Irwin, Inc., 1979. Chaps. 6–10.

Koontz, Harold, and **O'Donnell, Cyril.** *Management: A Systems and Contingency Analysis of Managerial Functions.* 6th ed. New York: McGraw-Hill Book Co., 1976. Part 4.

Longnecker, Justin G. *Principles of Management and Organizational Behavior.* 4th ed. Columbus, Ohio: Charles E. Merrill Publishing Co., 1977. Chap. 19.

McCormick, Ernest J., and **Tiffin, Joseph.** *Industrial Psychology.* 6th ed. Englewood Cliffs, N.J.: Prentice Hall, Inc., 1974. Chap. 4.

Megginson, Leon C. *Personnel and Human Resources Administration.* 3d ed. Homewood, Ill.: Richard D. Irwin, Inc., 1977. Chaps. 9, 10.

Terry, George R. *Principles of Management.* 7th ed. Homewood, Ill.: Richard D. Irwin, Inc., 1977. Chaps. 17, 21.

JOURNALS

Bassett, Glenn A. "Checking Job Applicants: How Much Do You Need to Know?" *Management Review,* vol. 54, no. 4 (April 1965):59–62.

Carratu, Vincent. "It's the Hot Season for Selling Secrets." *Industrial Management* vol. 64, no. 10 (October 1965):33–37.

Curcuru, Edmond H., and **Healey, James H.** "The Multiple Roles of the Manager." *Business Horizons* vol. 15, no. 4 (August 1972):15–24.

Ewell, James M. "The Effect of Change on an Organization." *Advanced Management Journal* vol. 36, no. 4 (October 1971):26–33.

Ewing, David W. "The Right to be Let Alone." *Across the Board* vol. 14, no. 10 (October 1977):62–73.

Foster, Harvey G. "Employee Screening." *Personnel Journal* vol. 44, no. 7 (July/August 1965):354–55.

Glueck, William F., and **Mittlestaedt, Robert A.** "Protecting Trade Secrets in the 70s." *California Management Review* vol. 16, no. 1 (Fall 1973):34–39.

Harrison, E. Frank, and **Rosenzweig, James E.** "Professional Norms and Organizational Goals." *California Management Review* vol. 14, no. 3 (Spring 1972):38–48.

Mallor, Jane. "Are Business Papers Safe from the Government." *Business Horizons* vol. 20, no. 3 (June 1977):57–60.

Management Review ed. "A 'Light-Cavalry' Approach to Decision Making." Vol. 62, no. 1 (January 1973):33–35.

Management Review ed. "Why Many Business Secrets are in Danger." Vol. 65, no. 5 (May 1976):50–52.

Milgrim, Robert W. "Trends in Trade Secret Litigation." *Management Review* vol. 65, no. 1 (January 1976):38–41.

Mitchell, William. "Personnel Security in the Atomic Energy Program." *Science* vol. 125, no. 3261 (June 28, 1957):1279–83.

Segal, Benjamin D., and **Kornbluh, Joyce L.** "Government Security and Private Industry." *The Reporter* vol. 16, no. 9 (May 2, 1957):25–27.

Sheridan, Peter J. "Aggressive Action against Trade Secret Thefts." *Management Review* vol. 63, no. 9 (September 1974):46–49.

35

SYSTEM–WIDE SOLUTIONS NEEDED

An integrated structure of company objectives, leadership, responding effectively to provocation, introducing changes

Incident

"WELL, IF YOU CAN'T SOLVE THE PROBLEMS in your department, what makes you think you can tell me how to run the entire company?" the president of Mid-State Machinery Company exploded to Craig Anderson, manager of the Data Processing Department at the end of a difficult hour-long meeting between the two. Anderson had joined the firm only one week earlier after five years of successful experience as a data-processing programmer, senior systems analyst, and associate manager of data processing in a firm that was larger and more complex than Mid-State. After coming to Mid-State he immediately began to assess the role, function, and performance of the data processing department. Anderson first talked with Bill Klein, a systems analyst and long-time employee of the company who was nearing retirement age. Anderson expected Klein to speak freely. He did!

Klein told Anderson the following:

With the emergence of the computer for business applications, Mid-State created a data processing department as a staff department but located it in the organizational structure at the same level as the operating departments that used its services. Since the data processing department was budgeted as an administrative overhead department, its services were available to the operating departments without direct charge. It was established with little guidance for the general purpose of developing computerized systems for the other departments within the company.

With this wide mission, we set out to "computerize" the company. The heads of other departments readily accepted this concept because electronic data processing looked like the answer to many of their management problems. Our data processing department ballooned in size—almost overnight, it seemed. Many systems had been designed, installed, and were running before we began to realize that company-wide objectives had never been formally established. Each department worked hard to achieve departmental objectives, but quite often the objectives of one department conflicted with those of other departments.

By this time, several operating departments were heavily dependent upon the data processing department to generate data and reports and to improve their systems as needed. Other departments had not contributed much to the development of the computer system. The computer could do clerical procedures faster and more accurately than clerks had done them. While fewer clerks were needed in the company after "computerization," a larger number of persons with higher skills were required to keep up with what the computer was doing and to correct errors in the input data. In short, our electronic data processing department had grown and developed by doing exactly what it thought *its* goal was. Of lesser concern to us was what the user departments actually needed or wanted.

Next, Anderson developed this list of characteristics of the data processing department as follows:

1. Employees of the data processing department are largely college graduates in mathematics and computer science. About half of the supervisors have been with the company a long time, while the other half are relative newcomers. This mixture has advantages, but conflicting ideas are frequently produced.

2. Most of the personnel joined the data processing department directly from college and with little previous work experience.

3. More than 50 percent of the personnel in the department are female. Data processing is an area that many women are interested in.

4. The previous manager of the department was an experienced line manager who had not kept up to date with the data processing field.

5. The majority of the women employees are at the lower levels

of the department. This is not a policy but a circumstance that should be adjusted with the passing of time.

6. The data-processing environment is a very disciplined one in which to work. There must be standards, rules, and guidelines in order to assure that the problems of the user department are addressed and solved. Work must be accomplished on schedule. As a result of continuing and rapid changes in technology, languages, systems, and procedures, the personnel in data processing are required to continually update their preparation in the field.

Anderson completed his analysis of the data processing department by identifying four crucial problems:

1. Requests from the user departments for data-processing services seldom were completed within a reasonable time and almost always *after* established due dates had passed. Some user departments had urgent needs for systems analysis and programming that were not being met. Much of the delay in starting and completing work seemed to be caused by a continuing scheduling battle between the Project Development Section and the Programming Section of the department.

2. The pressure of unmet schedules made most of the employees tense, lowered their morale, and increased their errors. Much poor work was being produced. Turnover was excessively high and required that a large proportion of new employees be hired and trained. The time spent in training the new employees further reduced the data output from the data-processing personnel, and in turn caused delays in completing regularly scheduled work.

3. The discouraging climate in the department had caused some otherwise dependable, productive employees to say they would no longer use initiative to solve the problems of the department but would only do what they were told to do.

4. Objectives for the company as a whole had been neither formally established nor communicated to managers within the company. A hierarchy of integrated objectives for units at various levels in the organizational structure was lacking. Apparently planning was done at the department level only—and done there only for the short run. No evidence

could be found to suggest the existence of a long-range strategic plan for the company as a whole.

Anderson tried to convince the president that the lack of an integrated, clearly established structure of objectives and performance standards at Mid-State was a problem that should be dealt with by the top management of the company. Moreover, he explained in detail why he felt that early attention to this problem would greatly facilitate, and should precede or at least be done concurrently with, the efforts by the data-processing department in developing effective interface linkages among the computerized systems in the various departments of the company. At present, system-wide solutions were not being generated; only departmental solutions were being produced.

As Craig Anderson sought to formulate a satisfactory course of action for his department and for his next meeting with the president, the challenging words of the president rang repeatedly in his ears: "Well, if you can't solve the problems in your department, what makes you think you can tell me how to run the entire company?"

Critiques

EDWARD R. CLAYTON
Professor of Management Science
Virginia Polytechnic Institute
and State University

In the first place, there seems to be a complete absence of appreciation of the capability of current computer technology on the part of top management in Mid-State Machinery. Forming a department called Data Processing, appointing a line manager who is not an expert in business applications of computer technology, and locating a staff department at the same organization level as operating departments is asking for trouble. Add to these errors a general mission to computerize the company on a departmental basis, computerizing whatever the operating departments want with no central guidance, and one should expect conflicts, duplication of effort, lots of complaints, and suboptimization. The problem of personnel turnover and lack of initiative is basically due to lack of leadership, both on the part of the manager of data processing and top management.

In Anderson's meeting with the president, he is in effect crying about problems of objectives, performance, system-wide solutions, effective interface linkages, and so on that the president probably does not understand or want to be concerned with. Should the president set up the company books and accounts? Of course not. Neither should he set up the computer system. Anderson is the expert. He was hired as the head and the manager. His job is to set up the system, provide the long-range plan and sell management on its implementation. Anderson should take the initiative, meet and work with the operating department heads to assess the requirements of the different departments, develop an integrative plan for the system, provide solutions to the problems, and keep the president informed of his progress.

When the data processing department starts operating like a staff position by providing guidance and advice to the president and operating departments, it will be fulfilling its mission. To computerize the company is a lot larger mission than the simple data-processing aspect. Its mission is also aimed at operation research activities to optimize the computer-based systems and calls for a high degree of interaction between the system analyst and the operating departments. In order to automate and improve operating systems the system analyst and operations researcher must completely understand the system to be automated and the results required by operating management.

Further, the overall company system and data base must be known. This requires highly skilled people with stability of tenure. Turnover of keypunch and machine operators is one thing, but turnover of system analysts and operations researchers is completely different and much more serious. Anderson must stop the loss of key emloyees by providing direction, leadership, and reasonable work schedules. The scheduling of routine data processing should present no major problems, but Anderson himself should be concerned with major system development, timing, and implementation.

GEORGE J. GORE

Professor of Management
University of Cincinnati

One gets the impression that Mid-State is a long-established, middle-sized firm that thrived because of advantages other than sophisticated management. It may be a profitable manufacturing operation with a relatively small proportion of college-trained personnel. Mid-State's president could be a founder or owner-manager whose rank and spontaneous style are essentially unchangeable.

According to Bill Klein, the computer installation took place during the first rush of applications to business and "with very little guidance." The manual systems at Mid-State were probably faulty and poorly integrated, but this rash start was not unusual in the early 1960s, when the emphasis was on hardware.

Anderson's predecessor, a former line manager, plunged headlong into justifying the department's existence with an initial focus on operating departments (which are most amenable to applications). But, as the field and tasks expanded, so did the function's size and problems. The manager was clearly inadequate, yet the president allowed the department's shortcomings to mount. Some staff members became disdainful toward those who did not know what they knew, and exit interviews may have speeded the arrival of a better qualified manager.

Craig Anderson had only five years' experience in a larger, more complex firm, but this was enough to establish his concept of normalcy. Was he hired for his initiative and with the objective of developing system-wide solutions or was Mid-State mostly seeking an order-taker who could get the department in hand? It seems probable that specialists before Anderson had either proposed more sophisticated schemes or had felt them *inadvisable* for this firm.

Regardless, the audacious newcomer angered the president by trying to tell him what to do. The boss was brittle and defensive. He concisely communicated his judgment that Anderson had overstepped his bounds and that attention should be shifted to the flaws of the malfunctioning department.

With his own house in better order, Anderson would be in a position to tactfully propose suitable goals. A comprehensive recommendation could be prepared in report form and management's reaction would determine the department's orientation. Meanwhile, effective meetings with other managers could gain support. A general management consultant would be an invaluable ally, and an executive development course might enlarge management's understanding.

Be that as it may, interminable delays could occur before dreams are realized at Mid-State—if they ever are. The company could probably be improved in scores of surefire management ways, but the president may have adroitly resisted plans that would curtail his freedom. Competent personnel in loosely run organizations can live wearisome lives, since correct procedures may be defied. Protracted clashes of objectives are untenable; so, if Anderson gets only token support, he may be limited to the less important work of perfecting suboptimal schemes.

Discussion items

1. Why does the work of the data processing department require close association with the operating departments of the firm? Should the organizational location of the data processing department be changed? In what way? Why?

2. What priorities would you assign to the four crucial problem areas of the data processing department that Anderson has identified?

3. Suggest an approach to dealing with each of the four crucial problem areas of the data processing department.

Suggested reading list

BOOKS

Carroll, Stephen J., and **Tosi, Henry L.** *Organizational Behavior.* Chicago: St. Clair Press, 1977. Chaps. 6, 7.

Davis, Keith. *Human Behavior at Work.* 5th ed. New York: McGraw-Hill Book Co., 1977. Part 3.

Donnelly, James H.; Gibson, James L.; and Ivancevich, John M. *Fundamentals of Management.* 3d ed. Dallas, Tex.: Business Publications, Inc., 1978. Chaps. 14–16.

Flippo, Edwin B., and Munsinger, Gary M. *Management.* 4th ed. Boston: Allyn and Bacon, Inc., 1978. Chap. 21.

Jucius, Michael J. *Personnel Management.* 9th ed. Homewood, Ill.: Richard D. Irwin, Inc., 1979. Chap. 3.

Kast, Fremont E., and Rosenzweig, James E. *Organizations and Management: A Systems Approach.* 3d ed. New York: McGraw-Hill Book Co., 1979. Chaps. 3–5.

Koontz, Harold, and O'Donnell, Cyril. *Management: A Systems and Contingency Analysis of Managerial Functions.* 6th ed. New York: McGraw-Hill Book Co., 1976. Part 2.

Longnecker, Justin G. *Principles of Management and Organizational Behavior.* 4th ed. Columbus, Ohio: Charles E. Merrill Publishing Co., 1977. Chaps. 3, 21.

Megginson, Leon C. *Personnel and Human Resources Administration.* 3d ed. Homewood, Ill.: Richard D. Irwin, Inc., 1977. Chap. 15.

Miner, John B. *The Management Process.* 2d ed. New York: Macmillan Publishing Co., Inc., 1978. Chap. 9.

Terry, George R. *Principles of Management.* 7th ed. Homewood, Ill.: Richard D. Irwin, Inc., 1977. Part 2, chap. 12.

JOURNALS

Boulton, William R. "The Changing Requirements for Managing Corporate Information Systems." *MSU Business Topics* vol. 26, no. 3 (Summer 1978):4–12.

Drucker, Peter F. "New Templates for Today's Organizations." *Harvard Business Review* vol. 52, no. 1 (January/February 1974):45–54.

Duel, Henry J. "Some Manager Problems in the Development of Information Systems." *Personnel Administration and Public Personnel Review* vol. 1, no. 2 (September/October 1972):51–55.

Edstrom, Anders. "Conceptualization of Design Problems for Management Information Systems." *Journal of Management Studies* vol. 10, no. 2 (May 1973):118–32.

Gibson, Cyrus F., and Nolan, Richard L. "Managing the Four Stages of EDP Growth." *Harvard Business Review* vol. 52, no. 1 (January/February 1974):76–88.

Hicks, Robert L. "Developing the Top Management in a Total Systems Organization." *Personnel Journal* vol. 50, no. 9 (September 1971):675–82.

Jenkins, Woodrow W. "What Top Management Doesn't Need to Know." *Journal of Systems Management* vol. 24, no. 2 (February 1973):8–12.

Kast, Fremont E., and **Rosenzweig, James E.** "General Systems Theory: Applications for Organization and Management." *Academy of Management Journal* vol. 15, no. 4 (December 1972):447–65.

Kromer, Ted L. "New Employee Orientation for Managers." *Personnel Journal* vol. 51, no. 6 (June 1972):434–38.

Lorsch, Jay W. "Organization Design: A Situational Perspective." *Organizational Dynamics* vol. 6, no. 2 (Fall 1977):2–14.

McFarlan, F. Warren. "Management Audit of the EDP Department." *Harvard Business Review* vol. 51, no. 3 (May/June 1973):131–42.

Nolan, Richard L. "Plight of the EDP Manager." *Harvard Business Review* vol. 51, no. 3 (May/June 1973):142–52.

Ouchi, William G., and **Price, Raymond L.** "Hierarchies, Clans and Theory Z: A New Perspective on Organization Development." *Organizational Dynamics* vol. 7, no. 2 (Fall 1978):24–44.

Schleh, Edward C. "Six Managerial Pitfalls for a Growing Company." *Management Review* vol. 62, no. 9 (September 1973):5–14.

Tebay, James E. "Planning That Begins and Ends with People." *Management Review* vol. 62, no. 1 (January 1973):47–51.

36

UNEXPECTED RELIEF

Special problems of task organization, communicating, motivating, gaining acceptance of change

Incident

A NEW RATE SCHEDULE from Medicare that required an unusual service-charge breakdown caused an overload in the insurance claims office of Regional Hospital. Even by scheduling all the overtime allowed by the budget, the section head was unable to keep the work from piling up. Mr. Barker, accounting division director, requested a procedure change as soon as possible to reduce the burdensome workload. In response to his request, Mr. Marks, an assistant hospital administrator whose specialty was conversion to computer operations, was assigned to analyze the problem. On the recommendation of Mr. Marks, a special project unit was set up near the insurance office to convert the problem procedure to data processing. Mr. Marks took charge of the special project, assisted by staff personnel and one claims supervisor. Completion of the special conversion project within six months was necessary in order to meet audit requirements and to qualify for a federal hospital grant.

On Wednesday, the day after the special unit was set up, Mr. Marks asked Mr. Barker to send three reliable clerks from his division. General supervision of the clerks would be retained in the division from which they had been borrowed, but the clerks would receive technical supervision in the special project unit.

One of the clerks selected for the special project unit was Ms. Lin Buxby, who had graduated from high school one year ago with a good achievement record. She had near-point vision corrected by contact lenses, a fact that was reflected on her personnel record. The supervisor to whom she was first assigned called personnel about the matter but he was assured that Ms. Buxby's eyesight problem should not handicap her for general clerical work. At her first formal appraisal six months after being hired, Ms. Buxby's overall performance was rated as "good" by the supervisor. Partly for this reason, she was selected as one of three clerks to go to the special project unit.

On Thursday, the three clerks were told about their temporary reassignment by Mr. Barker shortly before they were to undertake their new duties. The type of work was not mentioned in his brief announcement. The reassignment was unexpected by them. Two of them readily accepted the reassignment with comments such as "Our pay will be the same" and "We can still have lunch with our friends here because we're just going across the hall."

Lin Buxby, however, was noticeably upset by the turn of events. She asked Mr. Baxter, "Why can't I stay here? When can I return?" Her questions went unanswered.

When the three clerks arrived at the special project unit on Friday, one of the staff members explained the work to be done, desks were chosen, and work was assigned. During the first coffee break, Lin rushed back across the hall. Bursting into tears, she implored Mr. Barker to let her return and continue training in her original assignment. She said, "The confusion and pressure are too much. And we don't know what to expect next." Mr. Barker explained that the situation would soon settle down, that the experience would help her when she returned to her original training position, and that she might be able to make some overtime wages. Lin seemed convinced and went back to work in the special project unit.

Two working days later Mr. Marks called Mr. Barker and demanded that Lin be replaced immediately. Mr. Marks said that Lin was too slow, that she couldn't do anything right, and that Mr. Barker had sent an incompetent clerk for a top-priority project. This attracted Mr. Barker's attention because he did not want to make that kind of an impression on the assistant hospital administrator. He was upset and surprised and convinced that Lin's poor performance was intentional. A replacement for Lin was selected.

The next morning, Mr. Barker took Lin's replacement to the special project unit, brought Lin back, and talked to her. It appeared that Lin didn't know why she had been replaced. When he referred to her being so slow and making so many mistakes, Lin said, "No one said anything to me about making mistakes. But I know I was slow. The lines on the data sheet ran together due to the columns on the coding sheets being only one-fourth inch wide. Everything seemed to swim in front of my eyes. Trying to make sure I didn't make mistakes slowed me up. I told the supervisor about my trouble and she said, 'I'll see what I can do.' The next thing I knew was that you came over and brought me back."

Mr. Barker could not avoid the conclusion that everyone connected with the Lin Buxby incident was partially responsible.

Critiques

WILMAR F. BERNTHAL

Professor of Management and Organization
University of Colorado

The most obvious approach to analyzing the "Unexpected Relief" incident is to view it largely as a breakdown in interpersonal relations and communication. The solution would then be to train managers in interpersonal skills and sensitivity.

Another approach is to view the incident as an illustration of job enrichment, with a supervisor giving a worker doing a routine job an opportunity for personal growth and development on the job. The analysis would then point out the importance of considering individual differences when anticipating worker response to such a change and challenge.

A third view is that the incident may basically be a manifestation of a systems problem, in which managers act quite naturally in their given system roles, but the system may not provide adequately for dealing with individual and interpersonal consideration. While all three approaches have merit, I prefer to look at the systems elements first, to make sure we do not prematurely ascribe to managers' personalities what may be a result of structural arrangements in the organization.

In Regional Hospital the administration of business affairs, such as accounting and the processing of insurance claims, is highly routinized, with employees implementing standardized procedures. When a change is required by new environmental circumstances, such as the Medicare changes, the organization responds by having staff specialists, such as Mr. Marks's special projects unit, develop new procedures.

In this type of setting administrators tend to think in mechanistic terms. They use employees as interchangeable parts to serve system needs and train them to implement the prescribed new procedures. And they look to experts in the personnel department to help in selection and placement, to assure that employees are technically qualified to do the work. In such a system it is only natural that the supervisor checked only with personnel in determining whether Ms. Buxby could do the special project work.

This management system, however, neglects to consider other motivating factors that might affect employee behavior. Ms. Buxby, for example, may have special needs for a supportive work climate, in view of her visual handicap. To remove her from the security of a considerate training supervisor, routine work, and a happy relationship with fellow workers, and to place her in a temporary, nonroutine job assignment under less sympathetic direction may undermine the very self-confidence that she must develop to be able to function effectively.

The administrator thus faces a conflict between his right to assign workers (his bureaucratic role) and his need to live with the consequences of these decisions. The system provides him with initial screening of employees to be sure they are qualified to do a job, including working on the special project temporarily. However, it is only through sharing the problem with employees and permitting them to express their preferences for assignments that he can elicit information on those motivational factors that would cause one employee to seek out the variety or excitement or challenge of a special assignment while causing another to prefer the shelter and security of an old, routine assignment. This is particularly true in assigning work to a person, such as Ms. Buxby, who already feels handicapped in one way or another.

To the extent that most of the business administration work in

Regional Hospital is likely to be routine, compared to nursing or medical work, this part of the administrative system is likely to be bureaucratic. Yet when administrators are confronted with needed changes they can minimize the anxiety that the possible change may cause workers, facilitate adjustment by workers, and enhance the quality of their performance by sharing the nature of the problem with them and making it possible for them to bring their special sociopsychological needs to their attention. This is even more important on jobs that, by their routine and pro- grammed nature, do not in themselves provide a high level of motivation for most employees.

HERBERT G. HICKS

Professor of Management
Louisiana State University

This incident vividly illustrates several things about persons working in organizations:

1. Members of organizations have feelings or emotions that may affect their performance more than pay.
2. Although organizations exist to accomplish their organiza- tional objectives, these objectives may not be compatible with the objectives of individual members.
3. Informal organizations spring up in the "shadow" of formal organizations. These informal organizations exist to satisfy the needs of members that are not satisfied by formal orga- nizations.
4. The objectives of persons, as expressed in their membership in informal organizations, may be just as powerful as their objectives in belonging to the formal organization.
5. Managers frequently ignore all the above.

In the present case, the three clerks were treated as if they were emotionless machines with no social bonds in the organization.

Clearly, as a prescription, Mr. Barker should have discussed the proposed transfer with the three affected persons. He should have taken into account the points I have listed above.

It is quite likely that Ms. Buxby's increased visual difficulties in the new situation are partly psychosomatic in origin. That is, they may be due partly to the problems described above. On the other hand, her physical problem would have been uncovered with appropriate discussion.

I disagree with Mr. Barker's conclusion that everyone was responsible. There is no evidence that anyone performed incompetently before this incident. I pin the blame squarely on Mr. Barker for failing to communicate adequately with his employees to discover their feelings about the new work assignment.

Members of organizations are not unfeeling robots who can be mechanically manipulated. Every person has a unique personality, a unique set of abilities and limitations, and a unique set of needs and objectives. Further, many times a person's emotions may cause him or her to act in ways that may seem to defy rational understanding by someone else. But, to one's self, one's actions always "make sense," based upon some facet of his or her internal motivation.

Proper management in the present incident probably would have totally prevented the problem. Then, we never would have heard of Ms. Buxby's "eye trouble."

Discussion items

1. What were the primary objectives governing the behavior of the following persons in this incident: *(a)* Mr. Marks? *(b)* Mr. Barker? *(c)* Ms. Buxby?

2. At what points in the chain of events connecting Ms. Buxby's initial hiring and her unexpected replacement on the special task unit could intervention in the unfortunate cascade of events have been accomplished? By whose actions? Explain.

3. Compare the three ways that Professor Bernthal views the incident. Which do you think has the most validity? Explain.

Suggested reading list

BOOKS

Carroll, Stephen J., and **Tosi, Henry L.** *Organizational Behavior.* Chicago: St. Clair Press, 1977. Chap. 9.

Davis, Keith. *Human Behavior at Work.* 5th ed. New York: McGraw-Hill Book Co., 1977. Chaps. 3, 4, 10, 21, 22.

Flippo, Edwin B., and **Munsinger, Gary M.** *Management.* 4th ed. Boston: Allyn and Bacon, Inc., 1978. Chaps. 14, 17, 21.

Hicks, Herbert G., and **Gullett, C. Ray.** *The Management of Organizations.* 3d ed. New York: McGraw-Hill Book Co., 1976. Chaps. 16, 20.

Jucius, Michael J. *Personnel Management.* 9th ed. Homewood, Ill.: Richard D. Irwin, Inc., 1979. Chaps. 11–13, 26.

Koontz, Harold, and **O'Donnell, Cyril.** *Management: A Systems and Contingency Analysis of Managerial Functions.* 6th ed. New York: McGraw-Hill Book Co., 1976. Chaps. 24–26.

Longnecker, Justin G. *Principles of Management and Organizational Behavior.* 4th ed. Columbus, Ohio: Charles E. Merrill Publishing Co., 1977. Chaps. 20–23.

McCormick, Ernest J., and **Tiffin, Joseph.** *Industrial Psychology.* 6th ed. Englewood Cliffs, N.J.: Prentice Hall, Inc., 1974. Chap. 12.

Miner, John B. *The Management Process.* 2d ed. New York: Macmillan Publishing Co., Inc., 1978. Chap. 18.

Reitz, H. Joseph. *Behavior in Organizations.* Homewood, Ill.: Richard D. Irwin, Inc., 1977. Chaps. 3, 4, 14.

Terry, George R. *Principles of Management.* 7th ed. Homewood, Ill.: Richard D. Irwin, Inc., 1977. Part 5.

JOURNALS

Averch, Vernon R., and **Luke, Robert A.** "The Temporary Task Force: A Challenge to Organizational Structure." *Personnel* vol. 47, no. 3 (May/June 1970):16–19.

Bolinder, Erik, and **Gerhardsson, Gideon.** "A Better Environment for the Worker." *International Labor Review* vol. 105, no. 6 (June 1972):495–505.

Carter, Byrum. "Some Reflections on Merit." *Business Horizons* vol. 21, no. 6 (December 1978):3–6.

Fourmet, Glenn. "Job Satisfaction: Issues and Problems." *Personnel Psychology* vol. 19, no. 2 (Summer 1966):165–80.

Gibb, Jack R. "Communication and Productivity." *Personnel Administration* vol. 27, no. 1 (January/February 1964):8.

Michael, Jerrold M. "Problem Situations in Performance Counseling." *Personnel* vol. 42, no. 5 (September/October 1965):16–22.

Moore, Michael L., and **Dutton, Philip.** "Training Needs Analysis: Review Critique." *Academy of Management Review* vol. 3, no. 3 (July 1978):532–45.

Morano, Richard A. "How to Manage Change to Reduce Stress." *Management Review* vol. 66, no. 11 (November 1977):21–25.

Morgan, Chester A. "Up With Young Employees." *Business Horizons* vol. 21, no. 5 (October 1978):45–48.

Murray, J. Alex. "A Sociometric Approach to Organizational Analysis." *California Management Review* vol. 13, no. 3 (Spring 1971):59–67.

Prangley, Robert E.; Gannon, Martin J.; and **Poole, Brian A.** "Involuntary Job Rotation and Work Behavior." *Personnel Journal* vol. 51, no. 6 (June 1972):446–48.

Speroff, B. J. "Sociometry: A Key to the Informal Organization." *Personnel Journal* vol. 47, no. 2 (February 1968):121–23.

Stansbury, William F. "Reducing Clerical Turnover." *Personnel Journal* vol. 52, no. 3 (March 1973):209–12.

Student, Kurt R. "Managing Change: A Psychologist's Perspective." *Business Horizons* vol. 21, no. 6 (December 1978):28–33.

Warren, Joseph B. "EDP; Scapegoat for Human Errors." *Business Automation* vol. 17, (October 1970):46–51.

Weiss, Alan. "Are Your Stifling Your New Employees? *Supervisory Management* vol. 17, no. 6 (June 1972):9–14.

Young, Jerald W. "The Subordinates Exposure of Organization Vulnerability to Superior: Sex and Organizational Effects." *Academy of Management Journal* vol. 21, no. 1 (March 1978):113–22.

37

UNION'S DILEMMA

Union-management cooperation: union leadership and organizational structure

Incident

THE EXECUTIVE COMMITTEE of Local Union Number 16 of the American Machinists and Skilled Workers met in the local union hall for deliberation of a perplexing problem. The committee was concerned with promotion policies of the company. It seemed that every time the union elected a member of their ranks as shop steward in some production department, the company shortly thereafter promoted that individual to the rank of foreman or supervisor. Thus, overnight the shop steward became a member of management. Occasionally a shop steward who was not too effective in representing the employees was allowed to remain a shop steward. However, some of the best union members were now members of management.

The executive committee realized what it was up against. A person offered the position of foreman could hardly afford to turn down a pay raise of approximately one third. It was also true that the union could not afford to subsidize each employee who was offered such a job and turned it down. One member of the committee suggested that only the incompetent should be elected shop stewards, but a howl of laughter rejected this idea since they all agreed that the shop steward occupied the most important single post in the local union organization. Another suggestion was that the union bargain for and write into the next union-management contract a clause that would prevent management from promoting anyone who held the title of shop steward. Bill Peterson, president of the union, thought this was a sound idea except for the fact that the company would probably offer the best of the shop stewards a promotion after they gave up the post of shop steward. In a way the union would be training and selecting personnel for management positions.

Critiques

L. CURTISE WOOD
Professor of Administration
Wichita State University

The basic problem facing the executive board of Local Union Number 16 is as old as the union movement. Unions have always had a problem of attracting, developing, and maintaining competent leaders.

From the beginning, a stigma was attached to unions; the legitimacy of union leadership was suspect, the practices of employers of rarely promoting active union members or leaders, and the unceasing upward movement of the ambitious and able from the ranks all functioned to reduce the quality of union leadership.

The attitudes of members and inner workings of unions have also taken a toll on the quality of leadership. Representing the oppressed has long been considered a work of love; thus, union representatives have been expected to work long hours for the same wages as (or in many instances less than) members. Lower echelon representatives have also been faced with the problem of getting elected every year. Frequently, competent people have been judged by members on the basis of what they didn't accomplish today rather than on the basis of achievement through time.

In this particular situation, there is a real need for both company management and union management to review their policies. The company policy of promoting "managers of discontent" to company management may have improved the quality of company management, but the policy is now creating fear and uncertainty within the union. A fluid, unstable condition within the union may provide a breeding ground for ambitious radicals.

The executive committee should consider several courses of action. One alternative is to do nothing. After all, the number of openings for new foremen is limited. Further, while the union has lost competent stewards, the foreman ranks are now held by people who understand the union's point of view.

If the executive committee should try to act to prevent stewards from moving to foremen, the job of steward may become less attractive to the rank and file and a new kind of problem appears.

Another alternative emerges as one questions the matter of subsidizing stewards. Who is subsidizing whom? It appears that the stewards are now subsidizing the members. Well-paid workers of the 1980s cannot reasonably expect their more able fellows to represent them for love alone.

The executive board might well note that other unions have solved problems of this nature by increasing dues, paying stewards, and initiating training programs for potential stewards. Thus, a constant supply of competent stewards is available when a need arises.

MAX S. WORTMAN, JR.
Professor of Management
Virginia Polytechnic Institute and State University

Clearly, management is attempting a long-term effort to undermine the strength of the union. In the past few years it has become increasingly common for management (particularly in states that are not pro-union) to attempt to undermine the union. Such attempts range from covert efforts like those outlined in this incident to overt attempts to prevent representation elections by the commission of deliberate unfair labor practices as outlined by the National Labor Relations Act (for example, management efforts to prevent the unionization of J. P. Stevens).

Management is undermining the union strength in several ways. First, effective union stewards are almost always promoted to foremen, thus taking away the backbone of an effective union (both as present first-line leaders of the union and as future presidents and officers of the union). Second, "converted" foremen are usually much tougher on their former union colleagues than foremen who have never served in a trade union. For example, former union officials frequently make extremely tough employers' association executives. Third, management has an unusual pay policy of one third more than the pay of stewards for its foremen. Normally, foremen are paid on a salaried basis, while stewards are paid on an hourly basis plus a certain amount per hour for performing the duties of steward. If such a steward draws overtime, it is not uncommon for the individual to make more than a foreman. The seeming overpayment to the foremen in this incident is a clear symptom of an attempt to undermine the union. Fourth, management was willing to retain ineffective stewards in that position after it was determined that they were not effective. Clearly, this weakens union participation in the administration of the contract.

On the other hand, assuming that management is not trying to undermine the union, management may be weakening itself because of a potential pro-union stance of management from the continuous feed in from the neophyte union leaders. Furthermore, informal bargaining between pro-union foremen and stewards may occur at the supervisory level, thus setting precedents which will weaken the overall position of management in the long run. Lastly, management is relying upon the union for both selection and training of foremen. Such a reliance upon the union gives the union control rather than management over the type of foremen selected and trained.

What should the union do (assuming that management is trying to undermine it)? First, the union needs to strengthen the position of steward by negotiating a stronger clause on payment for the steward's duties. In this way there would not be as wide a differential in pay between stewards and foremen and there would not be as large an incentive to become a foreman. Second, the union should attempt to negotiate joint union steward-foreman training programs. Perhaps these training programs could be taught by a joint union-management team or by an unbiased team of faculty from a local community college or industrial relations center at a nearby college or university. Third, the union should attempt to negotiate as many joint labor-management committees as possible, including joint safety and health committees, joint benefits committees, and joint productivity improvement committees. Through these joint efforts, the union would strengthen its position.

What should management do? It should be looking at its entire selection and training program to determine if it has a pro-union bias, which has spread throughout the managerial hierarchy. Then it should attempt to establish a strong selection program which consists of entry-level supervisors from both internal and external sources. External sources could include management trainees from community colleges and universities. After they have been selected, a strong management development program should be instituted and continued. By gaining control of the input into foreman selection and training, management should eliminate its pro-union bias.

Discussion items

1. Should the union attempt to negotiate a clause in the union-management contract that would prevent management from promoting union stewards? Explain.

2. Explain the potential advantages to both the union and the company of having foremen who are ex-union stewards. Any disadvantages? Could this be considered an unfair labor practice on the part of management?

3. Should a union steward have privileges at work beyond those afforded the rank and file union member? Justify your position.

Suggested reading list

BOOKS

Burack, Elmer H., and **Smith, Robert D.** *Personnel Management.* New York: West Publishing Co., 1977. Chap. 13.

Carroll, Stephen J., and **Tosi, Henry L.** *Organizational Behavior.* Chicago: St. Clair Press, 1977. Chap. 6.

Davis, Keith. *Human Behavior at Work.* 5th ed. New York: McGraw-Hill Book Co., 1977. Chap. 17.

Dressler, Gary. *Personnel Management: Modern Concepts and Techniques.* Reston, Va.: Reston Publishing Co., 1978. Chap. 17.

Flippo, Edwin B., and **Munsinger, Gary M.** *Management.* 4th ed. Boston: Allyn and Bacon, Inc., 1978. Chap. 24.

Jucius, Michael J. *Personnel Management.* 9th ed. Homewood, Ill.: Richard D. Irwin, Inc., 1979. Chap. 25.

Koontz, Harold, and **O'Donnell, Cyril.** *Management: A Systems and Contingency Analysis of Managerial Functions.* 6th ed. New York: McGraw-Hill Book Co., 1976. Chap. 18.

Longnecker, Justin G. *Principles of Management and Organizational Behavior.* 4th ed. Columbus, Ohio: Charles E. Merrill Publishing Co., 1977. Chap. 11.

Megginson, Leon C. *Personnel and Human Resources Administration.* 3d ed. Homewood, Ill.: Richard D. Irwin, Inc., 1977. Chaps. 21, 22.

Miner. John B. *The Management Process.* 2d ed. New York: Macmillan Publishing Co., Inc., 1978. Chap. 10.

Terry, George R. *Principles of Management.* 7th ed. Homewood, Ill.: Richard D. Irwin, Inc., 1977. Chaps. 13, 26, 27.

JOURNALS

Batt, William L., Jr., and **Weinberg, Edgar.** "Labor Management Cooperation Today." *Harvard Business Review* vol. 56, no. 1 (January/February 1978):96–104.

Bonham, T. W. "Foreman in an Ambiguous Environment." *Personnel Journal* vol. 50, no. 11 (November 1971):841.

Foegen, J. H. "Super Role-Playing: Labor and Management." *Personnel Journal* vol. 50, no. 8 (August 1971):611–17.

———. "Duality in Unionism." *Personnel Journal* vol. 41, no. 5 (May 1962):220–25.

Gart, Murray J. "Labor's Rebellious Rank and File." *Fortune* vol. 74, no. 6 (November 1966):151–53, 256–63.

Hilgert, Raymond L. "An Arbitrator Looks at Grievance Arbitration." *Personnel Journal* vol. 57, no. 10 (October 1978):556–59, 578.

Kerr, Raymond L. "Dual Allegiance and Emotional Acceptance-Rejectance in Industry." *Personnel Psychology* vol. 7 (Spring 1954):59–64.

Mason, Sandra L. "Company Union and Non-Union Wages in Manufacturing." *Monthly Labor Review* vol. 94, no. 5 (May 1971):20–26.

Rosen, Hjalmar. "Dual Allegiance: A Critique and A Proposed Approach." *Personnel Psychology* vol. 7, no. 1 (Spring 1954):67–71.

Rosenfeld, Peter. "Training Trade Unionists for Today and Tomorrow." *Personnel Management* vol. 9, no. 6 (June 1977):37–41.

Shershin, Michael J., and **Boxx, W. Randy.** "Building Positive Union-Management Relations." *Personnel Journal* vol. 54, no. 6 (June 1975):326–31.

Sorcher, Melvin. "Cementing Union-Management Relationships at the Bottom." *Personnel Journal* vol. 46, no. 10 (November 1967):649–52.

Stagner, Ross. "Dual Allegiance to Union and Management." *Personnel Psychology* vol. 7, no. 1 (Spring 1954):41–47.

Stern, Irving, and **Pearse, Robert F.** "Collective Bargaining: A Union's Program for Reducing Conflict." *Personnel* vol. 45, no. 3 (May/June 1969):61–72.

Thompson, Duane E., and **Borglum, Richard P.** "A Case Study of Employee Attitudes and Labor Unrest." *Industrial and Labor Relations Review* vol. 27, no. 1 (October 1973):74–83.

Truell, George F. "Core Managerial Strategies Culled from Behavioral Research." *Supervisory Management* vol. 22, no. 1 (January 1977):10–17.

38

WIREWEAVE, INCORPORATED

Automation and its general effects

Incident

FIVE YEARS AGO, Wireweave, Incorporated, moved to a rural area 25 miles outside of a large southern city. The company, formerly situated in a midwestern industrial city, chose this location primarily because of the lower wage rates paid in the community and because of the favorable tax situation.

Wireweave is a manufacturer of wire products. One of its basic products, manufactured in large volume, is aluminum wire screen. Because of intense competition in the industry, the company realized several years ago that if it were to continue to manufacture aluminum wire screen and, in fact, stay in business, it would have to procure up-to-date equipment and become more automated.

Over a two-year period the procurement officer of Wireweave surveyed existing suppliers and users of the most modern and completely automated manufacturing equipment in use in the industry. In attempting to enter into negotiations with manufacturers of the automated equipment, the procurement officer of Wireweave ran into a series of problems that practically closed out the possibility of ever securing this equipment in the American market. The major hurdle pertained to patent rights of the company that developed and used the equipment. However, the following year the procurement director traveled to Europe, and in Sweden he visited a producer of wire screen manufacturing equipment that was similar but slightly superior to that manufactured in the United States. Under a different patent arrangement Wireweave was able to enter into a contract with the Swedish company and purchase equipment which, when installed and functioning, would replace 50 percent of the present obsolete

265

equipment and 65 employees. The 65 employees to be replaced represented about 33 percent of the total labor force.

The following spring, shortly after the installation of the new equipment, Mr. Dillard Jackson, president of Wireweave, called in Ms. Muriell Fincher, director of personnel. Mr. Jackson told Ms. Fincher that as of now, the company no longer needed, or could afford to employ, the 65 workers directly affected by the installation of the new machinery. It was Mr. Jackson's opinion that the sooner Ms. Fincher discharged the workers, the sooner the company would become a profitable operation.

Critiques

WILLIAM H. KEOWN
Professor Emeritus of Management
University of Oklahoma

Brief comments on the economic aspects of the two decisions already made may be helpful.

The decision to move. Firms move for many reasons, including the search for lower wage costs and/or lower taxes. Let us leave to each legislature the responsibility for encouraging the industrial development of its state by maintaining favorable tax schedules. Wage differentials based on geography have been reduced or even eliminated in many industries through collective bargaining (notably in auto, steel, and meat packing) and through the Fair Labor Standards Act and similar state statutes. (What was the minimum wage in 1938? What is it today? Has the coverage changed?) These forces are still extending the application of the concept of equal pay for equal work; in the years ahead, therefore, Wireweave and other firms are less likely to find cheaper labor by moving to another region.

The decision to automate. On the average our national productivity has been increasing about 3 percent annually. What factors have caused this? One is the capital investment that substitutes electromechanical power and machines for human strength and skill. In our society the pressures of technological advancement are irresistible. Firms may postpone the introduction of improvements, but in an "intensely competitive" industry even delay may be fatal. In the years ahead, these changes may be of greater magnitude and come at a faster rate.

Business managers certainly must recognize economic realities such as those mentioned above, but their responsibilities are even greater. No business enterprise can be merely an economic institution, nor can the decisions of business managers be based solely on economic considerations. The birth, growth, transformation, and death of a business enterprise have social consequences for the community in which it "lives and moves and has its being." One reason for this lies in the impossibility of separating labor from the laborer. Although business leaders generally seem to be becoming more aware of their social responsibilities, especially with respect to the employees, there is nothing to suggest that Mr. Dillard Jackson is one of them.

Mr. Jackson's opinion that 65 employees should be discharged forthwith.

FACT: The decision to automate was made more than two years ago.

FACT: During recent years the average monthly separation rate in the metal fabricating industry has been 4.6 per 100 employees.

FACT: Wireweave's total labor force is approximately 200.

If Wireweave's separation rate is no less than the industry average, how many employees have left since management made the decision to automate? How many of these persons were replaced? Typically, how many more would be expected to leave during the next year? Could some of the 65 be trained as replacements for other departments? Are there any other means now available to keep these 65 from joblessness? Is Ms. Fincher aware of the inadequacies of the present (unwritten) policy? Will Ms. Fincher discharge her responsibility to the company and give Mr. Jackson the advice he so desperately needs, or will she say "Yes, sir!" and discharge 65 employees?

Your answers to these questions will suggest how the incident might have been avoided. The philosophy underlying these answers and actions provides the basis for a policy for the future.

WALLACE D. TREVILLIAN

Professor and Dean of
Economics and Management
Clemson University

Modern management, not just modern machinery, is needed at Wireweave, Incorporated! Its president faced a two-fold problem: (1) management's *internal responsibility* to substitute a more efficient factor of production—in this case machines for employees—by a sound method of implementation; and (2) the *broader responsibility* for solving technological unemployment in a free enterprise economy.

Mr. Jackson definitely did his duty as a manager in substituting the machines for the workers. But he neglected the basic managerial function of *coordination,* and this stemmed from a lack of communication. He established no coordination whatever between the procurement director, the personnel director, and the production director. Yet he knew that unless up-to-date equipment were obtained, the company might go out of business; and his procurement officer spent two years seeking such equipment, and another year acquiring and installing it. So Ms. Fincher and the production team should have been made aware of the eventuality at the outset, and then definite action taken to prepare the workers in the interim. As employees left by normal attrition— moving away, finding better jobs, retiring—replacements should not have been hired unless absolutely essential, even if this meant some overtime. And employees in expendable jobs should have been retrained whenever possible for jobs in other areas of the plant. In short, every attempt should have been made to absorb the work force efficiently within the firm. By not doing this, Mr. Jackson produced a situation that is bound to backfire. If one third of the force is now discharged, the morale of those retained will be adversely affected. As these desired workers begin to feel insecure, rates of production will fall, inefficiencies will occur, and profits will suffer.

And what about the resulting technological unemployment? Machinery has been replacing manpower ever since the invention of the wheel. Today, however, automation is accelerated;

and so are other factors in the employment picture—population growth, specialized education, mobility of labor, relocation of industry, variables that do not always coincide. So society must share the responsibility for retraining displaced workers. Many states have technical schools for this purpose, and the federal government also has a variety of programs geared to training the unemployable. However there remains a vital role for creative management. Take Wireweave, Incorporated. With new automatic machinery superior to all its competitors, this firm should be planning for a larger share of the market, full modernization, greater production, and ultimately increased employment! Instead, its shortsighted president thinks only of discharging employees. The sooner he is replaced by a dynamic and efficient executive, the sooner the company will become a profitable operation and an asset to the small southern community.

Discussion items

1. If you were in the personnel director's position, would you follow orders and discharge the 65 employees forthwith or would you make recommendations for other action to reduce the work force of the company? If the latter, then give your recommendations.

2. What is your evaluation of the actions that the president proposes be taken?

3. Comment on Professor Trevillian's view that modern management is needed at Wireweave.

Suggested reading list

BOOKS

Burack, Elmer H. *Organization Analysis: Theory and Applications.* Hinsdale, Ill.: The Dryden Press, 1975. Chaps. 3, 4.

Carroll, Stephen J., and **Tosi, Henry L.** *Organizational Behavior.* Chicago: St. Clair Press, 1977. Chap. 18.

Davis, Keith. *Human Behavior at Work.* 5th ed. New York: McGraw-Hill Book Co., 1977. Chaps. 13, 14.

Donnelly, James H.; Gibson, James L.; and **Ivancevich, John M.** *Fundamentals of Management.* 3d ed. Dallas, Tex: Business Publications, Inc., 1978. Chap. 3.

Flippo, Edwin B., and **Munsinger, Gary M.** *Management.* 4th ed. Boston: Allyn and Bacon, Inc., 1978. Chap. 12.

Kast, Fremont E., and **Rosenzweig, James E.** *Organizations and Management: A Systems Approach.* 3d ed. New York: McGraw-Hill Book Co., 1979. Chaps. 6–8.

Koontz, Harold, and **O'Donnell, Cyril.** *Management: A Systems and Contingency Analysis of Managerial Functions.* 6th ed. New York: McGraw-Hill Book Co., 1976. Part 6.

Longnecker, Justin G. *Principles of Management and Organizational Behavior.* 4th ed. Columbus, Ohio: Charles E. Merrill Publishing Co., 1977. Chaps. 3, 26.

Megginson, Leon C. *Personnel and Human Resources Administration.* 3d ed. Homewood, Ill.: Richard D. Irwin, Inc., 1977. Chaps. 1–6.

Miner, John B. *The Management Process.* 2d ed. New York: Macmillan Publishing Co., Inc., 1978. Chaps. 10, 18, 19.

Terry, George R. *Principles of Management.* 7th ed. Homewood, Ill.: Richard D. Irwin, Inc., 1977. Part 7.

JOURNALS

Blough, Roger M. "Security—In an Age of Technological Change." *Advanced Management Journal* vol. 29, no. 2 (April 1964):22–28.

Buckingham, Walter. "Automation—Its Impact on People." *Advanced Management Journal* vol. 29, no. 2 (April 1964):34–38.

Fried, Louis. "Hostility in Organization Change." *Journal of Systems Management* vol. 23, no. 6 (June 1972):14–21.

Gallagher, William E., Jr., and **Firhorn, Hillel J.** "Motivation and Job Design." *Business Journal* vol. 49, no. 3 (July 1976):358–74.

Gerwin, Donald. "The Comparative Analysis of Structure and Technology: A Critical Appraisal." *Academy of Management Review* vol. 4, no. 1 (January 1979):41–62.

Gorman, Liam, and **Mullan, Cathal.** "Human Aspects of the Management of Technological Change: A Case Study." *Journal of Management Studies* vol. 10, no. 1 (February 1973):48–61.

Lasher, Albert C. "When You Automate: How to Avoid Labor Woes." *Dun's Review and Modern Industry* vol. 75, no. 4 (April 1960):42–44.

Lebergott, Stanley. "Productivity: Eight Questions and Seven Answers." *Management Review* vol. 55, no. 6 (June 1966):9–12.

Lindo, David K. "Looking Beyond Short-term Manpower Needs." *Advanced Management Journal* vol. 42, no. 1 (Winter 1977):36–46.

McCarthy, Russell C. "Automation and Unemployment: A Second Look." *Management Review* vol. 51, no. 5 (May 1962):35–43.

Mortensen, K. G. "Planning for Technological Change." *Personnel Practice Bulletin* vol. 27, no. 3 (September 1971):252–53.

Sawyer, George C. "Social Issues and Social Change: Impact on Strategic Decisions." *MSU Business Topics* vol. 21, no. 3 (Summer 1973):15–20.

Scherba, John. "Outplacement as a Personnel Responsibility." *Personnel* vol. 50, no. 3 (May/June 1973):40–44.

Sebring, Thomas H. "Planning for a Personnel Reduction." *Management Review* vol. 54, no. 6 (June 1965):62–68.

Singer, Henry A. "Human Values and Leadership." *Business Horizons* vol. 18, no. 4 (August 1975):85–88.

Snyder, John I., Jr. "Automation and Unemployment: Management's Quiet Crisis." *Management Review* vol. 52, no. 11 (November 1963):4–18.

Sokolik, Stanley L. "A Strategy For Planning." *MSU Business Topics* vol. 26, no. 2 (Spring 1978):57–64.

Wetjen, John E. "Implementing Change—10 Questions to Ask." *Management Review* vol. 61, no. 11 (November 1972):46–48.

39

ABANDONED PRIORITIES

CONDITIONS IN THE TYPING POOL of Computer Management Company were near the point of breaking down 14 months ago when Allison Little was placed in charge. Absenteeism, turnover, dissatisfaction, and work backlog were high. Skill levels, quality of work, wages, and morale were low. The pool was viewed by the persons in it as a sort of purgatory that one had to endure while seeking better placement in an office elsewhere in the company.

Allison, as supervisor of the pool, reported to Barbara Benchley, the vice president of personnel. She had accepted the supervisory position only after receiving assurances that she would receive strong support in her efforts to improve the working conditions and performance of the pool. She inaugurated many effective changes with the support of Ms. Benchley. The name of the unit was changed to "Communication Center," in order to supplant the "typing pool mentality" with pride of purpose and performance. Equipment and furnishings were modernized. Acoustics were improved. A priority system for sequencing work was installed. Wages were increased. Output and quality of product were increased markedly. She attributed much of this success to her supervisory concept of "consideration for others." Allison felt that of all the improvements, the system of work priorities had made the greatest contribution to achieving an orderly flow of work and to providing fair treatment of the many persons served by the Communication Center.

The Communication Center now was "humming." Most but not all of the 120 professionals served by it agreed that Allison was responsible for "turning the typing pool around."

On Friday morning Fred Hahn handed Allison a 30-page manuscript with instructions to type it immediately. She told him that the work load was at a peak and further that manucripts had only third priority after letters and reports. Fred responded,

"Don't tell me your troubles. Work overtime if you have to, but I want this manuscript completely typed for mailing by Monday morning." He then left.

Around 11:00 A.M. the following Monday, Fred returned to Allison's desk, saying that he had come for his manuscript. When she told him that it would not be ready until Wednesday, Fred began verbally to roast Allison. Though neither raised the volume of their voices, the intensity of the verbal exchange escalated rapidly to a point where Fred Hahn said threateningly, "Well then, I'll take this matter to the vice president of personnel." Allison observed aloud that no one was standing in his way.

Ms. Benchley, the vice president, walked through the door at the moment. Immediately she asked, "What is going on here?" Fred told her.

Ms. Benchley turned to Allison and, loud enough for all to hear, said witheringly, "What do we have to do to get some service out of this typing pool? Forget the priority system. Get this manuscript done!"

40

A COURSE IN SENSITIVITY TRAINING

THE PRESIDENT OF HILTON STEEL COMPANY, Mr. John Hudson, attended a ten-week advanced management seminar at Highview Lake Retreat. The seminar was sponsored by the Young Presidents' Club, of which he was a member. A much-emphasized feature of the seminar was the sponsoring of a sensitivity-training laboratory, better known as t-group. The stated purposes were as follows:

1. Assisting participants to learn more about themselves.
2. The development of an awareness of one's self and others.
3. Assistance in the exploration of one's values and their impact on others.
4. The creation of an awareness of the importance of developing meaningful relationships.
5. The development of reality-centered leadership traits.

Upon conclusion of the t-group sessions, President Hudson felt he had certainly profited from the experience. He felt a definite shift toward a set of values that would enable him to cope with interpersonal relationships he faced each day. In fact, he was so impressed with the results that he arranged for the same instructors to conduct a similar program for top executives in his own company. It was agreed that he would designate 15 of his most immediate subordinates to take the five-day course.

On the first class day there was mixed enthusiasm among the participating executives. During midafternoon of the second day, five members of the group walked out of the classroom and asked to see President Hudson. A spokesman for the group said there was much opposition to continuation of the course. As a group they contended this was merely a manipulative process conducted by a group of psychologists for the purpose of brainstorming them into thinking or feeling the way someone wanted without their realizing what was happening.

41

CASHIER NEEDED

SUNDAY WAS A PREFERRED DAY to work at Westgate Su-
permarket because of the time-and-a-half pay scale. Larry Shaw
had been a stock clerk at the store for two years. During this time
he had been called upon occasionally to run the cash register at a
checkout counter, of which there were nine in the store. He had
had a few bad experiences on the cash register and was now
paying off some shortages, as required by store policy. He had
told the store manager, Richard McLane, that he did not wish to
run a cash register any more, due to the money responsibility.

Larry was pleased that the assistant manager had asked him to
come in on Sunday and work stock. The time-and-a-half pay
would go far toward paying off his accumulated cash register
shortage. When he got to work, McLane told Larry to operate
register #6 because he needed a cashier more than he did a
stock clerk. When Larry reminded McLane of his previous request not to be used as a cashier anymore, McLane told him
either to work the cash register or not to work at all. Larry
promptly, but politely, left for the day.

The next day, before going to work, Larry went to the district
supervisor on his own initiative, related his reasons for refusing to
work the cash register, and asked for a clarification of the situation. The district supervisor told Larry that the store manager paid
his wages and, therefore, had the right to assign Larry to whatever duties were most pressing.

Mr. McLane also was considering his options. He had been
both disappointed and mildly angered by Larry's refusal to work
the cash register during the busy Sunday hours. Stock clerks typically considered it a privilege and a form of promotion to be
assigned to a cash register. One of the main characteristics
that McLane looked for in a stock clerk was a willingness to
"help out" in pressing situations. Larry had been unwilling.

43

ENERGY CONSERVATION DIRECTIVE

THE ENERGY CRISIS HIT BRUCE CRANDEL in an unexpected way. As director of a federal agency located in an urban area and employing 1,200 persons, he received a directive through federal administrative channels that set forth requirements for conserving energy in federal facilities. The energy conservation measures related to (a) federal motor vehicle management, (b) heating, cooling, and lighting of federal facilities, and (c) federal employee parking.

The intent of attachment (c), relating to federal employee parking, was "to implement energy conservation measures that extend every effort to encourage the most efficient use of passenger vehicles that carry federal employees to and from their place of work." Specifically, the major purpose was to encourage "carpooling" among employees by generally denying parking space to those who did not join car pools.

The directive required that first priority be given to official personnel, critical personnel, and visitors. Not more than 10 percent of the parking spaces would be allocated to handicapped employees and persons who work unusual hours. The remaining parking spaces would be available for assignment to employees who were regular members in a car pool. Any other parking spaces would be reported as "excess to the needs of the facility" and would *not* be used for parking. Bruce Crandel saw clearly that employees who preferred to drive their cars to work without car-pooling would be denied parking privileges even though an ample number of spaces existed.

Free parking had always been considered a fringe benefit of federal employment. The existing parking facility had been expanded and improved five years ago at considerable expense in order to provide adequate free parking for employees of the agency. Rigid enforcement of the energy conservation directive would deny parking to employees who could not conveniently car-pool or who desired not to car-pool for personal reasons.

As Bruce Crandel pondered the matter, four options appeared to be open to him:

1. He could enforce the directive to the letter. Increased absenteeism and a general decline in morale would be a likely consequence.
2. He could disregard the directive with the hope that the "central office" would not seriously enforce it.
3. He could comply with the directive except that employees not in car pools would continue to be allowed to park in the "surplus" parking spaces.
4. He could continue searching for better options.

He was not certain how to proceed. A complete report on the action taken in response to the energy conservation directive was due in the central office in ten days.

44

FRANK JONES: SUPERVISOR

FRANK JONES BECAME SUPERVISOR of plant maintenance after 15 years as operator of a local electrical appliance repair shop. Spindle Rayon Mill had moved to the small southern community in which Frank lived in 1963. Frank accepted a job on the construction crew and was later employed to install and maintain lights, air conditioning, generator, steam plant, and miscellaneous equipment.

By 1970, floor space had tripled and the work force increased by several hundred. Frank found that his responsibilities had grown commensurately. He was often required to work overtime and occasionally returned to the plant during the night to make necessary repairs. He performed his work in a conscientious manner and was considered to be a devoted and loyal employee. It was necessary to add workers to his crew, and in late 1978 he found himself with a salary, the title of director of physical plant, and responsibility for the efforts of 16 employees.

It was noted, however, that he still preferred to repair the machines personally rather than direct his subordinates to do so. The plant manager told him one man could no longer perform all the work required of his department and encouraged him to do less of the repair work himself, but instead to select, train, and direct capable subordinates.

Frank made an attempt to do so. He even dressed like the other supervisors and organized his crew in such a way that he could spend most of his time in the office. It was not long, however, before department heads were complaining that machinery needed repairs and work schedules were disrupted due to idle machines. It was reported that when physical-plant repairmen were summoned, more likely than not they were incapable of completing the repairs without calling Frank. After a brief interval Frank returned to his blue denims. One department head complained to the plant manager that Frank was possessive about the machinery and was deliberately not selecting and training qualified repairmen because he seemed to feel secure only if others regarded him as indispensable.

The plant manager took under advisement the action to be taken. He knew that Frank was not performing the supervisory function, yet he remembered the years and loyalty Frank had devoted to the company.

45

HUMAN OBSOLESCENCE

THE SPRINGSIDE MANUFACTURING COMPANY has employed six bookkeepers for many years to keep the accounts current. Recently, however, these bookkeeping procedures had been converted to electronic data-processing procedures. The need for the bookkeepers was extinguished and a managerial committee meeting was called to determine the disposition of the excess personnel.

During the meeting, decisions were made to send one of the bookkeepers to the data-processing school, to accept the resignation of one, and to grant a leave of absence to one. Moreover, it was decided to use one of the bookkeepers on a temporary assignment in the typist pool, since she had indicated her intention to leave to return to school in two months, and to discharge the fifth person with 30 days' pay, since he had been absent from work excessively during the past year.

The last person was Jack Anderson, a loyal and faithful employee of 18 years. He had celebrated his sixty-third birthday the previous week and was looking forward to retirement in two more years. Although Jack's availability and credentials had been circulated to all department heads in the company, no one was interested in accepting him.

One member of the committee, a vice president, suggested that Jack be discharged with 60 days' pay in order to have some compensation while seeking employment. Another member of the committee suggested that Jack be given some menial job with the company for another two years so that he could qualify for retirement. This committee member argued that it would be extremely unfair to discharge a man with Jack's length of service and so near to retirement. The response to this suggestion centered upon such topics as obligation to stockholders, obligation to employees, public relations, appropriate policy for dealing with human obsolescence, and responsibilities of management in the event of displacement.

46

JOB ROTATION

THE CHIEF DIETITIAN at the Longwood Veterans Administration Hospital initiated plans to rotate the job assignments of the three staff dietitians in the nutritional therapy section every six months. Job rotation was generally recommended as a technique of giving nonsupervisory dietitians training in various assignments as a means of preparing them to meet the qualifications for upgrading and promotion. The rotation plans were developed and announced to all concerned on December 1, with the rotation to begin 30 days later on January 1.

Around the middle of December the chief dietitian received a telephone call from Dr. Rednick, who was in charge of the Renal Dialysis Unit. Dr. Rednick said that he was not at all in favor of the dietitian on his unit being rotated; that he had not been consulted; that he wanted all staff presently assigned to his unit to be permanent; and that if the chief dietitian did not change her mind and concur with his wishes he would take the matter to "higher authorities," that is, the chief of staff. After trying to discuss the matter amicably with him, the chief dietitian told him she did not like being threatened and that she still planned to implement the rotation as scheduled. The doctor called the chief of staff who in turn called the chief dietitian and asked her to see Dr. Rednick to discuss the matter with him again.

The chief dietitian did this and explained to Dr. Rednick that she understood his feelings, but she pointed out that nothing is permanent and, in case the dietitian assigned to the unit should decide to leave, no one would be trained to provide his patients with the required complex, individualized diets. He retorted that this was a chance he would have to take. He told her in no uncertain terms that he could never agree to the dietitian on the unit being moved unless she told him she wanted to work elsewhere for her own personal reasons. Moreover, he said that he firmly believed that the traumatic nature of the illness of dialysis patients required a stable patient-care team to which they could relate and upon which they could depend.

As a result of this exchange, it was agreed the staff dietitian assigned to the Renal Dialysis Unit would not move. Rotation of other staff dietitians was postponed until April 15.

Several days later, the dietitian assigned to the renal unit visited the chief dietitian and said that she realized her need for training in other areas of her field, that she had explained this to Dr. Rednick, and that he had pleasantly acquiesced to her wishes. The chief dietitian was surprised but made plans for this dietitian to rotate with the others.

Rotation occurred as scheduled on the morning of April 15. At lunch, the replacement dietitian in the renal unit rushed into the office of the chief dietitian and reported that Dr. Rednick had denied ever agreeing to the dietitian rotation plan and that she had been treated rather rudely by the doctor. Other staff members and nurses in the renal unit had treated her coldly and with disdain, she said. But her major concern was that Dr. Rednick had made thinly veiled threats against the chief dietitian. She quoted Dr. Rednick as having said that he would "take care of things" since she had rotated his "permanent" dietitian after agreeing not to do so.

47

LINEAR ELECTRONICS

LINEAR ELECTRONICS COMPANY requested a management consulting firm to submit recommendations regarding steps that could be taken to upgrade first-level supervision in the company. One of the recommendations the firm made was to give first-line supervisors a course in human relations. It was decided to implement this recommendation by retaining the consulting firm to conduct such a course. Agreement was reached to offer the course in two six-week sessions with two weeks between. The course was to be taught by staff members of the consulting firm and held during working hours, on company property, and at company expense.

The course started with 15 supervisors as students. Tests measuring knowledge of good supervisory practices were administered prior to the course and again at the end of the first six-week period. A comparison of scores verified that the supervisors had made significant improvement during the first six weeks.

During the two week lapse, however, numerous complaints of difficulties between supervisors and employees were received. It was noted that a larger-than-average number of the complaints were traceable to supervisors who had attended the human relations training course.

The president of Linear Electronics, reminded that the second session would begin shortly, hastily appointed an investigative committee. Within hours the committee reported that instructors had spent most of the time in the first six-week session lecturing the supervisors on the techniques of good human relations. The following are examples of the techniques:

1. Show a sincere interest in the personal problems of your subordinates.
2. Treat complaints as suggestions.

3. Admit your mistakes.
4. Set a good example.
5. Learn the first names of your subordinates, their spouses, and their children.
6. Refrain from showing favoritism.
7. Treat employees fairly.

Most members of the investigative committee felt that no attempt should be made to resume the course since it was evident that the supervisor-students had failed to convert their success at memorizing platitudes to successful on-the-job behavior. A few members of the committee felt that good human relations is an inherent trait and cannot be taught. Others felt good human relations could be taught, but that the course did not use the correct approach. The president asked for an expression of ideas concerning what should be the content and instructional methodology of a course in human relations.

48

NO-WIN SITUATION

BUSINESS HAD BEEN GOOD during the past year, and Mr. Harvey Daniels, president of Systems and Mechanical Research Associates, Inc., confidently expected a 200-percent increase in business volume within two years. Knowing that many carefully selected professional persons would be required in the near future, Mr. Daniels authorized the director of personnel, William Seagle, to establish orderly procedures for formally recruiting and selecting professional personnel for the company.

Mr. Seagle, who had resolutely campaigned for a more centralized procedure for hiring professional personnel, was visibly pleased with the president's decision. Without delay he devised and applied a set of modern personnel practices that gave the personnel department an important role of authority and responsibility in the hiring of professionals. To his great disappointment, however, the operating managers, including Mr. Daniels, continued to hire professionals through informal means, and after the fact to ask the personnel department to set up personnel folders.

Recently, Mr. David Hall had been hired as chief research engineer after his name was submitted to the president by the vice president of engineering. Mr. Hall, who was unemployed at that time, was invited to the home office for a personal interview. After spending three full days with the man, the top management of the company unanimously agreed that he was an excellently qualified, technically competent person and was easy to get along with. Mr. Daniels then decided to telephone Mr. Hall's references. In every case but one, the candidate was given the best recommendation possible, and, in fact, two of the firms stated they would be delighted to employ him again. These comments substantiated Mr. Daniels' own impression of Mr. Hall. Without losing any more time, Mr. Daniels dictated a letter to Mr. Hall, formally extending a job offer. Mr. Hall accepted the proffered position and moved his family and possessions to a nearby city the following week.

After being on the job for three months, Mr. Hall's contributions were sufficiently impressive that Mr. Daniels wondered how the company had been able to get along without him.

About ten days later Mr. Seagle became worried about some irregularities in Mr. Hall's background. In a routine manner, his office had set up a personnel folder after being notified of Mr. Hall's hiring and had initiated the data confirmation process: (a) the College of Engineering were Mr. Hall said he had taken his undergraduate and graduate work in mechanical engineering was contacted, (b) an attempt was made to assemble copies of publications that Mr. Hall had listed in his employment application, and (c) an effort was made to confirm the "highest previous salary earned" that Mr. Hall had reported. The personnel director was amazed to discover that (a) Mr. Hall had never been enrolled in the institution from which he claimed two degress, (b) one listed publication had never been published, and (c) Mr. Hall had overstated his highest previous salary by seven thousand dollars.

Mr. Seagle was uncertain how to proceed. His position as personnel director had been seriously undercut by the operating managers; moreover he felt that the president had lost confidence in him. "What should I do?" he wondered as he reflected on his dilemma. On the one hand, Mr. Hall's credentials were unquestionably flawed and overstated, perhaps even fraudulently so. Yet, on the other hand, Mr. Hall had proven impressively that he could do the job for which he had been hired and, in so doing, had earned the professional respect of the president of the company. Mr. Seagle was disconsolate. He felt that any option he chose would leave him vulnerable and unprotected.

49
NOT-SO-SMOOTH OPERATOR

MAUDE GRUNDLE RETURNED TO THE SWITCHBOARD and began to work as her group supervisor, Alexandra Bell, watched intently. Alexandra had just asked Maude to resign for the fifth time in 15 months, and Maude had replied, "No, I keep telling you if you people want to get rid of me, you'll have to fire me."

Maude had been employed by the Middlevale Telephone and Telegraph Company for 25 years. Her health was very good, and she always reported to work promptly and observed work rules of the strongly unionized company. She was active in the local union and was liked by her associates. She was 43 years old, had less than a high school education, and the rapid growth and automation of the telephone industry had been hard for her to keep up with. Maude had the highest hourly wage and worked the choice hours, which also happened to be the busiest of the workday. Her performance, however, was very poor, and her error index (the number of billing errors per calls handled) was the highest on her unit.

According to the union contract, work schedule and pay scale were based soley on seniority. Included in the contract was the provision that if an employee was fired by the company after five years of employment, the company would have to pay an average week's salary for each year employed as severance pay. There were specified means of obtaining the average by using the salaries for the four weeks immediately prior to dismissal.

Maude made $235 a week (averaged as specified in the contract). Her errors had cost the company $900 over the last three-month period. If she were fired now, her severance pay would be $5,875. The company offered to give her $1,000 severance pay if she would resign, but she laughed and replied, "Fire me!"

50

PENINSULA MARINE INSURANCE COMPANY

SEVERAL MANAGERS ON THE BOARD of the Peninsula Marine Insurance Company had expressed concern over the attitude of office employees in all departments toward getting to work on time, taking extended coffee breaks, stretching out their lunch hours, and leaving work several minutes early. The managers agreed that the problem was due to failure to administer a clear-cut policy consistently in all departments.

Phillip Underwood, head of the claims department, was appointed to make a study of certain employee work practices. On reviewing the problem, he realized that something more would have to be done than just posting on the bulletin board a statement citing requirements and regulations for working hours. This had been done before, with little noticeable change in the habits of office employees. Some dramatic action should be taken, or threatened, that would awaken the office force.

One possibility would be to post the policy regarding working hours along with a warning that those guilty of violating the policy would be discharged immediately. A second possibility would be to dock the pay of those who habitually failed to conform to the working schedule and to reprimand them personally. A third possibility would be the installation and use of time clocks to determine accurately the amount of working time each employee put in. Their pay would then be based on actual hours worked. Perhaps other steps could be taken.

Underwood knew that each possible action had advantages and disadvantages. However, with approximately 500 office employees involved, something had to be done that would permanently establish managerial policy regarding work hours and that would change present widespread and deeply ingrained employee attitudes toward wasted time.

51

SENSITIVE EMPLOYMENT REFERENCE

AS DIRECTOR OF A LARGE, nonprofit research organization that has an active affiliation with a large university nearby, you have just transferred an experienced administrative officer to one of your largest and most active departments. The department has a substantial budget and is supported by numerous research grants, both governmental and nongovernmental, that are administered by the university. Many of the professional staff of this department, including its chief, hold faculty appointments at the university. Most of the technical support personnel are full-time employees of your organization. The two top-level technical personnel in the department are the administrative officer and the supervisory technician, both of whom are your employees.

Shortly after assuming her position, the new administrative officer discovered several suspicious operations involving the supervisory technician's areas of responsibility. This person was a 15-year veteran of the department who had advanced to his present position through six promotions. In addition, he had received numerous performance awards and commendations over the years. The supervisory technician has a very close personal relationship with the department chief and also with one of the primary contractors who provided most of the supplies for the department.

A committee of three was appointed to conduct an investigation of the irregularities. The committee was zealous and its investigation took on the appearance of an inquisition rather than an inquiry. The material developed by the committee is incomplete and inconclusive, however. It contains many assumptions, conclusions, and speculations that are neither supported nor denied by the facts. While the information looks bad for the supervisory technician, you do not have sufficient evidence to prosecute or to fire the employee outright.

When the supervisory technician is confronted with the evidence, he claims that he is being used as a scapegoat for the professionals at the university. He claims to be just following their orders. He threatens to "blow the whistle" on a "lot of important people" in the research organization and at the university if action is taken against him. You allow the supervisory technician to go on extended leave with pay, at the end of which he is to be permitted to resign. You replace the department chief.

While the supervisory technician is on leave prior to resigning, his attorney, a former U.S. Attorney and local political figure, contacts you concerning the kind of employment reference his client will receive. He states that his client is being used as a scapegoat and that his future employment should not be jeopardized by a bad employment reference, especially since nothing prejudicial was ever proven. The attorney feels it would be better for all concerned if his client were able to secure other employment smoothly.

Shortly after the attorney's visit, an investigator from a federal agency contacts you concerning a full-scale investigation they are conducting as a preliminary step in employing the supervisory technician in a "sensitive" position with their agency. He asks you for a confidential employment reference for the supervisory technician. What should your recommendation be?

52

SMOKING POLICY

A MEETING OF THE SAFETY COMMITTEE had been called to review and revise the policy on smoking at Lake Haven Veterans Hospital, which basically provides psychiatric health care. The present smoking policy clearly limits smoking to offices, day rooms, and lounges. "No Smoking" signs are prominently posted in other areas such as hallways, laboratories, and patient rooms.

During the committee meeting, it was revealed that both patients and employees often ignored the signs and smoked in the restricted areas. The chief of housekeeping services pointed out that tile floors were being ruined by cigarette burns. This was especially true, he said, outside the main dining room where patients waited for the dining room to open for each meal. He said that either the dietetic services or the nursing services personnel should stop the patients from lounging in the hallway and smoking while waiting for meals. The chief dietitian retorted that it wasn't her job to control the patients in the hallways. Likewise the head nurse said that a majority of the patients had "privileges" and therefore nurses could not control their smoking.

After this exchange, other suggestions for dealing with the smoking problem were heard. Someone suggested that wall-type ashtrays be installed in the problem areas, but this was objected to on the grounds that it did not appear logical to put ashtrays in areas posted with "No Smoking" signs. The fact that the canteen sold cigarettes was mentioned along with the suggestion that perhaps cigarette sales should be halted. Several members of the committee felt that the no-smoking policy should be abolished if it were not going to be enforced. Still others expressed the opinion that the official no-smoking policy should remain even though it was ineffective.

But the central question remained unanswered: "How to prevent smoking in the areas where it was potentially damaging or unsafe?"

53

SPAN OF CONTROL

THE OWNER AND CHIEF EXECUTIVE OFFICER of Electronic Systems, H. F. Olson, an avid reader of professional management literature, became intrigued with concepts emanating from the behavioral sciences. Particularly impressive were the ideas expressed by such men as Chris Argyris, A. H. Maslow, and Douglas McGregor. Recorded attempts to put into practice McGregor's so-called "Theory Y" were especially intriguing. Olson decided he should make an effort to modernize his company's style of management in accordance with these concepts. His first act was to retain the services of a consultant whose name he associated with these newer concepts of management.

The consultant made many suggestions regarding job enlargement, decentralization, delegation, participation, and reorganization of work patterns. Most of the recommendations seemed to relate in one way or another to the company's organization structure. The consultant noted that organizations structured in accordance with classical management theory provided for a narrow span of control. This is necessary because of the close supervision that must presumably be given subordinates. However, recent notions regarding a subordinate's ability and desire to exercise self-direction and control eliminate the necessity of close supervision. The span of control can be wide with fewer managerial levels.

Olson was not completely convinced that a wide span of control and fewer levels really reflected the views of the behavioral scientists, as opposed to the views of the traditionalists. Electronic Systems was at present organized in such a way that above the first-line supervisor level there were 20 department heads, 5 heads of divisions, 3 vice presidents, 1 executive vice president, and the president.

54

SUBLEASE CONTRACT CLAUSE

HENRY RATHBONE, vice president of student affairs at State University, was concerned at the firm stance taken by his director of housing, Charles Robinson, against the subletting of dormitory rooms. Rathbone and the university attorney had given final approval to the current procedures under which dormitory residents were required to sign a housing contract that could be broken only if a student married, dropped out of school, or successfully petitioned for release for reasons of health or financial necessity.

Some students claimed they felt trapped by this contract and urged that it be rewritten to allow dormitory dwellers to sublet their rooms so as not to lose a term's rent in the process. Student pressure for the sublease contract clause had escalated recently, in response to which Robinson was quoted as saying, "I'll keep my commitment to establish a task force of students and staff to study an alternative housing contract, but there's *no way* it'll (subleasing) happen."

Brian Corbishley, former director of off-campus housing, testified before the special task force that all 33 privately owned off-campus apartment complexes in the area offered their tenants a subletting option for an average fee of about $40. He said, moreover, that subletting is "a spinoff of the consumer movement" and, if allowed by the housing contract, would be a continuation of a trend toward greater freedom in dorm living.

Robinson restated his "no and never" posture against subletting and gave as his primary reasons: (1) subletting would defeat the educational experience of dormitory living, (2) it would be too costly to administer, (3) roommates would have no control over who would come to live in their room or suite, and besides, (4) university housing is not supposed to be a Holiday Inn where people come and go as they please.

A student editorial in the *Independent Astonisher,* a daily newspaper distributed to all campus locations, including the dormitories, which housed some 5,000 residents, stated: "In an amazing display of candidness and gall, if not insensitivity, Housing Director Charles Robinson already has promised that the subletting proposal will never see implementation—he says he won't turn our dormitories into motels. So there. What happened to the democratic process? What happened to the willingness of university officials to listen to students? If Robinson would only relax and listen, he might learn to like it."

Rathbone realized that the sublease issue had reached an impasse and was reflecting unfavorably upon a major area of his responsibility, since Robinson reported directly to him. Rathbone felt that intervention time had come. But how to do it? On which side of the question? With what consequences? Should he sit tight? As he pondered his options, searching for a managerial intervention that might resolve this vexing problem successfully, the phone rang. A moment later, his secretary signalled that the university president was on line one.

55

SUGGESTION SYSTEM PROBLEMS

OFFICE OF THE PRESIDENT

Memorandum

Date: Friday, November 29, 1979

From: Bob Adams, president

To: John Sullens, vice president for personnel

Employee suggestion systems have been around for a long time. The positive financial impact of suggestion systems is significant in some organizations, according to my reading. For example, the National Association of Suggestion Systems estimates that 80 percent of the 500 largest U.S. corporations have such programs, and that employee suggestions save the nation's companies more than $500 million a year.

The other side of the suggestion system coin is that employees may become disgruntled over the way the company runs the system. You may recall that two United Airlines employees charged in court that United stole their suggestion for a reduced-fare plan for employees of all airlines, that United successfully implemented the reduced-fare plan, and that United thereby cheated them out of hundreds of thousands of dollars that they had coming under the company's suggestion system. The suggestors cited a provision of United Airline's suggestion program rules which stated that, "An employee is entitled to 10 percent of a typical year's profits resulting from an idea submitted through the suggestion system and successfully implemented."

During the trial, expert witnesses testified that in a typical year of operations under the reduced-fare plan, United had earned $3 million attributable to the plan, of which 10 percent, or $300,000, rightfully belonged to the two employees who initially submitted the suggestion. The jury found that the company acted in bad faith by failing to pay off under the suggestion system and assessed $1.8 million in damages against the airline, which later was reduced by a judge to $368,000.

We can't afford to risk such financial peril! It's critical, therefore, that you promptly review our suggestion system rules and policies and get back to me with your recommendations on the following issues. Include advantages and disadvantages as you see them.

1. *Calculation of award amount:* Should we offer a flat amount of money for each suggestion accepted or should the award be based on a percentage of the savings (earnings) during some period of time? What percent? What period of time?

2. *Maximum award:* Should we have a maximum limit on the payoff for any single suggestion (perhaps $10,000), or should it be open-ended?

3. *Time of award payment:* Should we pay the award in full at the time the suggestion is accepted or as the savings (earnings) are realized annually?

4. *Joint award allocation:* When two or more employees combine on a suggestion, how should we allocate the award among them?

5. *Originality:* Should we pay off for suggestions that help us, even if they aren't original with the employee(s) making the suggestion?

6. *Impetus award:* Are you in favor of an "impetus award" in the range of $100-$500 to recognize the contribution of a suggestion that speeds up an action that was initiated by the company before receipt of the suggestion?

7. *Written rules:* Do you think we need to spell out in writing every aspect of our suggestion system, or will an informal approach be more conducive to employee participation?

8. *Proof of knowledge:* Should we require all employees to sign a form stating that they have read and understand the rules of our suggestion system (if we decide to write them up)?

9. *Another limitation:* Should an employee be limited to suggestions relating only to his area of the organization?

10. *An exclusion:* Should our marketing function and finan-

cial policy (including product and service pricing) be excluded from the suggestion system?

11. *Evaluation:* Do you have any suggestions on a procedure for evaluating suggestions?

12. *Abandonment:* Maybe dropping the suggestion system would be the simplest thing to do. What do you think?

Let me hear from you soon. Treat this as a "hot" item.

56

UNCERTAIN JOB PROSPECTS

GLENN DICKEY SAT IN HIS OFFICE reviewing the occurrences of the last few days. As executive vice president of Deep Comfort Mattress Company, he faced a difficult decision.

Three weeks before, Eric Demuth, manager of sales, came to his office and announced he was leaving the organization to join a competitive firm. The reason for his decision was that the other company had offered a significant increase in salary plus a percentage of profits above a certain gross sales figure. The competitive firm's president had made the offer, but he had put nothing in writing.

Mr. Dickey was shocked and offended to learn of Demuth's decision to leave the company. He said he would try to work out a better financial arrangement if Demuth wanted more money. Demuth told Dickey that if he were worth more money now because of the pending resignation, he should have been paid more money before he received the offer. At the end of the week Eric Demuth left the firm.

Several days later Dickey read in the business section of his newspaper that the firm that was to employ Demuth had been acquired by a large conglomerate. Yesterday Dickey had another visit from Demuth. Demuth recounted that after he had left Deep Comfort and before he had had a chance to formalize his contractual arrangement as director of marketing with the competitive firm, it had been sold to the conglomerate. The conglomerate immediately imposed upon its newly-acquired company a 90-day moratorium on hiring, during which an analysis of personnel needs within the company would be made. As a result, Demuth said, he did not now have a job. Moreover, his prospects of ever getting the position as director of marketing were unlikely, given the conglomerate's history of bringing in members of its own management team to run new acquisitions.

Demuth told Dickey he would appreciate having his old job back.

57

UNREALIZED EXPECTATIONS

ON A HOT TUESDAY AFTERNOON the county auto inspection station was operating with only two of its eight inspection lanes open. Tuesday was typically a high volume day because the station was closed each Saturday afternoon, Sunday, and Monday. This combination of many automobiles to be inspected and only two open lanes resulted in waiting lines that averaged 16 automobiles each—and as many hot drivers, in varying states of irritation.

Ms. Miller arrived at the station and selected the shorter of the two waiting lines (which happened to contain 14 cars at the time) and slowly proceeded toward the station in increments of 20 feet per advance. Her journey required 55 minutes in the hot sun, but she was confident that her car would easily pass the inspection. Her confidence was justified. Only yesterday she had asked her local service station operator to check the car thoroughly and prepare it for the inspection. This he did at a cost to Ms. Miller of $58. These facts were documented by an itemized bill lying beside her on the front seat.

Except for a faulty low beam on the right headlight, Ms. Miller's car passed the inspection. Because of this defect, Jake Wheeling, the lane inspector, explained, her car failed to pass the inspection. Therefore, she would have to replace the faulty light and return later for a reinspection.

At this news, Ms. Miller shut off the engine, removed the ignition key, and jumped from her car waving the service station bill, which reported the headlights to be in perfect working order. She demanded to see the station supervisor, Blake Meadows.

Blake Meadows listened to her story but refused to overrule Jake Wheeling's decision. He also told her that the decision was in accord with official policy. Ms. Miller yelled that she could wait as long as they could and sat down on a nearby chair, leaving her car to block the inspection lane.

As the minutes passed, the drivers waiting behind Ms. Miller's car grew hotter, and several left their cars to see what was delaying them. Blake Meadows felt that something had to be done—and quickly.

58

WALKER BLANKET COMPANY

THE WALKER BLANKET COMPANY is one of four textile mills located in a small southern community. Responsibility for the management of the family-owned enterprise has been in the hands of Joe Walker for 29 years. Joe Walker is now 63 years old, and some employees have accused him of being senile. Various members of the Walker family, suspecting that Joe needed assistance and realizing the need for a successor, persuaded him to employ as executive vice president a young textile executive from out of state, Lou Winthrop.

Winthrop had been with Walker Blanket Company six months when the question of a Christmas bonus for the employees arose. It was a tradition for the textile mills in the community to give their employees some form of Christmas bonus such as money, fruit, or a company product. For 29 years Joe Walker had given his workers a blanket. This year Lou Winthrop requested that each employee receive a week's salary since he felt the traditional blanket had lost its meaning. He was convinced that it was becoming a joke in the community and that the Walker employees were the subject of ridicule. Joe Walker became indignant at the suggestion and insisted the employees were grateful for all he had done for them. A rumor circulated among the employees that they were to receive a week's salary, and when Walker presented them blankets on Christmas Eve upon completion of the last shift, they plainly showed their disappointment and irritation.

Around midnight the community volunteer fire department was called to the scene of a fire on the community house lawn. Upon arriving they found approximately 300 employees of Walker Blanket Company. Many of them were obviously inebriated and were dancing and shouting around a huge fire fueled by Walker Christmas blankets. Almost half of the blankets given by Joe Walker just hours before were burned that evening and 32 Walker employees were jailed for disturbing the peace. On

December 26 Lou Winthrop was summoned to the Walker home where members of the family were assembled. Winthrop learned that Joe Walker suffered a heart attack upon hearing of the behavior of his employees, and he would probably be away from his desk for at least six months. Winthrop was told that he was being considered as a replacement for Walker, but first, members of the family desired to know what action he would take as a result of the fire and how he proposed to pay a $8,500 bill submitted to Walker Blanket Company by the city fathers for damages to city property.

ABOUT OUR CONTRIBUTING
PROFESSORS

Wilmar F. Bernthal, D.B.A. (Indiana University), is Professor of Management and Organization at the University of Colorado. He has taught at Valparaiso University and Indiana University. He has published numerous articles in management journals such as the *Academy of Management Journal.* Hs is consulting editor for Wiley/Hamilton management series, and is a fellow in the Academy of Management. His major fields of professional interest are organization theory, organizational behavior, and business and society.

Bernard J. Bienvenu, D.B.A. (Harvard University), is Professor and Head of the Department of Management and Adminstrative Studies at the University of Southwestern Louisiana. He has published numerous articles and is author of the book *New Priorities in Training—A Guide for Industry,* published by the American Management Association. He has served as a visiting professor at France's leading business school and has lectured on management in many African countries. He is past president of the Southwestern and Southern Management Associations. His major areas of professional interest are policy and strategy, motivation and morale, management development, and management of educational and public institutions.

Robert Boissoneau, Ph.D. (Ohio State), is Dean and Professor, College of Human Services at Eastern Michigan University in Ypsilanti, Michigan. He has spoken at many national health meetings and published widely in allied health and health administration literature. He has received numerous grants and served as a consultant to HEW's Bureau of Health Manpower and the Michigan Department of Mental Health. He has had experience as a hospital administrator at Detroit Memorial Hospital and The Ohio State University Hospitals and was a full time faculty member in the health administration programs at Ohio State and

306

the University of Missouri-Columbia. In his present position as Dean of Eastern Michigan's College of Human Services, he works with programs in dietetics, gerontology, health administration, home economics, medical technology, nuclear medicine technology, nursing, occupational therapy and social work. His major areas of interest are health administration, education in the health professions, and internal hospital organization and management.

Elwood S. Buffa, Ph.D. (University of California), is Professor of Business Administration, University of California at Los Angeles. He previously taught at the University of Illinois and was associated with the Eastman Kodak Company in an engineering capacity. Significant publications include *Modern Production Management* (5th ed., 1977), *Production-Inventory Systems,* coauthor (rev. ed., 1972), *Operations Management: The Management of Productive Systems* (1976), and *Management Science/Operations Research,* coauthor (1977). His major fields of interest are operations management and management science.

Elmer H. Burack, Ph.D. (Northwestern), is Professor of Management and Management Head, College of Business, University of Illinois at Chicago Circle. At various times he has taught at Illinois Institute of Technology, Northwestern University, and San Diego State University. He has published numerous articles in professional journals and approximately ten books including *Managing Change* (1979); *Growing: Careers for Women* (1979); *Human Resource Planning* (1979); *Personnel Management* (1977); and *Organization Analysis* (1975). He has been on the editorial review board of the Academy of Management Journal and has served as chairman or president of: personnel division and health care division of the Academy, Industrial Relations Association of Chicago, and the Illinois Management Training Institute for CETA. Currently he is vice chairman of the Governor's Advisory Council on Employment in Illinois and is a consultant to various institutions.

John M. Champion, Ph.D. (Purdue), is Professor of Management and Professor of Health and Hospital Administration at the University of Florida. Prior to returning to full time teaching and research he held an administrative position as chairman of the university's gradute program in Health and Hospital Administration. He has also held teaching positions at Purdue University and Georgia State University. He serves as management consultant to a number of hospitals and business firms and has conducted and particpated in many training and management development programs. In addition to the publication of numerous journal articles, he is author of *General Hospital/A Model* (University Park Press) and coauthor of *Critical Incidents in Management* (Irwin). He is a member of the American Psychological Association, the Academy of Management, the Southern Management Association, and other professional organizations and fraternities.

Edward R. Clayton, Ph.D. (Clemson University), is Professor of Management Science at Virginia Polytechnic Institute and State University. He is the author of numerous papers and articles on subjects of operations research and information systems. He is active as a consultant to several firms on business applications of computer systems and mathematical programming. He is a coauthor with L. S. Moore of *GERT Modeling and Simulation Fundamentals and Applications* (1978). His major fields of interest are simulation, mathematical programming, and computer applications to business problems.

Robert G. Cook, D.B.A. (Indiana), is Professor of Management, College of Business and Public Administration, University of Missouri at Columbia. His previous posts at the University include chairman of the Management Department, assistant director of Research Administration in the Graduate School, and Office of the Chancellor. Formerly, he taught at the Air Force Institute of Technology and at Indiana University. Prior business associations include work with I.B.M. Corp., Bendix Aviation Corp., and Revere Copper and Brass, Inc. He is a member of the board of directors of several corporations and public service organizations, and has been a management consultant in both business and hospital administration. His major fields of professional interest are executive development, production management, business and management history, policy and administration, and systems analysis.

Larry L. Cummings, D.B.A. (Indiana), is Professor of Organizational Behavior and Director of the Center for the Study of Organizational Performance, Graduate School of Business, University of Wisconsin, Madison. He has taught at Indiana University, Columbia University, and the University of British Columbia. He has published over 50 articles and is coauthor of three books: *Readings in Organizational Behavior and Human Performance* (1969, 1973), *Organizational Decision Making* (1970), *Performance in Organizations* (1973). He is consulting editor, Richard D. Irwin Series in Management and the Behavioral Sciences. He is a fellow of the Academy of Management and past chairman of the Academy's Division of Organizational Behavior. He also is a fellow in the Division of Industrial and Organizational Psychology of the

American Psychological Association. He serves as the editor of the *Academy of Management Journal* and as one of the associate editors of *Decision Sciences*.

James H. Davis, Ph.D. (Ohio State), is Professor of Business Administration in the College of Administrative Science at Ohio State University in Columbus, Ohio. He has published a number of significant publications including the *Handbook of Sales Training* (1954) and *Sales Management* (1954 coauthor). He serves as a consultant to a number of government agencies and industrial firms.

Keith Davis, Ph.D. (Ohio State), is Professor of Management, Arizona State University. He has taught at The Ohio State University, Indiana University, and the University of Texas. He has published over 150 professional articles, and his books include *Human Behavior at Work* (5th edition, 1977), *Organizational Behavior: A Book of Readings* (5th edition, 1977), *Business and Society* (3rd edition, 1975; winner of an Academy of Management Book Award in its first edition), and *Cases in Management* (3rd edition, 1962). He is consulting editor, McGraw-Hill Series in Management, a fellow in the Academy of Management, and a contributor to over 80 books. He was a National Beta Gamma Sigma Distinguished Scholar in 1975–76 and Visiting Professor at the University of Western Australia in 1974.

André L. Delbecq, D.B.A. (Indiana), is Professor of Administration and Director of the Center for Evaluation Research in the School of Social Work at the University of Wisconsin, Madison. He also holds a faculty appointment with the Health Services Administration Program. He serves on the Editorial Board of the *Academy of Management Review*. He is coauthor of a readings book in management published by Richard D. Irwin, Inc.; a book dealing with organization decision making published by McGraw-Hill; and a book concerned with nominal and delphi techniques for planning published by Scott, Foresman and has written more than 60 articles. He is a fellow of the Academy of Management. His research has received recognition from the Academy of Management, the American Sociological Association, the American Public Health Association, and the American Institute of Decision Sciences.

W. Jack Duncan, Ph.D. (Louisiana State University), is Professor of Management and Associate Dean for Graduate Studies and Research in the School of Business at the University of Alabama in Birmingham. He is a fellow of the Academy of Management, past chairperson of the Management Eduation and Development Division of the Academy, and treasurer of the Southern Management Association. He is the author of *Decision Making and Social Issues* (1972), *Essentials of Management,* 2nd ed. (1978), and *Organizational Behavior* (1978). He has published widely in journals such as the *Academy of Management Journal, Management Science, Management International Review, American Journal of Economics and Sociology.* His major areas of professional interest are administrative theory, organizational analysis, and business and society.

Robert E. Engel, Ph.D. (Iowa), is Associate Professor and chairman of the Division of Postsecondary and Continuing Education at the University of Iowa's College of Education. Other administrative positions that he has held at the University of Iowa have been assistant dean of liberal arts, assistant director of the summer session, associate dean for academic affairs, and assistant to the president. He has served on the board of trustees of Rust College, and is currently a member of the board of trustees of Cornell College, and of its executive committee. His publications include *Preparing for Planning: An Outline for Smaller Colleges and Universities* (with John D. Kraus, Jr.), Association of American Colleges, December 1978, and numerous other articles and monographs.

Alan C. Filley, Ph.D. (Ohio State), is Professor of Management, University of Wisconsin, Madison. He has taught at the University of Georgia as Distinguished Visiting Scholar, The Ohio State University, and the University of North Dakota. He is a contributor to major journals in the field of business and is the author of *The Compleat Manager* (1978) and *Interpersonal Conflict Resolution* (1975), and coauthor of *Managerial Process and Organizational Behavior* (1976). He has co-edited *Management in Perspective* (1965), and *Studies in Managerial Process and Organizational Behavior* (1972). His major fields of professional interest are organizational behavior, organization theory, and organizational intervention.

J. D. Forbes, Ph.D. (Harvard), is Professor of Business History at the Darden Graduate School of Business Administration, University of Virginia. He has served on the faculties of the University of Kansas City, Bennington College, and Wabash College. His significant publications include *Israel Thorndike, Federalist Financier* (1953), *Victorian Architect* (1953), *Stettinius, Sr., Portrait of a Morgan Partner* (1974). His professional interests are in the areas of business biography and literacy style in business writing.

William M. Fox, Ph.D. (Ohio State), is Professor of Industrial Relations and Management, University of Florida. He has held faculty positions at Ohio State, Texas Tech, and the University of Washington. He was a Fulbright Lecturer in Japan 1958–59 and a Senior Fulbright Research Scholar in Japan 1974–75. In addition to publishing numerous articles, he edited *Readings in Personnel Management from Fortune* (1957 and 1963), and wrote *The Management Process: An Integrated Functional Approach* (1963). He conducted studies in leadership under contract to the Office of Naval Research during 1970–74. He is past president of the Southern Management Association and past chairman of the Organization and Management Theory Division of the Academy of Management.

William C. Frederick, Ph.D. (Texas), is Professor of Business Administration in the Graduate School of Business at the University of Pittsburgh, where he teaches courses dealing with the relations between business and society and conducts research on corporate social policy. He has served as a management education consultant to private foundations and business corporations in the United States and abroad.

Robert Freedman, Jr., Ph.D. (Yale), is Professor of Economics, Colgate University. He has been on the faculty at Colgate since 1950. He is the author of *Marxist Social Thought* (1968). His major fields of professional interest are urban economics and comparative economic systems.

C. B. Gambrell, Jr., Ph.D. (Purdue), is Vice President for Academic Affairs at the University of Central Florida in Orlando. His previous teaching experiences were at Purdue University, Lamar University, Arizona State University, and Clemson University. He has published numerous articles in business and professional journals and is an active consultant to government and industry. His major areas of professional interest are organization and management, economic analysis, human factors, and work study and productivity.

Thomas Q. Gilson, Ph.D. (M.I.T.), is Associate Dean and Professor of Industrial Relations in the College of Business Administration at the University of Hawaii. Previously he was professor and chairman of the Management Department at Rutgers University. He also has served on the faculties of Massachusetts Institute of Technology, Clark University, and Newark College of Engineering. He has had business experience as a personnel director and as a training director. He is a labor arbitrator and is the author of several books and many journal articles. His major areas of professional interest are management development, collective bargaining, organizational behavior, and personnel administration.

Robert T. Golembiewski, Ph.D. (Yale), is Research Professor of Political Science and Management, University of Georgia. He previously taught at Princeton and Illinois, and was visiting lecturer in industrial administration at Yale. His significant publications include *Behavior and Organization* (1962), *The Small Group* (1962), *Men, Management, and Morality* (1965), *Organizing Men and Power* (1967), *Managerial Behavior and Organization Demands* (1967), *Perspectives in Public Management* (1968), *Sensitivity Training and the Laboratory Approach* (1970, 1973, and 1977), *Renewing Organizations* (1972), *Cases in Public Management* (1973 and 1976), *Individual Learning and Change in Groups* (1976), *Public Administration as a Developing Discipline,* 2 vols. (1978), and *Approaches to Planned Change,* 2 vols. (1978).

Paul J. Gordon, Ph.D. (Syracuse), is Professor of Management, Indiana University, and 1969 President of the Academy of Management. He is listed both in the 1973–74 issues of *Who's Who in the World and Who's Who in America.* He serves on the editorial boards of the *Academy of Management Journal, Business Horizons,* and *Hospital Administration.* His major professional interests include organizational, managerial, and policy studies in complex organizations.

George J. Gore, Ph.D. (Michigan), is Professor of Management, University of Cincinnati. An electrical engineer with three graduate degrees in management, his work experience includes full-time employment by General Electric and DuPont; 19 years of full-time university teaching in management; as well as extensive consulting for business, industrial, governmental, and health care organizations. A specialist in business policy and production/operations systems, he has written over 50 articles and directs executive development programs. In the Academy of Management he is a fellow, former vice president, and recent chairman of both the Consulting and Production/Operations Management professional divisions.

Walter T. Greaney, Jr., L.L.M., Ph.D. (Harvard), is Professor and Chairman of the Finance Department in the School of Management, Boston College. He is practicing attorney as well as a teacher. He is a member of the Massachusetts and Federal bars. His special fields of study are taxation and public finance, banking, and corporate finance.

Robert M. Guion, Ph.D. (Purdue), is Professor of Psychology, Bowling Green State University, and was 1972–73 president of Division Fourteen of the American Psychological Association. He is the author of *Personnel Testing* (1965). He is a member of the American Psychological Association and a licensed psychologist. He has taught and conducted research at the University of California, University of New Mexico, and the Educational Testing Service. He is an active consultant and contributor to journals in the field of personnel, psychology, and general business. His major fields of interest are employee selection, employee motivation, and measurement theory.

Ogden H. Hall, Ph.D. (Louisiana State University), is Professor of Management at the University of New Orleans. He previously taught at Virginia Polytechnic Institute. He has served as president of both the Eastern and Southern Management Associations. He has been active in the Academy of Management and the American Institute for Decision Sciences. His consulting activities include industrial, educational, and health services organizations. His major fields of interest are organizational and interpersonal communications, management in learning systems, and management training and development.

Dorothy N. Harlow, Ph.D. (Kansas), is Professor of Management, University of South Florida. She has taught at Wichita State University and at the University of Houston, Clearlake as the L. J. Buchan Distinguished Visiting Professor. She served on the editorial board of the *Academy of Management Review,* is vice president-elect (president during 1980) of the Southern Management Association, and has presented more than ten cases at workshops of the Southern Case Research Association. She is the author or coauthor of over 30 journal articles and papers presented at professional meetings and is senior author of a book in her main teaching and research interest area of organizational behavior, *Behavior in Organizations: Text, Cases and Readings,* published by Little, Brown and Co. in 1975. She has been extensively involved with management training programs for industry and government agencies. Her major professional areas of interest are organizational behavior, management of professional and technical employees, and women's role in the work force.

Richard I. Hartman, D.B.A. (Indiana), is Professor and Chairman of the Department of Business Management and Administration at Bradley University. Formerly he taught at the University of Georgia and Indiana University. He has published in *Human Resource Management, Per-*

sonnel *Journal, The Personnel Administrator, Industrial Management,* and *Industrial Engineering.* He is also coauthor of two books and a number of business cases. His major fields of interest are organization theory, personnel management, and business policy.

Robert D. Hay, Ph.D. (Ohio State), is Professor of Management, University of Arkansas. He is the coauthor of *Business Report Writing* (1957), and author of *Written Communications for Business Administration* (1965), *Introduction to Business* (1968), and *Business and Society* (1976). His major fields of professional interest are business policy, management history, social responsibility, and athletic administration.

James O. Hepner, Ph.D. (University of Iowa), is Professor and Director of the Washington University Health Administration and Planning Program. He is an experienced hospital administrator and presently serves as a national consultant in health services administration to the surgeon general of the United States Air Force. He is a fellow in the American College of Hospital Administrators, the American Public Health Association, and an honorary fellow in the American Academy of Medical Administrators. He also has served on major committees of, and is currently a consultant to, the Department of Health, Education, and Welfare. He is the author of four books: *The Health Strategy Game* (1973), *Personnel Administration and Labor Relations in Health Care Facilities* (1969), *Health Planning for Emerging Multi-Hospital Systems* (1978), and *Hospital Administrator-Physician Relationships* (1979).

Herbert G. Hicks, Ph.D. (Alabama), is Professor of Management, Louisiana State University. In addition to numerous articles, his books include *The Management of Organizations* (3d. ed., 1976), *Management Organizations and Human Resources* (2d. ed., 1976), *Modern Business Management* (1974), *Organizations: Theory and Behavior* (1975), and *Business: An Involvement Approach* (1975). He has served as president of the Southern Management Association, the Southwestern Division of the Academy of Management, and the Academy of Management. He is a fellow in the Academy of Management. His major fields of professional interest are organization theory, administrative theory, and basic management.

A. T. Hollingsworth, Ph.D. (Michigan State University), is Professor of Management, University of South Carolina. He has held faculty positions at Southern Illinois University in Carbondale and Florida Atlantic University in Boca Raton, Florida. He has published articles in journals such as *Journal of Retailing, Business Horizons, Journal of Small Business Management, Personnel Journal,* and *Journal of Applied Psychology.* He has also coauthored *A Practical Approach to the Management of Small Business* and other books. He has conducted extensive consulting work with a variety of organizations.

Sheila Davis Inderlied, Ed.D. (University of Massachusetts at Amherst), is Assistant Professor, Department of Human Resources Management, School of Business Administration, California State University, Long Beach. She has authored several articles and papers concerning women in management, sex role stereotyping, and conducts research on leader behavior and sex roles. Dr. Inderlied is an active member of the Academy of Management as program chairperson and chair-elect of the Status of Women Interest Group. She is also a member of the American Psychological Association and the Organizational Behavior Teaching Society. At present she is also a management consultant in the Southern California area to government agencies and private industry. Dr. Inderlied is director of the Women's Studies Program in the School of Social and Behavioral Sciences at California State University, Long Beach.

John H. James, D.B.A. (Indiana), is Associate Professor of Management at the University of Florida. His publications include *Critical Incidents in Management* (coauthor, 4th ed., 1980), *Long-Range Planning for Small Business* (coauthor, 1964), and articles. Professional activities include having been chairman of the Constitution and By-Laws Committee of the Academy of Management, and chairman of the South-eastern Chapter of the Institute of Management Sciences. In addition to teaching at both the graduate and undergraduate levels, he has participated in a number of management development and supervisory training programs for managers in business, government and health care organizations.

Harold D. Janes, Ph.D. (Alabama), is Professor of Industrial Relations, University of Alabama. Formerly, he was personnel manager of the Wadsworth Watch Case Company and director of personnel and industrial relations, Elgin National Watch Company. He is the author of "A Survey of Industries' Opinions on 'How to Apply for a Job'" (1952), as well as numerous cases, book reviews, and several articles published in the *Personnel Journal.* He is an active consultant and serves as an arbitrator for the American Arbitration Association. His major areas of professional interest are personnel administration, wage and salary administration, and arbitration.

Max B. Jones, Ph.D. (North Carolina), is Professor of Management, Old Dominion University and was 1971 president of the Southern Management Association. He has taught at North Carolina State University at Raleigh, The University of North Carolina, and the College of William and Mary. He is currently on the Roster of Arbitrators for the Federal Mediation and Conciliation Service and has served as consultant to both public and private sector organizations.

Michael J. Jucius, Ph.D. (Chicago), is Professor of Management at the University of Arizona. He is the author of *Personnel Management* (9th ed., 1979), *Purchasing* (coauthor, 1947), *Elements of Managerial Action* (coauthor, 3d ed., 1973), and *Introduction to Business* (coauthor, 3d ed., 1966). Formerly, he taught at The Ohio State University and the University of Kansas. In 1958 and 1959 he was visiting professor, Turin, Italy. His major fields of professional interest are organization, personnel management, and industrial management.

William H. Keown, Ph.D. (Wisconsin), is Professor Emeritus of Management at the University of Oklahoma in Norman. Formerly, he was on the faculty of the University of Wisconsin and director of industrial relations for the Louisville Railway Company.

James P. Logan, Ph.D. (Columbia), is Professor of Management at the University of Arizona, Tuscon. Formerly he was a visiting fellow, Western Australian Institute of Technology, Perth. He served on the faculty of the Graduate School of Business, Columbia University, and as visiting professor at IMEDE in Lausanne, Switzerland. His publications include being coauthor of *Strategy, Policy and Central Management* (7th ed., 1976) and *Management of Expanding Enterprises* (1955). His major fields of interest are business policy, strategic planning, and organizational behavior.

Vincent P. Luchsinger, Ph.D. (Texas Tech) is Professor of Administration and Human Resources, Texas Tech College of Business Administration, Lubbock, Texas. He served a number of years in the Air Force and is currently a colonel in the Air Force Reserve. His major areas of expertise are organization behavior and development and international and comparative management systems. He is licensed as a psychologist in the state of Texas.

Fred Luthans, Ph.D. (Iowa), is Regents Professor of Management, University of Nebraska. He taught at the United States Military Academy, West Point while serving in the United States Army. He has published over 50 articles and is the author or coauthor of numerous books including *Emerging Concepts in Management* (1969, 1975), *Organizational Behavior Modification* (1975), *Social Issues in Business* (1972, 1976, 1980), *Organizational Behavior* (1973, 1977), *Introduction to Management: A Contingency Approach* (1976), and *The Practice of Supervision and Management* (1979). He is on the editorial boards of *Organizational Behavior Management Journal, Academy of Management Review,* and *Akron Business and Economics Journal* and is consulting co-editor for the McGraw-Hill Series in Management. Dr. Luthans is an active member of the Academy of Management where he is currently vice president of the Midwest Division.

Joseph F. McGraw, M.S. (University of Colorado), is presently an instructor with the Department of Business, Troy State University at Montgomery, Alabama. His past experience includes a partnership in a manufacturing concern and 27 years of experience as a personnel officer with the United States Air Force.

Quinn G. McKay, D.B.A. (Harvard), is Senior Vice President/Human Resource Development of Skaggs Companies, Inc., and holds the David L. Tandy Chair of American Enterprise Management at Texas Christian University. During 1971– 72 he was a visiting professor at IMEDE (an international management institute) in Lausanne, Switzerland. From 1965– 69, he was the dean of the School of Business and Economics at Weber State in Ogden, Utah. His major academic interests are in the fields of organizational behavior, corporate strategy, executive development, and social responsibility or corporate ethics.

Karl O. Mann, Ph.D. (Cornell), is Professor of Industrial Relations at Rider College. Previously he served as a faculty member at the American University, Duquesne University, and the University of Toledo. He is an Accredited Personnel Diplomate as well as a member of the Academy of Management. His many publications in personnel management and labor relations include a book of *Readings in Labor Relations* which was published in 1974 by Dow Jones Books. His major areas of professional interest are personnel management, labor relations and collective bargaining, and compensation administration.

Jack W. Martin, M.B.A. (Northwestern), is Professor Emeritus of Management, University of Denver. He attended the Harvard Case Seminar and is an officer in Planning and Development Associates (Industrial Economists). His special fields of study have included business organization and policies.

Thomas E. Miller, Ph.D. (Northwestern), is Professor of Business Administration and Human Relations, University of Missouri at Kansas City. Formerly, he taught at Northwestern University and the University of Kansas. His major fields of interest are communications and human relations.

Thomas A. Natiello, Ph.D. (Michigan State), is Professor of Management and Health Administration and Director of the Institute for Health Administration and Research at the University of Miami where he heads the Graduate Health Administration Program. He has conducted research on health and other organizations and was chairman and founder of the Health Care Administration Division of the Academy of Management. He has served as a consultant to various agencies of the U.S. Department of Health, Education, and Welfare and to other public and private organizations. His major fields of professional interest are organization structure and design, evaluation of health care and other human services, organizational policy, and contingency theory.

Frank P. Numer, M.S. (Duquesne), J.D. (University of Miami), is Professor of Business Administration at Robert Morris College in Pittsburgh. His industrial experience includes being manager of management development for the R.C.A. Service Company, Cape Kennedy, Florida, as well as positions with Westinghouse, Inc., and the H. J. Heinz Company. He is a management consultant having given management development seminars in Pennsylvania, Ohio, Indiana, Illinois, Florida, New York, and Kentucky. His major areas of professional interest are business policy, labor management relations, law, and management development.

Lynn H. Peters, LL.B, Ph.D. (Wisconsin) is Professor of Management, San Diego State University. He is author of *Management and Society,* and is listed in both *Who's Who in America* and *American Men and Women of Science.* His extensive consulting activities include being the "in-house" organizational design consultant at San Diego State. He has been an officer of the Academy of Management and is currently a member of the Academic Senate of the California State University and Colleges. His major areas of professional interest are business and society, organization theory, and organizational change.

Rosemary Pledger, D.B.A. (Texas Tech) and **Linda McGee Calvert,** Ph.D. (LSU), are both on the faculty of the University of Houston at Clear Lake City where Dr. Pledger is the Dean of the School of Professional Studies and Dr. Calvert is Assistant Professor of Management. Dr.

Pledger and Dr. Calvert collaborated in writing a critique for the "Fiery Provocation" incident. Dr. Pledger is presently president of the Academy of Management (1979) and Dr. Calvert is actively engaged in the Organizational Behavior and Management Consultation divisions of the Academy of Management. They both describe their major areas of professional interest as management theory, organizational behavior, personnel management, and women in management.

Lyman W. Porter, Ph.D. (Yale), is Dean of the Graduate School of Administration at the University of California, Irvine. He also holds the title of Professor of Administration and Psychology. Prior to joining UCI in 1967, he served 11 years on the faculty of the University of California, Berkeley. He has published widely, and is the coauthor of two books. He is co-editor of *Annual Review of Psychology* and is a member of the editorial boards of several journals. He served as president of the Academy of Management in 1973–74, and president, Division of Industrial/Organizational Psychology of the American Psychological Association in 1975–76. He is a fellow in the American Psychological Association. His major fields of interest are job attitudes, organization communication, and organization politics.

William A. Preshing, Ph.D. (Illinois) has held a variety of positions including that of director of Institutional Research and Planning at the University of Alberta and as president of William A. Preshing and Associates Ltd., Development Consultants. He is author of *Introduction to Canadian Business Management* (1974), coauthor of *Concepts and Canadian Cases in Marketing* (1973), author of *Cases for Managerial Decisions* (1964), and author of over 100 articles in marketing and management.

Harold F. Puff, D.B.A. (Indiana), is Professor of Management, Miami University, Oxford, Ohio. He has taught at Indiana University, Earlham College, University of Michigan, California State College at Long Beach, and was visiting scholar at the University of California in Los Angeles. His latest publication is "Cost Improvement Programs," *Encyclopedia of Professional Management,* McGraw-Hill Book Co. (1978). His major fields of professional interest are personnel management, purchasing and materials management, and industrial relations.

Jonathon S. Rakich, Ph.D. (St. Louis University), is Professor of Management and Director of Graduate Programs in Business at the University of Akron. He has held faculty positions at the University of Detroit and The University of Akron. He currently serves with an Ohio

Health Systems Agency and held a federal faculty fellowship with the Department of Health, Education and Welfare (1973). His books (coauthor) include *Managing Health Care Organizations* (1977) and *Hospital Organization and Management: Text and Readings* (1978). He has written numerous articles in the health services administration field on unionization, planning, and national health insurance. His major fields of professional interest are business strategy, policy formulation, and health services management.

Dennis F. Ray, Ph.D. (Florida), is Professor and Head, Department of Management at Mississippi State University. Prior to his appointment at Mississippi State in 1966 he held teaching positions at the University of Alabama and the University of Florida. He is presently editor of the *Journal of Management,* business manager of the Academy of Management Publications, member of the board of governors of the Academy of Management, and secretary-treasurer of the Academy of Management. He serves as consultant to numerous government agencies including the U.S. Department of Agriculture. His major areas of professional interest are organizational behavior and management theory.

Daniel D. Roman, Ph.D. (University of Southern California), is Professor of Management Science, The George Washington University, Washington, D.C. He has taught at the American University, Florida State University, California State, Northridge, and the University of Southern California. He has published many articles on the management of science and technology. He is the author of *R&D Management: The Economics and Administration of Technology* (1968) and *Science Technology and Motivation: A Systems Approach* (1979). He has served as a consultant to many industrial organizations and government agencies as well as such international organizations as UNESCO (Paris), International Institute for Management of Technology (Milan), Organization of American States (Brazil, Peru), and the Bradford Management Center, Bradford, England. He is past national chairman of the Academic Advisory Committee for the National Association for Purchasing Management. His major fields of interest are management theory and practice, production, and the management of science, technology, and innovation.

Frank J. Schilagi, Ph.D. (University of Georgia), is Dean and Professor, Babcock Graduate School of Management, Wake Forest University. He has served as a consultant to government agencies and universities and is currently on the board of directors of three corporations. He is currently a partner in a management company employing over 900 people. His major areas of professional interest are organization/individual behavior and leadership-power.

Lawrence L. Schkade, Ph.D. (Louisiana State), is Professor of Systems Analysis and Urban Affairs, University of Texas at Arlington. He has served on the faculties of the University of Texas at Austin, Louisiana State University, and as Ford Foundation Professor at the Instituto Tecnologico de Monterrey, Mexico. Recent publications include *Statistical Analysis for Administrative Decisions* (1979) and research articles in several journals. He is past president and a fellow of the American Institute for Decision Sciences, a fellow of the American Association for the Advancement of Science, and the recipient of a Distinguished Scholar Award from Beta Gamma Sigma and the American Assembly of Collegiate Schools of Business. His special fields include system theory, organization behavior, decision making, and urban affairs.

Albert N. Schrieber, M.B.A. (Harvard), is Professor of Business Policy and Operations Management at the Graduate School of Business Administration of the University of Washington, Seattle. He has had a variety of business experiences, serving as president to Pacific Plastics Company, 1954–55, and as a consultant to numerous companies, including the Boeing Company. Among his numerous publications are: *Defense Procurement and Small Business* (1961), *Cases in Manufacturing Management* (1965), and *Corporate Simulation Models* (1970). In 1965 and 1966 he taught at IMEDE, the international management institute in Lausanne, Switzerland. In 1967, he was at Oxford University and in 1968 at Cranfield University, both in England, as a visiting professor in advanced management seminars.

Louis J. Shuster, Ph.D. (Washington), is Professor of Management, College of Business, California State College at Bakersfield. He previously taught at the University of Missouri in St. Louis, Sacramento State University, University of Santa Clara, and Northern Illinois University. His publications include articles in the *Academy of Management Journal* and the *Journal of College Placement*. His ten years of industrial experience include consulting activities with the Pacific Telephone and Telegraph Company and the Aerojet-General Corporation. His major fields of professional interest are organizational theory, personnel management, and business policy.

Henry Clay Smith, Ph.D. (Johns Hopkins), is Professor of Psychology at Michigan State University. He previously held faculty positions at Knox College and at Hamilton College. During World War II he was director of training and research, Western Electric Company, Baltimore, Maryland. His books include *Psychology of Industrial Behavior* (1972), *Sensitivity Training* (1973), and *Personality Development* (1974).

Allen R. Solem, Ph.D. (Michigan), is Professor of Management, School of Business Administration, University of Minnesota. Formerly he directed the Behavioral Sciences Program at the University of Rochester's College of Business Administration and, earlier, undergraduate and graduate training in the University of Maryland's Industrial Psychology Program. He was visiting associate professor of psychology at the University of Michigan during the 1959–60 academic year. Professor Solem is a coauthor of *Supervisory and Executive Development* (1957) and has contributed to numerous professional journals.

Robert T. Sprouse, Ph.D. (Minnesota), is Vice Chairman of the Financial Accounting Standards Board (FASB), Stamford, Connecticut. Prior to joining the FASB in 1973, Mr. Sprouse was professor of accounting at the Stanford University Graduate School of Business. At Stanford he received the 1969 Salgo-Noren Award for Distinguished Teaching. He also has taught at the University of Minnesota and the University of California. From 1962 to 1965 he was visiting lecturer of business administration, Harvard University. He has published many articles in professional journals as well as having been coauthor of "A Tentative Set of Broad Accounting Principles for Business Enterprises," Accounting Research Study No. 3; *Accounting Flows: Income, Funds and Cash;* and *Essentials of Financial Statement Analysis.* His major fields of interest are corporate financial reporting and management accounting and control.

David B. Starkweather, Dr. P.H. (UCLA), is Professor of Hospital Administration, University of California, Berkeley. His previous positions include those of associate director and later director, Palo Alto Stanford Hospital Center. His publications include numerous cases and articles in professional journals. His current research is centered upon hospital mergers and health facilities planning. He is a trustee of Herrick Memorial Hospital in Berkeley, California, and chairman of the Accreditation Commission for Graduate Education in Health Services Administration.

Harold W. Stevenson, Ph.D. (Michigan), is Professor of Finance, Arizona State University. He has taught at Michigan State University,

Northwestern University, and the University of Minnesota. From 1950 to 1953 he was senior analyst, National Bank of Detroit. Significant publications include *Equity and Long-Term Financing for Small Manufacturing Firms in Minnesota* (1962) and *Profits of the Modern Economy* (1967), of which he is coauthor. His special fields of interest are investments, banking, public utility financing, and corporation finance.

George R. Terry, Ph.D. (Ball State University), until his recent death was an educator, writer, management consultant, and Distinguished Professor of General Business Administration at Ball State University in Muncie, Indiana. Among his widely accepted books are *Office Management and Control* (7th ed., 1975), *Principles of Management* (7th ed., 1977), and *Supervisory Management* (rev. ed., 1978). He was an active member and held offices in many of the leading professional business and management organizations. His major areas of professional interest were management theory and practice, strategic planning, human relations and motivation, and organizational development.

Alfred L. Thimm, Ph.D. (New York University), is Professor of Industrial Administration at Union College in Schenectady, New York. In 1972 he was a guest professor at the University of Munich. Formerly he taught at Clarkson College of Technology, New York University, and St. Lawrence University. In 1967–68 he was a Fulbright Professor at Groizer Technische Hochschule. He is coauthor of *Economists and Society* (1973). In addition, he has contributed numerous articles to journals in the field of management and was a contributing author to the text *Introduction to Modern Economics* (1952). His special areas of professional interest include mathematical statistics, operations research, and management science.

Henry L. Tosi, Ph.D. (Ohio State), is Professor and Chairman of the Department of Management, University of Florida. He has held other faculty positions at the University of Maryland, University of California-Irvine, and Michigan State University. He is a fellow of the Academy of Management, has been president of the Midwest Division (1972), and has served as chairman of the Organization Behavior Division. His books include *Management by Objectives: Research and Applications* (1974), *Management: Contingency, Structure and Process* (1976), and *Organizational Behavior* (1977). He has written over 40 articles covering a range of diverse topics that have appeared in the *Academy of Management Journal, Journal of Business, Administrative Science Quarterly,* and other journals. He is a member of the editorial review board of *The Academy of Management Review, Journal of Business*

Research, and *Business Topics.* He has consulted with organizations such as Pontiac, Black and Decker, Commercial Credit Corporation, IBM, Ford, Playboy, and Sperry-Vickers.

Ralph N. Traxler, Jr., Ph.D. (Chicago), is Dean of the School of Management and Business Sciences at Oklahoma City University. Previously he served on the faculties of Emory and Henry College, the University of Florida, ad Emory University. He was Dean, College of Business and Management Studies, University of South Alabama. He is active as a consultant with a specialized interest in management development. His other fields of interest are business history, business organization, and policies.

Wallace D. Trevillian, Ph.D. (Virginia), is Professor of Economics and Dean of the College of Industrial Management and Textile Science at Clemson University. He is a member of the Southern Economic Association, Academy of Management, American Association of Collegiate Schools of Business, Beta Gamma Sigma, and Phi Psi. He is also president of the National Council for Textile Education and is secretary to the Commission for Business Professions, National Association of State Universities and Land-Grant Colleges. His major fields of interest are managerial economics, personnel management, and textile education.

W. T. Tucker, Ph.D. (Illinois), is Professor of Marketing Administration at the University of Texas. Previously, he taught at Georgia State College and the University of Illinois. His numerous publications include two books: *Foundations for a Theory of Consumer Behavior* (1967), and *The Social Context of Economic Behavior* (1964).

William J. Wasmuth, D.B.A. (Indiana), is Professor of Human Resources and Personnel Management, New York State School of Industrial and Labor Relations, Cornell University, Ithaca, New York. He is director of a regional rehabilitation management training project. His books include *Human Resources Administration: Problems of Growth and Change* (1970), *Organizational Cases and Intrigues: Dynamics of Superivision* (1974), and *Effective Supervision: Developing Your Skills Through Critical Incidents* (1979). He is an active management consultant and is a member of the Academy of Management, the Industrial Relations Research Association, and the American Association of University Professors. His major fields of interest are organization growth and change, personnel management, training and development, and supervision.

Stuart A. Wesbury, Jr., Ph.D. (Florida), is President of the American College of Hospital Administrators. Prior to that appointment he was director and professor, Section of Health Services Management, School of Medicine, University of Missouri, Columbia. He has had hospital administration experience as director of the University of Florida's Shands Teaching Hospital and Clinics. He is a fellow in the American College of Hospital Administrators and a former member of the Advisory Editorial Board of *Hospitals and Health Services Administration*. He is immediate past chairman of the board of directors of the Association of University Programs in Health Administration.

L. Curtise Wood, Ph.D. (State University of Iowa), is Professor of Administration at Wichita State University. He is an active consultant to public and private organizations. His major fields of interest are labor relations, business policy, and public organizations.

Max S. Wortman, Jr., Ph.D. (Minnesota), is Professor of Management, Virginia Polytechnic Institute and State University. He previously taught at Iowa State University, University of Minnesota, University of Iowa, and University of Massachusetts. He has been editor, *Academy of Management Review;* associate editor, *Academy of Management Review;* and has served on the editorial review boards of the *Journal of Management, Journal of Collective Negotiations in the Public Sector,* and *Human Resources Planning.* He has written over 100 articles and papers and written or edited nine books including: *Administrative Policy,* (1975, 1980); *Defining the Manager's Job,* (1975); and *Emerging Concepts in Management,* (1975). He was a Ford Faculty Research fellow in 1963– 64. He has served as a consultant to federal, state, and local governments including the U.S. Equal Employment Opportunity Commission, U.S. Civil Service Commission, and the U.S. Navy. He has served in many different capacities in the Academy of Management and the International Personnel Management Association.

DATE DUE

GAYLORD			PRINTED IN U.S.A